FLEETING AGENCIES

This book offers a bold new perspective on the concept of agency and history of long-silenced coolie women—their role in the colonial economy and transnational movements.

The history of transnational labor has refused to acknowledge the importance and agency of women workers. In this landmark study, the author revises and decolonizes the history of transnational female plantation labor. This is the first book to examine the history of Indian coolie women who migrated to British Malaya and contributed to the Rubber Empire's making.

The author disrupts the male-dominated narratives by focusing on gendered patterns of migration and showing how South Asian women labor migrants engaged with migration, interacted with other migrants, and negotiated colonial laws. In exploring the politicization of labor migration trends and gender relations in the colonial plantation society of British Malaya, it shows how the immigrant Indian coolie women manipulated colonial legal and administrative perceptions of Indian women, the gender-perspective roles within Indian societies, relations within patriarchal marriage institutions, and even the emerging Indian national independence movement in India and Malaya, all to ensure their survival, escape from unfavourable relations and situations, and improve their lives. Through this study, the author introduces the concept of *situational or fleeting agency* to provide a nuanced understanding of the term "agency" within the contexts of subaltern and colonial histories.

Meticulously researched, *Fleeting Agencies* is a major contribution to labor migration history, inter-Asia history, and British Empire history.

Arunima Datta is Assistant Professor of History at Idaho State University, USA, where her research focuses on transnational labor migration, gender, and women's history and Asian history.

T0381696

GLOBAL SOUTH ASIANS

Throughout the modern era, South Asia and South Asians have been entangled with global flows of goods, people and ideas. In the context of these globalised conditions, migrants from the subcontinent of India created some of the world's most extensive and influential transnational networks. While operating within the constraints of imperial systems, they nevertheless made distinctive and important contributions to international trade, global cultures and transnational circuits of knowledge. This series seeks to explore these phenomena, placing labourers, traders, thinkers and activists at the centre of the analysis. Beginning with volumes that seek to radically reappraise indenture, the series will continue with books on the mobility of elite actors, including intellectuals, and their contributions to the global circulation of ideas and the evolution of political practice. It will highlight the creativity and agency of diasporic South Asians and illuminate the crucial role they played in the making of global histories. As such it sets out to challenge popular misconceptions and established scholarly narratives that too often cast South Asians as passive observers.

FLEETING AGENCIES

A Social History of Indian Coolie Women
in British Malaya

ARUNIMA DATTA

CAMBRIDGE
UNIVERSITY PRESS

Shaftesbury Road, Cambridge CB2 8EA, United Kingdom

One Liberty Plaza, 20th Floor, New York, NY 10006, USA

477 Williamstown Road, Port Melbourne, VIC 3207, Australia

314–321, 3rd Floor, Plot 3, Splendor Forum, Jasola District Centre, New Delhi – 110025, India

103 Penang Road, #05–06/07, Visioncrest Commercial, Singapore 238467

Cambridge University Press is part of Cambridge University Press & Assessment, a department of the University of Cambridge.

We share the University's mission to contribute to society through the pursuit of education, learning and research at the highest international levels of excellence.

www.cambridge.org
Information on this title: www.cambridge.org/9781009415491

First published 2021
First paperback edition 2023

A catalogue record for this publication is available from the British Library

ISBN   978-1-108-83738-5   Hardback
ISBN   978-1-009-41549-1   Paperback

For
Mimi, Papa, and Adi

CONTENTS

TABLES

FIGURES

ABBREVIATIONS

AGIM	Agent of the Government of India in Malaya
AN	Arkib Negara, Kuala Lumpur
BL	British Library
CO	Colonial Office Records
CUKL	Cornell University Kroch Library
FMS	Federated Malay States
IIC	Indian Immigration Committee
INA	Indian National Army
IOR	India Office Records
MIC	Malaysian Indian Congress
NAI	National Archives of India, New Delhi
NAUK	National Archives of United Kingdom, London
NAS	National Archives of Singapore
NLI	National Library of India, Kolkata
NLS	National Library of Singapore
OHI	Oral History Interviews
PAM	Planters Association of Malaya
RJR	Rani of Jhansi Regiment
SS	Straits Settlement
TNSA	Tamil Nadu State Archives
UMS	Unfederated Malaya States
UPAM	United Planters Association of Malaya

ACKNOWLEDGMENTS

This book began with my curiosity about the silence in scholarly literature concerning "coolie" women, though they were regularly recruited in British India for being transported to various British plantation colonies for both labor production and labor reproduction. That curiosity has been encouraged, nurtured, and supported by many scholars, archivists, colleagues, friends, and family.

My biggest debt of gratitude is owed to my mentors and colleagues, who over the years have patiently listened to my ideas, read drafts, provided valuable feedback, answered innumerable questions, and, most importantly, stood by me as pillars of wisdom and strength. In particular, I would like to thank Vineeta Sinha (Ammu), Sunil Amrith, Barbara Andaya, Leonard Andaya, Siddharthan Maunaguru, Kelvin E. Y. Low, Noorman Abdullah, Paul Kratoska, Indrani Chatterjee, Erika Rappaport, Catherine Hoyser, Louise Williams, Laura Seddelmeyer, Eadaoin Agnew, Kate Imy, Daniel Grey, Jonathan Saha, and Sumita Mukherjee—thank you for always supporting me, motivating me, and helping me develop my ideas. Words cannot define how thankful I am for your unwavering support and encouragement. Ammu, Barbara, Daniel, Indrani, Sid, and Sunil—I cannot express in words how grateful I am to you for always being there for me whenever the path became difficult. I also want to extend heartfelt thanks and gratitude to Elaine Farrell for being an amazing friend and mentor who helped me deal with trying situations in research and writing—in a task that seemed insurmountable. Kate Imy and Laura Seddelmeyer—thank you for always being there, always having time for me and being an amazing source of strength during trying times. Elaine, Kate, and Laura—I am lucky to have your friendship: it is hard to find friends like you in today's world and I would have never believed it is possible to build such friendships in academia until I met you. I also want to extend special thanks to Gordon Ramsey—without your help and constant readings and comments, this manuscript would not have reached its final stages. Finally, I would like to thank my wonderful colleagues at Idaho State University, especially in the Department of History, who have constantly been a great support through the process of finishing this book.

A few chapters are revised versions of the following articles: parts of Chapter 4 appeared in "Immorality, Nationalism and the Colonial State in British Malaya: Indian 'Coolie' Women's Intimate Lives as Ideological Battleground," *Journal of Women's History Review* 25, no. 4 (2016): 584–601; Chapter 5 is a revised version of "Social Memory and Indian Women from Malaya and Singapore in the Rani of Jhansi Regiment," *Journal of Malaysian Branch of the Royal Asiatic Society* 88, Part 2, no. 309 (2015): 77–103. I owe grateful acknowledgment to the journals and publishers for allowing me to build on this earlier work.

Many institutions, libraries, and archives have made this project possible: multiple research grants from the National University of Singapore; research fellowship at the Institute of Commonwealth Studies, University of London; and the Asia Research Institute research grants helped in the research for this book. Accessing the stories of the heroes of my book—the "coolie" women—would not have been possible without the hard work and support of many archivists around the world. In the UK, I am grateful to the staff at the British Library, the National Archives, and the Women's Library. I am especially grateful to the British Library staff—Annabelle Gallop, Arlene C. B., Charles Bonnah, Dorota Walker, Gary Carter, Haque Sarker, Jeff Kattenhorn, John Chignoli (Chop Chop), Lorena Garcia, Richard Bingle, Richard Morel, and Robert Boyling—most of whom have become as close as family to me over the years. In Singapore, I am grateful to the staff at the National Archives Singapore, the National Library, National University Library, in particular to Fiona Tan, Janice Loo, Yap Fuan Tim, Han Ming Guang, Herman Felani, Winnifred Wong, Letha Raveendran, Miskiah Bte Rahmat, and all the counter staff (especially Shanta, Letchmi, Sumati, Ramli) who have helped me locate rare books and microfilms, in inter-library loans, and, most importantly, have always been ready to help with a smile and go an extra mile to make research easier for me. Special thanks to Mr Tim at NUS library—without your guidance and help this research would not have been possible and I would be lost in the special collections. In Malaysia, I am grateful for all the support I received from the staff at Arkib

Negara, Kuala Lumpur. In India I am grateful for all the support and help I got from the archivists and staff at the National Archives of India, Delhi; Tamil Nadu Archives, Chennai; West Bengal State Archives, Kolkata. I would also like to thank the two anonymous readers and the series editor at CUP, Crispin Bates, who offered perceptive comments that generated crucial revisions to the manuscript. I am also grateful for the constant support and guidance I received from the CUP team—Ms Qudsiya Ahmed, Ms Sohini Ghosh, Mr Aniruddha De, and their team.

I also thank the various conference organizers and panelists between 2010 and 2015 who have given me the incredible opportunity to share my research and whose insightful comments have helped me develop my arguments. Your time, comments, and suggestions were extremely valuable.

I would also like to acknowledge with gratitude the love and support I have received from friends and family. First of all, Raghava Bhaiya, Mira, Riya, and Xiaoyang (Stella), thank you for being my family and home away from home. Thank you for patiently listening to all my challenges and giving me the courage to go on. Heather Ott, I cannot thank you enough for your kindness and amazing friendship.

Most importantly, I am ever grateful for the unconditional love and unquestioning support from the most important people in my life—my parents, Debasish Datta (Papa) and Rumjhum Datta (Mimi), and my amazingly supportive husband, Shiladitya Mukherjee (Adi). Papa, Mimi, and Adi, thank you for always being ready to read my work and providing valuable feedback on it—even though you were reading it for the fifteenth time. Adi, thank you for constantly encouraging me by reminding me that the blessings of the unsung heroes of my book, the "coolie" women, will always be with me. Papa, Mimi, and Adi—without your constant support, patience, willingness to postpone plans, willingness to travel, and constant encouragement, I would not have been able to complete this book. Come challenges, illness, or doubts, you three were always there and always believed that I would do fine. I dedicate this book to my parents and my husband!

INTRODUCTION

This book explores the lives of socially, politically, economically, and *archivally* marginalized Indian "coolie" women who migrated from British India, particularly south India, to British Malaya during the late nineteenth and early twentieth centuries to labor on Malaya's rubber plantations, especially in the Federated Malay States (FMS). The conventional historical narrative of South Asian labor migration under the British Empire emphasizes the experiences of coolie men and their instrumental role in the success of plantation colonies. This study, in contrast, traces coolie women's experiences and their crucial contributions to the plantation colony in British Malaya. *Fleeting Agencies* goes beyond the add-and-stir approach, however. It does not merely append the history of coolie women to existing labor migration histories. Rather, in exploring the gendered everyday experiences of coolie women in spaces of work and home and in their social, political, and intimate relations, the book exposes how gender was used in shaping colonial policies regarding migration, labor production, and reproduction, and also reveals the gendered spaces and strategies of nationalist movements. It explores the relationships and experiences of coolie women across plantation societies. In so doing, it also shows how coolie women capitalized on gendered understandings of labor, morality, and patriotism to carve out channels within which they could negotiate for their own interests.

As might be expected, plantation societies, colonial politics, and nationalist movements were all designed and conceptualized largely by men in positions of authority, and consequently often favored men's roles and voices over those of women, especially women laborers. *Fleeting Agencies* shows how colonial administrators, planters, managerial staff on estates, and Indian nationalists all deployed racialized and stereotyped images of South Asian coolie women in support of their own political agendas and the complex ways in which women responded to such stereotypes. As the chapters in this book show, women laborers actively engaged with, adapted, negotiated, rejected, and sometimes indirectly influenced stereotypes produced in these male-dominated spaces and institutions, and used them to form relations and find channels to make their voices heard in a world divided by political interests, to ensure their ability to make choices, and at times to ensure their daily survival. *Fleeting Agencies* is the first study to interrogate how coolie women in Malaya experienced and responded to colonial and nationalist efforts to categorize and control their identities. This book, therefore, provides important correctives to male-centered histories of colonial labor, of transnational labor migrations, and of transnational nationalist movements, which often hide the nuanced and textured sociopolitical and economic realities of colonial politics and plantation societies. It recognizes that gender was crucial and was embedded in social relations, economic institutions, and political interactions in the larger context of colonial plantation societies. *Fleeting Agencies*, thus, presents a case for centering the everyday experiences of migrant women laborers in national, transnational, migration, and colonial histories, consistently placing their everyday lives within the contexts of events in colonial politics, market economics, transnational nationalist movements, and world war.

The central argument of *Fleeting Agencies* is that coolie women played crucial roles in the rubber plantations of Malaya as producers and reproducers of labor, and that despite being exploited, oppressed, and used by more powerful actors, including colonial planters and administrators, middle-class Indian nationalists, and their own husbands or sexual partners, they did not consent to be passive victims but exercised agency in navigating the complex dilemmas of plantation life in protean ways ranging from strategic compliance to armed resistance. In so doing, coolie women in Malaya played diverse and vital roles in local and transnational histories: roles which have not, to date, been fully explored by historians.

Fleeting Agencies, thus, catechizes colonialism, Indian nationalism, and, most importantly, the concepts of *agency* from a subaltern perspective and places labor, migration, and gender at the center of history.[1] Drawing on archival records and oral history interviews, *Fleeting Agencies* explores the ways in which coolie women articulated moments of agency and acts of *survivance* within extended periods of exploitation and subjugation.[2] It highlights the artistry and creativity of coolie women in negotiating with various hierarchies and power structures, unveiling the ways they actively engaged with the contexts they found themselves in and deployed different modes of agency that they understood to be appropriate to particular situations. Coolie women's determined efforts to carve out better spaces and roles for themselves in realms ranging from employment to marriage suggest a conscious awareness of the complex power dynamics in which they lived and a degree of strategic thought and action that has been largely overlooked in previous accounts of colonial plantation societies.

In its efforts to re-evaluate established understandings of the term "agency," this study—through an exploration of coolie women's engagement with patriarchy, colonialism, and colonial migration policies, estate economies, and social arrangements—unravels the complex ways in which individual decision-making was related to constraints of gender, class, race, and temporality in everyday history. The work shows how coolie women negotiated these hierarchical social structures both in times of comparative stability and in times of upheaval and chaos. It offers a fresh perspective on agency by identifying and critically examining how temporally fleeting discourses and actions emerge within the extended contexts of colonialism, nationalism, patriarchy, and war. In so doing, the book develops an innovative theoretical framework, *situational agency*, to explore and understand the ways migrant women negotiated the complex textures of temporality, gender, race, class, and migration. So, whilst the issues raised in this book are rooted within the late nineteenth and early twentieth centuries, they have contemporary social and political relevance. *Fleeting Agencies* is, above all, about those working-class women whose agency and importance are yet to be acknowledged in the pages of history.

Through this book, I weave together a wide range of snapshots of different phases in coolie women's lives to tell *a* history of their everyday work, and their social, intimate, and political lives within colonial estate societies.[3] To this end, the work not only investigates coolie women's engagements with their immediate environment of estate society, but also travels deeper to explore their engagements with British colonialism, Indian nationalism, and Japanese occupation during World War II. To achieve this, the book uses archival fragments documenting coolie women's "marginal" lives to explore the significance of a wide range of interactions between coolie women and other individuals, spaces, and infrastructure. In the process, the book throws light on a kaleidoscopic range of everyday relations between coolie women and coolie men, colonial administrators, planters, estate managers, and Indian nationalist leaders.

Focusing on the implicit and fleeting moments of agency exhibited by coolie women, this study delineates a route toward understanding the roles, experiences, and struggles of colonial labor migrants, and thereby provides an *entrée* into larger questions: How did subaltern subjects navigate colonial policies of labor and migration? How did coolie women perceive their roles in plantation societies, and how did they use those perceptions to negotiate for what they desired? To what extent did migration transform social and intimate relations of labor migrants? How did migrant laborers respond to colonial and nationalist constructions of the "coolie imaginary"? How did colonial and nationalist intrusions into the everyday lives of migrants shape their experiences, perceptions, and strategies, and how did migrant laborers contribute to the making and unmaking of colonial and nationalist agendas in the realm of colonial politics? In other words, how did migrant laborers engage with colonial understandings of morality, domesticity, and victimhood in a distant colony away from their homeland, and how did they perceive and engage with the Indian nationalist agenda of patriotism and "national" solidarity?

In exploring these questions, this study decenters colonial and nationalist discourses about migrant labor in colonial plantation societies by showing how gendered behaviors of migrant laborers, their workspace interactions, and everyday life choices have, at times, facilitated or frustrated both colonial and nationalist agendas.

Given the conflicting political interests of colonial and nationalist actors, ideas produced about coolie women were neither uniform nor simple. Yet, if there was one common theme in colonial and nationalist attitudes toward coolie women, it was that they were useful pawns to be categorized, stereotyped, and deployed in the realm of colonial power politics. This work shows, however, that coolie women were anything but passive subjects. Slicing open various insidious stereotypes and categories into which coolie women have often been homogeneously packed, *Fleeting Agencies* analyzes the politics behind the construction of such categories, the ways coolie women made

4

sense of such identities, and, in different contexts, appropriated, strategically deployed, or rejected them. Investigating and analyzing gendered stereotypes of "coolie women" and coolie communities, this book raises important questions concerning the construction of stereotypical categories, suggesting that real identities may be far more transient than these categories imply. This book, thus, emphasizes that a single dominant narrative cannot effectively represent the history of Indian labor migration in Southeast Asia. Instead, it shows that under the most accessible but often deceptive layers of history, which are easily available in the archives maintained by the dominant forces in a society, may be found far more complex and tangled stories. It is the responsibility of historians to engage with such diverse entanglements and seek to draw them into the light, rather than simply accept the dominant narrative that emerges from a surface-reading of the archives. That is what this study seeks to do.

Reconceiving the images of coolie women presented by the dominant narratives has important implications for understanding gender, labor, migration, nation, and community, not only in colonial Malaya and India but across the British Empire. Such a re-historicization allows us to foreground the significance of gender in interlinking various regional and transnational histories during the colonial past. On another level, exploring colonial history through coolie women's lives illuminates how gender and migration became an important ground of debate in colonial and postcolonial imaginations. The subjugation of coolie women and silencing of their stories did not necessarily end with the demise of colonial rule in Malaya.

This chapter begins with a discussion of the term "coolie." Thereafter, it situates its subject, coolie women, within larger frameworks of gender, migration, and colonial history and discusses how histories of migrant groups such as coolie women offer us lenses to (re)vision, reinterpret, and connect various regional histories, particularly those of South and Southeast Asia within colonial contexts. Next, it introduces the concept of *situational agency*, which forms the connecting tissue through which the following chapters in this book remain linked. It then moves to discuss the challenges and rewards of archival research, particularly concerning subaltern subjects whose "voice" may be hard to discern in the archives. Herein, the chapter discusses the rich variety of materials upon which this research has drawn, from over ten archives in India, Malaysia, Singapore, the United Kingdom, and the United

States of America. In the process, it also considers the challenges of curating archival records in migration history and shows how silences in the archives can be placed in a productive dialogue with presences to evoke more nuanced readings, enabling analysis of less-explored themes of colonial and subaltern histories. Finally, an outline of the following chapters is presented.

NOTES ON THE TERM "COOLIE"

The social stereotypes, prejudices, and presumptions surrounding the term "coolie" give me additional themes and textures to work with. "Coolie" does not have any given meaning attached to it; rather it is the economic, political, social, and racial concerns that influenced the evolution of derogatory ideas about "coolies" which have conditioned our understanding and perception of those to whom the term was applied. Hence, before proceeding further it is necessary to (re)visit and reexamine the concept of a "coolie," which, left unexamined, may limit our understandings concerning laboring women in colonial history.

There are various claims regarding the origins of the term "coolie." The most commonly heard, at least in Malayan history, is that it derives from the Tamil word *kuliah*, which refers to a person of low caste who performs menial and hard physical labor. Most rubber-estate coolies in colonial Malaya were Tamils, and in this study, whenever the term "coolie" is mentioned, it refers to Indian Tamil coolies, both men and women, unless otherwise indicated. I use the term "coolie" consciously but in a non-derogatory manner to refer to the professional category that is the subject of this book. I understand that using the term "coolie" as a professional category, as archival records suggest, is contentious since the term in the present day carries a heavy derogatory baggage. But the chapters in this study unpack some of the prejudices attached to the term, showing how such conceptions resulted from social constructs used both in the past and the present to (re)inscribe power, racial, and class hierarchies. Using the term "coolie" to describe the professional category, *Fleeting Agencies* thus suggests a (re)visioning of the term and a restoration of the term to working-class people, some of whom still identify with it.

Nineteenth- and twentieth-century colonial administrative records, including registers of migration and employment, use the term "coolie" to refer to Asian laborers, Indians, Chinese, and Javanese alike, engaged in any form of manual labor—whether on rubber estates, public-works departments, railways, or mines. With regard to Indian migrant laborers, the term "coolie", used as a professional category, was widespread within the British Empire and beyond: plantations in India, Fiji, Trinidad, Guiana, Suriname, Mauritius, the Maldives, and other European colonies had much earlier set the trend of referring to Indian migrant laborers, particularly on plantations, as "coolies."

In my interviews with Indian ex-coolies and descendants of Indian coolies in present-day Malaysia, I came to understand that the surviving coolie women and men often distanced themselves from the term as a result of contemporary connotations of racial and class identity in which they did not wish to invest. Nonetheless, a few individuals continue to identify as former "coolies" or descendants of "coolies." For them, the term had nostalgic connotations, and they took some pride in the fact that they or their ancestors were part of the "coolie army" that built modern Malaysia.[4]

Pushpa, daughter of a coolie couple who migrated to Malaya in the 1920s, and Pachaimmal, daughter of a coolie couple and a coolie herself in Malaya, referred to themselves as descendants of coolies or ex-coolies.[5] When asked whether the term "coolie" offended them, both explained that the term itself did not necessarily mean anything negative to them, but when the term is used to disrespect their profession or the community to which they belonged, it becomes offensive. During the conversations, they claimed that they were proud of their coolie connection and for them the term "coolie" meant hardworking laborers who were self-made men and women. Pushpa and Pachaimmal may be exceptional today in their appropriation of their coolie connection. In most of my personal interactions with second- and third-generation Indians in Malaysia, whose parents had immigrated to Malaya as coolies, they referred to their parents as "rubber-estate workers" and seemed to consciously avoid using the term "coolie."[6] Nonetheless, the qualified appropriation of the term by Pushpa and Pachaimmal unveils complex connotations of racial, class, caste, and gender histories.

Both present-day consciousness and pride in coolie connections and class identity by some and efforts to ignore and distance themselves from coolie histories and identities by others serve as a reminder of a related class consciousness that was used by Indian nationalists for whom the cause of overseas Indian coolies was a significant issue. The plight of coolies served as a clarion call for the masses to raise their voices against the British Empire. Gopal Krishna Gokhale of the Indian National Congress, for instance, who was a member of the Bombay Legislative Council, while requesting the Council to abolish the indenturing of Indians to other British plantation colonies, on 4 March 1912 argued:

> It is degrading to the people of India from a national point of view.... Wherever this system exists, the Indians are known only as *coolies* [emphasis mine], no matter what their position may be. Now, Sir, there are disabilities enough in all conscience attaching to our position in this country. And I ask, why must this additional brand be put upon our brow before the rest of the civilized world? I am sure, if only the Government will exercise a little imagination and realize our feeling in the matter, it will see the necessity of abolishing the system as soon as possible.[7]

Elite and upper-middle-class Indian nationalists like Gokhale used the oppression of coolies as a bargaining tool with the colonial government, but they simultaneously made efforts to other the coolie population to ensure that *all* overseas Indians were not identified as "coolies" by other ethnicities in the overseas colonies. The politics of othering coolies was, thus, prevalent in colonial politics on the grounds of race, caste, and class. The efforts of present-day Malaysian-Indians to distance their identity from the coolie community or even to erase their own "coolie" past, thus, continues long-established trends of othering. Even though many ex-coolies and their descendants reject the term "coolie," the term is loaded with historical significance beginning from the immigration policies and records of British Malaya, to the lives of migrant men and women as recorded in colonial discourses as well as in nationalist discourses in India and Malaya. As Gaiutra Bahadur, in her recent ethnohistorical book focusing on a coolie woman of Guyana, convincingly asserts, the term "coolie" carries "burdens of history."[8]

Along with class, race, and caste connotations, the term "coolie" has also reflected a gendered labeling and understanding of labor migration history. To date, the term "coolie" remains a code word for male plantation laborers, although plantations constantly depended on considerable numbers of coolie women for production of various resources from the plantations. By the

1930s, immigrant Indian women formed 30 to 40 percent of the total coolie force on European rubber estates in Malaya, but their active engagement in the socioeconomic and political life of the estates has been occluded and sometimes misrepresented in labor studies, and in Indian as well as Malaysian history.[9] Using the term "coolie" to include both women and men, this study democratizes its scope on the grounds of gender.

Using the term "coolie," in a non-derogatory way, to acknowledge the contributions of individuals, particularly women, who made the rubber empire of Malaya, *Fleeting Agencies* thus seeks to respect and celebrate the rich history of migrant laborers in the country.

SITUATING THE HISTORY OF COOLIE WOMEN

In narrating what I perceive as only a part of the untold, unexplored many-hued histories of coolie women's lives, *Fleeting Agencies* has engaged with two significant turns in history—the *gender turn* and the more recent *transnational migration turn*. At its heart, transnational labor migration histories have focused mostly on men's stories. An overwhelming number of migration histories have deployed Eric Hobsbawm's idea of "men moving,"[10] and have gone into extreme depths of archives to find histories of migrant men laboring in different regions in the colonial past.[11] But such rigor, while not entirely absent, has been much less common when it comes to exploring histories of women labor migrants.[12] More disturbing than mere neglect is that while some of us have pushed for recognition of coolie women's histories, other parallel studies of coolie migration have recycled the fallacies of earlier scholarship, failing to engage meaningfully with gendered issues or coolie women's histories.[13] Undeniably, coolie women's histories are much more difficult to find in the archives, and the trend of ignoring the gender politics and gender relations of coolie histories may suggest a degree of fear, disinterest, or even aversion by historians, particularly labor-migration historians, to addressing the silences, gaps, and absences in the archives.

Neglect of women in labor migration histories has not only silenced women's stories, but has also partially, perhaps almost completely, occluded the histories of gender relations and the key role of gender as a tool in colonial negotiations and debates, much of which remains visible in present-day patterns of labor migration.[14] Several excellent scholarly works have highlighted the importance of women's labor in colonial plantation societies. G. Roger Knight has shown how crucial women's labor was to colonial capitalism. Knight, through his study of sugar plantations in colonial Indonesia, reveals that the policy of increasing the numbers of women plantation workers on sugar estates from the 1880s, to the point that they eventually comprised half the labor force, was a well-thought-out gendered labor policy to ensure that planters could employ more laboring hands for less cost, as women's labor was markedly cheaper than men's.[15] The increased labor force ensured elaborate but cheap routines of weeding and fertilization of young sugar plants, which, in turn, ensured increased quality and quantity of production and hence profit for the Dutch estate companies. Similarly, a recent and important study by Elise van Nederveen has shown the crucial role of women estate workers in the global colonial economy—both at the metropole and in the colonies.[16] Scholarship by Rhoda Rheddock and Sobita Jain has shown how crucial migrant women's labor was to colonial plantation economies across the world—in Fiji, Jamaica, Mauritius, Sri Lanka, Cameroon, and Trinidad. By placing women workers center stage, they highlight how, in most colonial plantations around the world, plantation labor remained one of the lowest-paid occupational categories, invariably including large numbers of women. They show how such gendered labor arrangements influenced women's control of familial resources, patterns of authority in domestic spaces, forms of marriage, and the ability of women to negotiate their positions in plantation systems.[17] Following the path initiated by these scholars, *Fleeting Agencies* not only considers the crucial importance of coolie women to the rubber plantations and the colonial economy in Malaya, but also shows how coolie women shaped colonial and nationalistic imaginings of migrant labor in plantation societies. Some coolie women, for instance, embraced colonial stereotypical categorizations to gain sympathy from planters, judges, and even coolie society while performing "immorality," while others revolted against stereotypical identities to claim labor rights as estate workers. Yet others participated in anti-colonial movements, not necessarily on patriotic grounds propagated by nationalist leaders, but to ensure survival and protection in a context of chaos and uncertainty. Studying the multidimensional everyday histories of migrant Indian coolie women in British Malaya and the four years of Japanese occupation, this study, thus, brings together the themes of gender, transnational migration, colonialism, and long-distance nationalism to reevaluate notions of migrants' work, domestic life, social relations, and adaptations to colonial politics and wartime chaos.

In the past few decades, scholars have noted the importance of Indian coolies in the making of Empire, but have largely ignored the significance of coolie women within this community. For instance, the seminal work of Amarjit Kaur has examined how the labor of migrant Indian coolies guaranteed economic growth in Southeast Asia after 1840, transforming colonies like Malaysia, Singapore, and Burma into the British Empire's production capitals for rubber and tin. Kaur explores how transnational labor recruitment and gendered labor systems shaped labor organization and labor rights amongst immigrant communities in Southeast Asia.[18] However, she does not go on to explore how such heavy reliance on immigrant labor transformed not only the political but also the social and moral fabric of immigrant communities in Southeast Asian colonies, or how, in due course, it influenced the governing tactics of the colonial administration. At the same time, pioneering works by K. S. Sandhu, Selvakumar Ramachandran, and Usha Mahajani have thoroughly examined the pivotal role of migrant coolies in the building of Britain's Malayan rubber empire, but have solely focused on coolie men, treating coolie women as a mere auxiliary labor force, which this work will show is an inadequate view of the important roles played by women coolies.[19]

Consequently, colonial gender politics, a key motivator in engaging coolie women as migrant laborers, remains to be explored. Most of the attention that has been devoted to Indian coolie migration has uncritically accepted the stereotypes of coolie women purveyed in colonial or nationalist discourses as "dependent" migrants, morally weak, victims of either colonialism or native patriarchy.[20] Bringing into focus the racial, gendered, and class politics that lay behind such stereotyping, *Fleeting Agencies* provides a lens to expose the historical instability of categories based on race, class, and gender and highlights the ways politically informed ideologies of masculinity, femininity, agency, and victimhood enabled both colonial and Indian nationalist elites to justify and exploit their particular versions of paternalism.

By focusing on coolie women's experiences of various race- and gender-based stereotypical identity categories and emphasizing the situational crossing of identity boundaries, such as those between agent and victim, collaborator and perpetrator, the study permits new questions to be asked and develops new imaginations regarding stereotypes and identity categories. By "imaginations," I do not refer to an escape path, but rather the development of curiosity leading to alternate ways of engaging with fluidities and temporalities hidden in stereotypical categories and identities. *Fleeting Agencies*, thus, seeks to thaw our understanding of agent and victim identities and searches for new concepts and understandings that capture the fluidities inherent in such identities.

As scholars engaging with subaltern histories, including women's histories, have long since established, subaltern subjects, during their enduring experiences of institutionalized suppression, oppression, and exploitation, have produced a protean range of responses, reactions, and resistance, often more implicit than explicit. Migration and gender historian Marina Carter has noted that women's assertion of their rights and resistance to oppression in colonial societies has been recorded in various acts ranging from escape or larceny to overt protests and acts of violence.[21] Similarly, historian Clare Anderson, in her seminal work on subaltern migration history, has shown how subaltern migrants, including convicts and indentured servants and laborers, negotiated ways to ensure survival or avail of various opportunities through non-conventional methods that avoided theatrics or open confrontation and have often been overlooked by historians due to their lack of visibility.[22] Consequently, subalterns, in this case, migrant laboring women, became easily stereotyped as passive individuals and hapless victims.

Studies of Indian women plantation laborers migrating within South Asia, particularly within India under British rule, have flourished. Such studies demonstrate implicit forms of agency through which women laborers navigated various stereotypical identity categories in colonial contexts.[23] Piya Chatterjee, in her study of coolie women in Assam's tea plantations, presents a provocative examination of the factors that influence the variation in forms of resistance by women laborers: from individualistic efforts to improve personal situations to united struggles against different hegemonies.[24] Similarly, Samita Sen, in her study of women migrant laborers in the colonial jute industry of Bengal, has shown how expanding colonial capitalist investments accompanied by intrusive colonial policies regarding Indian marriages changed women's role and status in the society, at times to their advantage.[25] In her intriguing study, Sen has revealed how lower-caste women used loopholes in colonial laws to escape the penalties for "husband desertion" when they absconded in order to extract themselves from abusive marriages, find work elsewhere, or, in the worst cases, escape abuse by both colonial and colonized men.

Sen and Chatterjee, within the geopolitical boundaries of colonial India, have given long-overdue recognition to the everyday acts of self-determination exhibited by lower-class and lower-caste colonized women in pursuit of survival, economic mobility, and greater personal autonomy.[26] However, studies exploring similar aspects of the agency of Indian women labor migrants to overseas British colonies remain limited to date. Moreover, the majority of such studies have represented the dominant voices in colonial and nationalist discourses, which endemically erase the agency of coolie women. For instance, Jo Beall, in her study of Indian indentured women in sugar estates in Natal, implies that the women under indenture were absolutely devoid of any agency, portraying them as passive objects under the control of colonial and patriarchal structures.[27] Studies by Rhoda Rheddock and the very recent works of Gauitra Bahadur and Kalpana Hiralal have explored Indian coolie women's history in Fiji, the Caribbean, Natal, and Guiana.[28] While important in expanding our understanding of gender, migration, and Empire, this scholarship has nonetheless favored more *visible* forms of agency enacted by migrant coolie women, ignoring less obvious, but arguably more common, everyday form of agency. Moreover, even these rare but significant works have been criticized for "not adding anything new to the existing literature."[29]

The absence of attention to everyday and implicit forms of agency is not the only omission from the literature: geographically, there is a complete absence of literature on Indian coolie women in colonial Southeast Asia. This is particularly noticeable as Southeast Asia was geographically closer to the labor-exporting colony of India, a proximity which influenced the frequency of labor migration. Furthermore, the absence is all the more noticeable in the case of Malaya, as until 1867, it was administered through the East India Company in Bengal and this, in turn, influenced labor recruitment practices and migration policies between the two colonies. Even more troubling is that those studies which do focus on the history of Indians in colonial Malaya not only neglect women, but effectively deny their independent existence. Studies in both Malaysian and Indian history focusing on indentured labor or coolie migration from India pay attention to the lives, experiences, and agency of coolie men, but not coolie women. If coolie women are mentioned at all, they remain stereotyped as "dependents" who migrated with their male relatives.[30] While historians of Malaysian history have studied other subaltern groups in colonial Malaya, including Chinese rickshaw coolies, Japanese prostitutes,[31] Chinese tin-mining coolies (both men and women),[32] Chinese *amah*s,[33] Indian coolie men and Indian railway coolies,[34] studies of Indian coolie women remain absent. Even a volume capturing the social history of subalterns in colonial Malaya, *The Underside of Malayan History*, did not explore the history of Indian coolie women in the estates of Malaya. Gender and ethnicity were not the limiting factors in the choice of studies included in this volume, as it has a balanced representation of both Indian and Chinese ethnicities, and men (railway workers, rickshaw coolies, estate coolies) and women (prostitutes, tin mining women, *amah*s) subalterns.[35] Yet there remains a yawning gap in colonial labor histories of Malaya regarding the histories of Indian coolie women.

Fleeting Agencies seeks to address both these areas: first, the temporalities and everyday-implicit agencies of coolie women and, second, the history of Indian coolie women in Malaya. In so doing, it connects the local and regional history of South Asian women workers in Southeast Asia with the transnational history of women workers under colonialism. It illuminates how the experiences of South Asian migrant laboring women became an important ground of debate in Indian nationalism and colonial politics, showing that the history of South Asia itself cannot be completely understood if the histories of global South Asians or South Asian women are neglected. Furthermore, this book shows that writing a history of coolie women itself involves a rewriting of many other related histories. By foregrounding the roles of migrant women laborers in sociopolitical and economic structures, tissues of connection between the histories of different spaces, the borders of which have been enforced on our imagination by imperial actors, are brought into view. The lens of migrant coolie women's histories and more broadly global South Asians' history can bring to light many hidden yet connected histories of different colonies. Examples brought to light in this work include the sudden turn in trans-colonial labor migration policies, which began focusing on migration of coolie women and coolie families to Malaya, the ways in which stereotypes were created to serve particular agendas, and Indian nationalist leader Subash

Chandra Bose's use of gender in his war against the British. This history from below, then, can recognize ignored aspects of colonialism and anti-colonialism and address the long-overdue need for regionally specific histories to not only look inward, but to simultaneously look outward and include vital connections beyond perceived borders. In other words, it emphasizes that the histories of a space, a nation, or a region are not only made within its "imagined" boundaries, but also beyond them.

This focus on connection allows an examination of the crucial part that transnational South Asian labor migrants played in influencing the matrix of interconnections that developed, not only between the metropole and South Asia, but also between the British Empire's South and Southeast Asian colonies. It, therefore, allows us to reexamine not only *what* we know about South and Southeast Asian history, but also *how* we know it and, thus, to open up discussions regarding the complexities of British imperialism in South and Southeast Asia. Moreover, using transnational labor migration history to study South Asian, Southeast Asian, and colonial histories open up opportunities for dialogue between these and other disciplinary areas.

SITUATIONAL AGENCY: (RE)CONCEIVING AGENCY

The term "agency" has often been associated with radical, theatrical acts of resistance, challenging authorities in ways that allow a victim to be seen as becoming an agent. Scholarship on subaltern agencies has mostly favored spectacular and unique displays of agency, such as death or suicide.[36] Although some scholars have noted the shortcomings of such limited conceptions of agency, they have often shied away from proposing a new layer to the concept. Historians, such as Rosiland O'Hanlon, have observed the frustrating expectation that the agency of a subaltern subject will be visible in demonstrations of will or theatrical displays of power, which has limited more nuanced definitions and understanding of the various ways in which subaltern subjects have sought to achieve their various aims.[37] Like many others, however, O'Hanlon has not pursued the opportunity to explore the covert and implicit agencies of subaltern subjects. Scholars have also missed opportunities to acknowledge the rich histories of subaltern agency by favoring success, permanency, and longevity of the effects of an agential act over fleeting, episodic acts, which may or may not have "succeeded."[38]

Fleeting Agencies (re)visions such understandings of the term "agency" by including within its definition short-term, implicit, and less overt acts of self-determination and simultaneously highlighting the inherent temporality in any act of agency. Toward this aim, it introduces the term *situational agency*, which broadens the scope and significance of the concept of agency. *Situational agency* focuses on conscious acts of individuals, seeking to reconstruct the history of social relations and daily engagements of subaltern subjects with different hierarchies and structures of power. As Sumi Madhok, Durba Ghosh, Lila Abu-Lughod, Sherry B. Ortner, Judith Butler, and James Scott have argued in their respective studies, even in extremely oppressive situations, a subject does not necessarily become a passive victim.[39] *Fleeting Agencies*, thus, emphasizes that the term "agency" needs reevaluation.

Before defining *situational agency*, it is important to understand what barriers and boundaries it tries to break. Restrictive ways of defining agency as a radical act with a permanent or long-lasting positive effect have often led to the agency of subjugated individuals being completely ignored. Moreover, because only theatrical or confrontational forms of resistance, such as participation in riots, have been acknowledged, an unbalanced picture of the reality of subaltern lives has been presented. Consequently, the pioneering efforts of Rhoda Rheddock and Shobita Jain to explore the agency of coolie women in colonial plantations through rioting and other overt acts of resistance have often been criticized by feminist historians[40] for underplaying the subjugation and oppression under which these women suffered.[41] Similarly, Shaista Shameen's and Vereene Shepherd's work exploring the history of Indian women's labor on colonial Fijian and Jamaican plantations has privileged militancy and theatrical form of resistance in highlighting the role of women laborers in resisting capitalism, colonialism, and patriarchy.[42] These studies, like the earlier ones, tend to privilege collective participation in such acts of resistance over more individual and less visible forms of agency. Other contemporary studies of women laborers in plantations, like Shobita Jain's work on Assam and Rachel Kurian's work on Tamil women laborers in Sri Lankan plantations, similarly privilege militant collective resistance to plantation authorities.[43]

Much of the existing literature on agency, then, idealizes it as an eventful and theatrical act of disruption, contest, or transgression. Coolie women's agencies, however, were not always, or even often, theatrical, long-lasting, or permanent. Coolie women living in extremely oppressive conditions were agential in their multifarious relations within the oppressive constructs of colonial estate societies. They devised subaltern forms of agency, which were not necessarily "visible" and as a result have been overlooked by most labor and migration historians because such efforts did not appear radical or explicitly resistant to authority. It is these everyday, temporally limited or fleeting, covert or implicit forms of agency with which the concept of situational agency seeks to engage.

Situational agency recognizes the constraints on agency imposed by the material, social, and ideological structures within which coolie women had to negotiate their existence. One of the most significant of such constraints is temporal. Women whose personal safety, health, or survival was in doubt in the short term were in no position to prioritize long-term objectives such as those of the British imperial project or the Indian nationalist movement. Yet, by aligning themselves with the situational discourses emanating from such long-term projects, they could sometimes secure at least temporary relief from the oppressive situations in which they found themselves. *Situational agency*, therefore, was often the fleeting agency featured in the title of this book. Often, in such moments, the concerned individuals managed to escape victimhood in one instance only to find themselves subsequently victimized again. As the case studies in this book show, frequently, by risking action, oppressed individuals invited further oppression and hence their victimhood continued. Coolie women, while being victims of various forms of suppression and abuse, frequently chose to voice, sometimes explicitly and sometimes implicitly, the wrongs done against them, while being fully aware that by exhibiting such agency or efforts to negate others' agency, they could invite further violence and even death for themselves. The temporality of coolie women's escape from victimhood does not discount the fact that they chose to act despite the risks. *Fleeting Agencies* thus shows how individuals in oppressed situations often vacillated between agent and victim identities and at times even experienced both simultaneously. Such brief and episodic moments of agency, without transformative goals, can be best described as *situational agency*, wherein individuals use their agency to escape victimhood, even if only temporarily, with varying degrees of success. Such agencies were reflected not so much in challenging social order or colonialism, but rather in individual situational choices and in actions to negate the power of others over them for a brief period. Importantly, the fact that agencies were fleeting, episodic, and often motivated by short-term aims does not mean that they did not have long-term consequences which might extend far beyond the individuals involved. In fact, the actions of coolie women can be seen to have had significant long-term economic and political consequences for the modern postcolonial nations of Malaysia and India even if that was not their primary aim at the time. The term "situational agency," thus, captures the coexistence of traits of complicity, resistance, and "survivance" within an individual's agential act.[44]

Acknowledging the episodic and fleeting agency of subaltern individuals, which were often transitory and cyclical in nature, this study also emphasizes the co-existence and simultaneity of victimhood and agency, rather than considering them as mutually exclusive identities. In other words, it argues that the presence of agency or victimhood does not necessarily negate the other. As scholars like Sherry Ortner, Saba Mahamood, Indrani Chatterjee, Lila Abu-Lughod, Samita Sen, and Anindita Ghosh have shown, agencies become visible in uncelebrated spaces of everyday life and in such instances, agency may be a response to victimhood, meaning that the two have a complementary rather than a mutually exclusive relationship.[45]

Situational agency also allows us to acknowledge implicit means and modes through which an individual's agency comes to the surface. As mentioned earlier, another limiting aspect of the term "agency" is that, by emphasizing the act of doing, it acknowledges the efforts of the individual who acts but not those who choose to collaborate in performing the specific act. Historian Padma Anagol argues that the preoccupation of contemporary definitions of agency with purity and individual centeredness "is a dead-end question" that obscures agencies of many subaltern subjects, particularly women.[46] Recognition is long overdue to individuals who in oppressed situations expressed their agency implicitly and at times even through the explicit agency of others. For instance, some coolie women took advantage of flawed marriage-registration procedures in colonial Malaya and made efforts to escape abusive marriages or relationships with which they were dissatisfied. On eventually being caught by their husbands, however, they often presented themselves as victims of enticement by other men. They consciously took advantage of a biased colonial judiciary, which assigned agency entirely to men. In reality, an explicit act of "enticement" by an "other man" does not negate the implicit act of participation and collaboration by the concerned coolie woman.

Another feature that the concept of situational agency brings to light is situational collaborations between agents, which may or may not last. While participating in labor politics and demanding labor rights and benefits from oppressive planters and colonial administrators, coolie women collaborated with coolie men. In other instances, however, coolie women enlisted the aid of planters and overseers to discipline coolie men, particularly in cases of theft or physical hurt caused by the latter. There were also instances when coolie women collaborated with perpetrators to guarantee situational gains or escape unfavorable situations. This reality shows that agential collaborations were not necessarily permanent in nature; rather, they were often transitional alliances that coolie women crafted to fit their best interests as the situation demanded.

Broadening the definition and understanding of the term "agency," *Fleeting Agencies* thus revises biased presumptions that coolie women were merely passive victims in estate societies.[47] It addresses them as active members of the labor force, as household members, as members of estate society, as wives, as mistresses, and as political actors who crafted various strategies to ensure their survival or secure, often temporary, advantages. In focusing on gender relations amongst coolie women, it allows us to obtain a broader understanding regarding larger contexts of power relations, which can be applied to women and other subalterns, including underprivileged male subjects, children, and aged people living in conditions of structural constraint across time and space.

FINDING AND NARRATING A HISTORY OF COOLIE WOMEN

The attempt to reveal the stories of coolie women enforced the use of a variety of source materials as these women have been customarily underrepresented in records, archives, documents, and memoirs. Historians' choice of methodology remains influenced by how they choose to frame their questions, which influences both their selection of sources and how they choose to read the sources. Scholars who have denied that coolie women had a voice, and have represented the coolie women *only* as passive figures, did not choose to ask questions related to coolie women's presence in the archives, to their active engagement with colonial history in plantation colonies, or to the process of colonial labor migration. Rather, such studies have rendered coolie women as individuals who were outside such larger histories. As historian Elizabeth Kolsky has shown in her study of colonial justice in British India, what we choose to write influences how we write histories.[48] Many of the sources used here have also been used by earlier studies, but the different interpretations arrived at show how the intentions and approaches of historians shape the stories they write about past lives.

Weaving together the fragments of coolie women's lives from archives scattered across India (Chennai, Delhi, and Kolkata), Malaysia (Kuala Lumpur and Ipoh), Singapore, the United Kingdom (London) and the United States of America (Ithaca), I have explored everyday histories of colonial labor migration, the construction of stereotypical identity categories, and the ways migrants engaged with such stereotypes. Across the rich tapestry of case studies, one common thread appeared to link all the stories with each other: in their engagements with various actors, structures, and sociopolitical and economic contexts, coolie women constantly displayed situational agency. Like a dim and flickering light in a dark room, hints of coolie women's agency appeared, reappeared, and disappeared intermittently in the available archival records. Moreover, they appeared in less obvious and less visible spaces and through opaque discussions, which made them even more difficult to capture. Following the traces of coolie women's lives in a labyrinth of archival records, I felt like Alice going down the rabbit hole into a world where little was straightforward. Information concerning coolie women would often appear briefly in one department's file only to fade away within a few pages, if not paragraphs. Sometimes, changes in administrative structures within the British Empire resulted in sudden changes in document formats, which meant that I had to look for different kinds of documents in various departments to trace and retrace mentions of coolie women. Moreover, certain inconsistencies (sometimes deliberate and sometimes a result of carelessness) in filing information about subaltern subjects also meant that certain years of particular kinds of departmental records were found in Malaysia or India and other years in the United Kingdom. Fragments and silences, however, were not the only challenge I faced in this study; the sources were scattered in various forms of archives, various departmental records, and various geographical spaces, that is, they were scattered across archives in the United Kingdom, India, Singapore, and Malaysia.[49]

Most narratives in this book highlight incidents and episodes in coolie women's lives which do not offer us glimpses into the beginning and ending of their life histories. Furthermore, most of the incidents are accessed through narratives that coolie women did not themselves produce. If we look beyond the postcolonial gazes, however, we can create dialogues between voices present and voices absent in the archives, which allow us to imagine and explore innovative ways of thinking about histories of migration and Empire. This process of creation reveals a variety of paths to *decolonize* or *queer* history and explore the variegated stories that non-conventional sources and archival silences open up to historians.

An important decolonizing method was active engagement with the silences with which the archives often confronted me regarding coolie women's lives.[50] As historians Anjali Arondekar, James Francis Warren, Ann Laura Stoler, and Antoinette Burton have emphasized, historians need to read against the grain,[51] read the silences,[52] engage in "innovative investigative work"[53] to analyze past stories, and "re-define historical archives."[54] In this book, I piece together the fragments of coolie women's presences reflected through the "cracks"[55] of archival records, and show how these fleeting reflections help historians analyze the situational agency of coolie women within the constraints of gender, race, and class in estate societies.

Initially, my efforts to find documents relating to coolie women were frustrating, as these women had never been the focus of colonial or nationalist records, let alone of scholarship in Malayan or Indian history. As a result, I was soon made aware by the nature of the records themselves that to *find* these women I had to first *create* an archive which would enable me to negotiate my way around the voices and silences of a diverse range of sources. Creating an archive comprised the collection of fragments of material relating to coolie women from a diversity of official records, nationalist documents, newspapers, letters, and oral history recordings. However, locating these resources presented an additional challenge. I was dealing with materials some of which had been categorized as *destroyed archives*;[56] as a result of this I sometimes crossed time zones to access sources that offered no more than a few pages.

Whilst it was more difficult to find records on Malaya, especially records related to coolie women, compared to records from older colonies of the Raj like India, Fiji, and Mauritius, my research proves that it is not impossible. Limitations of colonial archives can often be mitigated either by the use of non-official archival records or, as Spivak prescribes, in situations where the subaltern's voice cannot be retrieved from the colonial archives and elite nationalist history records, subaltern histories can at least be "re-inscribed" through a critique of dominant historical representation.[57] There is no denying that research on coolie women was challenging: these women did not have the resources to leave their own records of struggle and were effectively silenced by the "privileging [of] men as main actors" in colonial archival records.[58] Furthermore, subaltern women's presence in the archives was recorded in the form of mediations by the colonial state. In other words, the most common images of coolie women that appear in the colonial archives are colonial stereotypical constructions, which present, at best, a partial and potentially distorted picture. These records were frequently framed to support colonial aims by highlighting the backwardness and uncivilized nature of the colonized society. As Spivak argues, subaltern women appear in colonial archives only when the colonial administrators deemed them necessary to produce a particular kind of idea about the colonized or colonial community.[59]

I have offset the fact that coolie women were not the focus of official records by using a variety of sources including censuses, migration reports, colonial correspondence, and various government department records—especially the reports of the Labor Department of Malaya, reports of the Prison and Crime Department in Malaya, the Health Department of Malaya records, annual reports of the Agent of the Government of India in Malaya, colonial law journals, newspapers, planters' memoirs, Indian lawyer S. N. Veerasamy's speeches at the bar,[60] oral history archives, and personal interviews with survivors of the period, some of whom were coolie women themselves, and their descendants. In drawing upon these diverse sources, I actively engaged with silences in the archives by placing various sources in dialogue with each other to illuminate histories of the coolie women of the period.[61]

Due to the range of aspects of coolie women's lives covered in the present study, the primary sources used for the book are multiple—within and between chapters. The first two chapters rely on migration records, census reports, labor department reports, labor committee reports, and official correspondences between the governments of India and Malaya. Chapters 3 and 4 draw mainly upon newspaper archives and records of judicial proceedings, which are put into dialogue with annual reports from the Crime, Prison, and Health Departments, Agent of the Government of India in Malaya, and reports of various committees appointed by the Colonial Office to enquire into the condition of overseas Indian laborers in various colonies. The fifth chapter is built upon oral history archives, memoirs, and personal interviews with ex-coolies, descendants of coolies, and others who witnessed the lives of coolie women during the Japanese occupation of Malaya.

CHARTING UNCHARTED HISTORIES

This study uses three stages of analysis in each chapter. First, an initial discourse analysis highlights popular memories and perceptions of coolie women, largely grounded in colonial and nationalist tropes. Next, each chapter creates a dialogue between the broad situations and contexts in which coolie women found themselves and the documented ways in which they responded to these situations. Finally, each chapter ends by analyzing how different contexts and moments in history conditioned and created opportunities for coolie women to exercise agency, often of a fleeting character which remained largely hidden in everyday life. This framework enables us to overcome essentialist depictions of coolie women as passive subjects or victims of colonialism, patriarchy, and war. Instead, it views coolie women and all other like-subjects in past and present societies as gendered agents who demonstrate the ability to deploy different forms of agency in varying degrees and through myriad modes and means, within different temporal moments of history.

The first chapter of this book describes the colonial backdrop against which the class of coolie women emerged, particularly in British Malaya. It outlines the sociopolitical and economic concerns that drove administrators and planters to transform their predominantly male labor recruitment policies by incentivizing female labor migration on which they ultimately came to depend. While such policies led to a more balanced sex ratio amongst Indian coolies, the percentage of women nonetheless remained less than that of men. Subsequent chapters illustrate how such an unbalanced sex ratio influenced colonial imagination and identification of coolies, and how coolie women and men imagined and made sense of such identities, and engaged with and articulated the boundaries of agency, gender, and ethnic categories. The chapter also analyzes the myriad push and pull factors in India and Malaya to explore what motivated coolie women to migrate.

Chapter 2 demonstrates the central place of coolie women within processes of labor production and reproduction on colonial rubber estates in Malaya. Although coolie women were not paid wages equal to coolie men, even when undertaking the same work, they were aware of their roles on the estates and they negotiated for what they considered to be their rightful compensation. The chapter explores how coolie women, as rubber tappers and weeders, consciously struggled, sometimes individually and sometimes in alliance with other coolie women, against the gendered labor regime, to ensure their labor rights were acknowledged by planters and plantation staff.

This chapter thus moves beyond the binary capitalist, gendered, and racial understanding of relationships between employer and employee. It considers the ways in which Indian coolie women used broader but gendered perceptions and understanding of health, morality, and vulnerability to influence employers and improve their situations. In the process, this chapter also explores everyday work on rubber estates as a space where coolie women, planters, and colonial administrators engaged with each other, although on unequal terms resulting from their differing situational agencies.

Chapter 3 turns to the domestic lives of coolie women. Colonial administrative reports and correspondences frequently construct Indian coolie households in plantation colonies, including Malaya, as chaotic spaces within which women are depicted as burdened and passive victims of skewed native patriarchy, while the men are presented as irresponsible and violent partners. Such sweeping depictions homogenized all coolie women into a single category of victims, and likewise all coolie men as perpetrators of abuse against their wives. Colonial constructions of coolie households and intimate relations amongst coolies disregarded the diverse designs of coolie households and the plethora of relations in which men and women within these households engaged. This chapter looks at the neglected intimacies and entrepreneurial adventures of Indian coolie households in British Malaya. It illuminates the struggles of women and men linked by complex marital and material partnerships. At the same time, it raises questions about the colonial purpose in exhibiting coolie households and judging coolies and the crimes committed within domestic spaces on the basis of a Victorian morality rooted in a material infrastructure providing privacy and firm family boundaries that was unavailable to the coolies. While violence periodically occurred in coolie households, it was not necessarily because of marital issues, nor were the perpetrators of violence always coolie men. Such generalized depictions silenced realities wherein both coolie men and women, as husbands and wives, often engaged in collaborative enterprises to ensure better living standards for their family. This chapter, thus, goes beyond the simplistic depictions of national and imperial histories to reveal the complicated nature of "domestic space" and intimacies of coolie households in the context of colonial estate societies.

Chapter 4 reconstructs the intimate lives of coolie women and revises predominant depictions of them, in colonial and nationalist discourses alike, as victims of moral failings. The cases settled by colonial courts in British Malaya often revolved around issues of gender, class, race, and colonial law. The discussion in this chapter is particularly oriented to understanding how coolie women reacted to stereotypical views of Indian women in colonial courts, and how, instead of challenging such tropes, they frequently appropriated gendered understanding of criminality in colonial law, as well as gendered social perceptions about coolie intimacies, to serve their own individual interests. The chapter provides detailed investigations of alleged offences committed by the husbands or partners of "deviant" women, and illustrates the factors influencing the attitudes of colonial courts, newspapers, members of the coolie community, and Indian nationalists toward such incidents. In seeking to escape unsuitable marriages or oppressive relationships, women exhibited fleeting signs of agency, but this was never acknowledged by either colonial administrators or nationalist leaders. On many occasions, however, coolie women capitalized on such gendered presumptions to escape social and legal consequences for their actions. Here, I challenge the conventional historical wisdom asserting that coolie women were entirely victims of enticement and violence by coolie men. Rather, I demonstrate that they acted consciously in crafting various intimacies in given situations and, when faced with social and legal consequences, they attempted to covertly influence the social and colonial infrastructures with their own gendered understandings of morality, immorality, vulnerability, and victimhood. In so doing, the chapter provides a nuanced and complex interpretation of social control as well as the agency of subjugated individuals in colonial plantation contexts.

Moving on to coolie women's roles and experiences in nationalist politics during World War II, Chapter 5 examines the lives of coolie women following the Japanese occupation of Malaya. The chapter considers the gendering of politics and martial strategies in times of war and explores the ways subaltern women negotiated these complex situations. It describes how and why coolie women in Malaya enlisted in the Rani of Jhansi Regiment (RJR) to fight British imperialism under the leadership of Subash Chandra Bose. The RJR is scarcely visible in the social memory of the Japanese occupation in Southeast Asia or of the activities of Subhash Chandra Bose on behalf of the Indian nationalist movement. The few memoirs that do exist were written by well-educated elite RJR veterans, and they celebrate a sense of unity among Indians from various backgrounds who supported Bose's efforts, including the soldiers who came to the RJR from working-class backgrounds in Malaya and Singapore. I challenge elite nationalist explanations of why coolie women joined Bose's nationalist movement and how they experienced the war. Using recollections from witnesses to and participants in the Indian nationalist movement in Japanese-occupied Malaya and Singapore, this chapter illustrates the importance of gender and socioeconomic boundaries in Bose's nationalist movement. It also argues that differences in class and caste estranged subaltern Indian coolie women from elite nationalist leaders during the occupation.

The Conclusion sums up the arguments developed in the preceding chapters, presents answers to the questions posed in the Introduction, and discusses the implications of these answers for the study of migrants and other marginalized or subordinated groups. The Conclusion is followed by a brief Epilogue, which relates the histories of coolie women explored in this book to the situation of female Indian agricultural laborers in contemporary Malaysia, thus demonstrating that such histories from below are not only matters of academic interest, but are vital in understanding the realities of life for marginalized groups in modern postcolonial contexts.

1

COOLIE WOMEN IN THE EMPIRE'S RUBBER GARDEN

HISTORICAL AND CONTEXTUAL BACKGROUND

As in all other plantation colonies, Indian labor migration to Malaya in the initial phase was primarily short-term and overwhelmingly male. It was clearly a period of "men moving," a term used by Eric Hobsbawm in his study *The Age of Capitalism* to describe the nineteenth-century cross-regional bulk movement of men, primarily of the laboring class.[1] This gendered migration to Malaya soon changed. Rising Indian nationalist movements highlighted the skewed gender ratio amongst laborers recruited from India, which they asserted was the cause of "immorality," including a range of social and moral vices, among Indian coolies overseas. Based on this argument, some nationalists pushed for a complete ban on overseas labor migration from India while others argued for a more balanced gender ratio.[2] Such nationalist voices led planters in Malaya to fear the loss of their regular labor source from India. British planters and administrators, therefore, promoted a gender-based strategy for labor recruitment, not merely to appease nationalists but, more significantly, to ensure a local means of reproducing labor in the future. Consequently, the fears of the planters led to an incentivized migration of coolie women and coolie families. Whilst the primary aim of this policy was to ensure a secure future labor supply, it was officially presented as establishing morality and ideal family life amongst overseas Indian laborers in plantation colonies, thus seeking to deprive nationalists of an emotive mobilizing issue by showing that their concerns were being addressed.[3] Indian women wishing to migrate out of India for a myriad of socioeconomic and cultural reasons often capitalized on such gendered incentivization of coolie migration. Even though many planters throughout Malaya valued coolie women both as laborers and as the source of future labor reproduction, which would decrease the planters' reliance on imported labor from India, plantation and migration lore has constantly celebrated coolie men and erased the narratives of coolie women.

This chapter investigates why colonial administrators and European planters in British Malaya promoted Indian coolie women's migration to Malaya and simultaneously reveals how coolie women themselves actively engaged with such opportunities. The chapter thus modifies the prevalent view presented in labor and migration histories concerning Indians in colonial Malaya, which presumes that the coolie women *only* migrated as dependents of migrating coolie men, thus discounting the choice of Indian women to migrate and become coolies. It focuses on coolie women who migrated to Malaya, with or without male relatives, as migrant laborers in their own right. Finally, this chapter provides the historical and contextual background crucial for understanding the everyday lives of coolie women on the estates, which is the subject of analysis in the chapters to follow.

THE LABOR CONNECTION BETWEEN INDIA AND MALAYA

Indian migration to Malaya began as early as eleventh century BC, although such migration was primarily transitory in nature and did not involve labor migration.[4] Regular migration and settlement of Indian labor in Malaya began only after Malaya became incorporated into the British Empire from the eighteenth century onward. The transition of Indian labor migrants from temporary sojourners to settlers commenced only in the late nineteenth century with the growth of the rubber industry in Malaya.[5]

Following the 1833 abolition of slavery within the British Empire, imperial economies underwent major transformations. Colonial capitalists and planters from the Empire's Caribbean colonies, whose output had dropped dramatically following abolition, became eager to engage in planting ventures elsewhere and their interest turned to the hitherto neglected fertile lands of Malaya.[6] Prior to the 1830s, Indian labor in Malaya primarily consisted of convict work-gangs, mostly from Bengal, who were sent to Malaya to serve their terms by laboring on railway and road construction sites.[7] Upon completion of their sentence, they were usually repatriated to India. Thus, no settled pool of Indian labor was available in Malaya. Most convict laborers were men. The first female convict, the only woman amongst 173 convicts, was shipped to Malaya in 1825. Within a few weeks, another woman was sent to Malaya amongst a group of 121 convicts.[8] In 1826, 80 convict men with 3 convict women were sent to Malaya. By 1865, there were 187 women convicts and 3,152 male convicts in Malaya.[9]

With the boom of the rubber industry in Malaya after 1900, planters began communicating with various recruiting agents in India to seek advice and help in recruiting Indian labor for their estates. Planters from Malaya soon realized, however, that they were late in entering the labor recruitment enterprise in India. By then, most established sources of labor in north India were already dominated by labor recruiters and agencies established by the older plantation colonies of Fiji, Suriname, British Guyana, Jamaica, and Mauritius. In 1902, W. T. Taylor, Colonial Secretary to Singapore, had written to R. P. Gibbes, the Trinidad Government Emigration Agency in Calcutta, seeking advice on Taylor's plan to set up an agency to recruit coolies in north India for the estates in FMS and the Straits Settlements (SS). Taylor, in this same letter, also requested Gibbes' agency to recruit for FMS and SS on behalf of Taylor and his agency. In his response, Gibbes wrote: "I regret that it would be not possible for this Agency to act on behalf of the Straits Government in addition to the Colonies which it already represents." Furthermore, Gibbes wrote that the competition for labor in north India was fierce and the chances of Malaya being able to recruit labor from north India were "very remote indeed." Gibbes explained that the great bulk of north Indian labor was already being recruited for Assam, Natal, Mauritius, Fiji, British Guyana, Jamaica, and even Dutch Guiana, and hence it would be impossible for agents from Malaya to find a place in labor-recruiting networks.[10] Colonial administrators and planters of Malaya, reading such signs of non-cooperation from other British colonial officers, were forced to look for other alternatives and hence turned to Madras, in south India. The geographical proximity of the Madras Presidency to Malaya kept travel time and associated costs for planters to a minimum. However, even in south India, other labor recruitment agencies had preceded them, recruiting for the jute industry in Bengal and the tea industry in Assam. Frequent correspondence between the United Planters Association of Malaya (UPAM) and the British Resident General in FMS during 1902 reflected the anxiety of planters at the stiff competition they faced in labor recruitment in India. In one such correspondence, E. V. Carey, the chairman of UPAM, wrote to the Resident-General, FMS, claiming that cheap tickets should be provided for coolies, who visit their villages and are eager to bring family and relatives to Malaya. He further insisted,

> Having before us the undoubted fact that the country is still very much understocked as regards to Tamil labor, it would appear to be impolitic to put any obstacles in the way of immigration if sufficient cause can be shewn [sic], for a departure from the orthodox system, in certain special cases.[11]

By seeking incentives for laborers to bring their families and relatives, the planters were aiming for a settled and reproductive labor population in Malaya so that they did not face perennial anxieties with regard to labor supply for their estates.

During the initial phase from 1833 onwards, most laborers migrated voluntarily and paid for their own passage to Malaya to seek work on coffee and sugar plantations. After the establishment of the Raj in 1858, the traffic in the Bay of Bengal was regulated by the Government of India, and voyages from India to Malaya became expensive. Consequently, laborers could no longer afford to pay for their own passage.[12] Following this, the indentured labor system, or, as Hugh Tinker calls it, the "new system of slavery," was introduced in Malaya to help rubber planters recruit laborers from India.[13] The indenture system came into force as early as 1834 in British colonies, following the abolition of the slave system. Under the indenture system of labor, the concerned coolie was indentured for three–five years to the employer who paid for his passage to the plantation colony. The planters either went to south Indian villages to recruit themselves or used agents in south India to recruit coolies to work for a predetermined number of years on estates in Malaya. The main sites of recruitment were markets, railway stations, and temples where the recruiters were reported to find vagrants and destitute subjects.[14]

Coolies arrived in Malaya in debt to their new employer for the cost of their tickets. This debt was discharged by labor. Fixed wages were paid to coolies under this system, but planters repeatedly extended the indebtedness period of laborers and simultaneously kept the wages of the laborers low. Consequently, coolies found themselves entrapped in debt and remained bonded to the planters for long periods.[15] While theoretically this was not slavery, in practice the experience of indentured coolies on estates resembled that of slaves. As the nineteenth century progressed, the indenture system came to be criticized, therefore, both by colonial administrators in India and other colonies who regarded it as inhumane and, toward the end of the century, by the growing Indian nationalist movement. High mortality rates amongst laborers and extensive abuse of power were the primary issues focused upon by critics.[16] The indenture system was abolished in Malaya in 1910 and was replaced with a *kangany* (meaning overseer or leader in Tamil) system, which became the only form of legal labor-recruitment process up until 1938.[17] In this system, a *kangany* or foreman, sometimes a laborer who had served at least three months on his employer's estate, was sent back to his village in south India and entrusted with the job of recruiting more coolies for the estate. The logistics of recruitment were paid for and the *kangany* was literally posed as a "walking exhibit" to aspirant coolies in his home village.[18] Upon gathering a gang of interested coolies, *kanganies* had to seek permission from the village *munsifs* (headmen) for the recruits to migrate overseas. Thereafter, these recruits had to be presented before the Emigration Commissioner and his staff at the depot for final health and eligibility screening. The *kangany* system was perceived as a more personal and "organized" system of recruitment, which was expected to eliminate concerns around the indenture system. Eventually, however, the *kangany* system too was critiqued by Indian nationalists, who alleged that it "always" used kidnapping and deceitful methods of recruiting coolies.[19]

NEED FOR COOLIE WOMEN ON ESTATES IN MALAYA

During the period of the indenture system, the rising volume of labor migration continued to be transient and male dominated. After the abolition of indenture, planters began to deliberately recruit women and families. Rubber planting, particularly tapping and weeding, required a large and reliable labor supply.[20] The transient, primarily male labor force, in place at the end of the indenture left European planters anxious regarding the future supply of laborers. Economic fluctuations, competition from recruiting agencies for other colonies, and an increasing political power struggle between the colonial governments of India and Malaya following their separation added to their concerns. Moreover, the development of an anti-colonial movement in India put pressure on the colonial Government of India to regulate unskilled labor migration from the country to the potential detriment of planters in Malaya. Consequently, planters felt the need for a locally settled Indian coolie population in Malaya, which would reduce their dependence on the *kanganie*s and the Government of India. As a result, planters began introducing gendered labor migration schemes for Malaya, whereby more women would be recruited as labor units and would also serve as the means for labor reproduction, thereby anchoring the previously transient labor force. Such gendered labor-recruitment policies were not a novelty initiated by the planters in Malaya. As Piya Chatterjee and Janaki Nair reveal in their studies, planters in tea plantations of Assam had previously used such gendered labor policies to ensure the availability of local labor.[21]

It is crucial to understand the various socioeconomic and political concerns of planters and administrators in Malaya that led to the recruitment of women and families to rubber estates, as these factors offer new textures to our understanding of the dynamics of gender-based labor migration policies within the British Empire. I here present a detailed examination of the economic issues, political issues, and inter-planter competition that led to new labor recruitment policies.

ECONOMIC CONCERNS OF PLANTERS

Because Malaya was closer to India than other plantation colonies, the return journey to India was affordable for coolies, and as coolies (primarily male during this phase) were not highly paid in Malaya, nor did they have any opportunity to establish a family, they had few incentives to remain. Consequently, most repatriated at the end of their three–five-year contracts. With every batch of returning migrants, the planters lost trained and experienced laborers. Although rubber tapping and weeding were not particularly skilled jobs, some training was essential to ensure efficiency in production. The transience of their labor force increased costs for planters, for whom the license fees for registering recruiters and the recruiting agents' own fees were ongoing costs, added to by the logistics involved in the recruitment process. Planters soon realized the unstable character of an overwhelmingly male labor force.[22] Consequently, the encouragement of female and family migration was seen by colonial planters and administrators as a means of ensuring a settled labor population in Malaya which would reproduce itself locally, obviating the need for ongoing recruiting costs.[23] In fact, once female coolies began settling in Malaya, child labor on estates became an increasingly visible sight on colonial plantations. Although by colonial law, no child under the age of sixteen years was to be formally recruited as a laborer; children were often found helping their parents by collecting rubber from latex-collection cups and cleaning them. Thus, growing up on the estates and watching others engaged in various estate work, coolie children developed skills and knowledge regarding estate work, reducing training expenses for planters. Issues of child labor and the effective entrapment of coolies in plantation life deserve attention as a separate project and hence are not taken up in this study.

POLITICAL CONCERNS OF PLANTERS

In addition to the economic factors contributing to the planters' desire for a more settled labor force, planters in Malaya also had pressing political concerns arising from inter-colonial governmental politics between British India and British Malaya. Since the establishment of the Raj, the Indian colonial government had heavily regulated labor recruiting and migration processes for Malayan plantations, placing both legal and logistical obstacles in the route of planters who, under East India Company rule, had long benefitted from being under the same administration. The Planters' Association of Malaya (PAM), which later came to be known as the United Planters' Association of Malaya (UPAM), began collectively lobbying through the Government of Malaya for more favorable treatment from the Indian government with regard to labor recruitment. Initially, PAM had some success in this regard. For instance, FMS and SS along with Ceylon continued to be exempted for a long period from the Indian government's gender restrictions on Indian emigration, enforced by the Indian Emigration Acts of 1864 and 1922,[24] whereas other colonies such as Fiji and Mauritius were strictly subjected to the Acts. But a trend for the

Indian government to become increasingly restrictive in allowing emigration of Indian laborers to plantation colonies alerted the planters in Malaya to the need to plan for alternative labor supplies. PAM knew well enough that they were largely at the mercy of an Indian government which had no need to respond to their concerns; hence, they saw the need to develop a labor supply within Malaya.

By 1917, planters in Malaya were well aware that they could not rely on the colonial administrators in British India being sympathetic to their labor needs. The Government of Madras, in 1917, had telegrammed the Colonial Office in London and the Rubber Growers' Association to inform them that from

> 1918 onwards in accordance of the India Act, the Government of India, as advised by its military authorities, considered it necessary that, in view of the large supply of Indian labor required for military purposes, the recruitment of all indentured labor should stop immediately and that the labor essentially required in Ceylon and the Federated Malay States should be reduced to the lowest minimum.[25]

Once this decision of the Government of India was communicated to colonial administrators and planters in Malaya, there began a series of requests from the High Commissioner of the Malay States to the Colonial Office in London for the Colonial Office to intervene to insist that the Government of India allow at least 82,000 laborers to be sent to Malaya every year. Both the Government of India and the Colonial Office balked at such numbers, however, and rather argued that the Government of Malaya should cooperate with India as the former had continuously received favorable treatment from India regarding the supply of Indian labor.[26] This clearly signaled to the planters and colonial administrators in Malaya that they had to fend for themselves in catering to the growing labor needs of the rubber industry.

During the 1920s and 1930s, the situation was made worse for planters in Malaya by a rubber slump which coincided with the rise of anti-colonial movements in India, demanding the absolute stoppage of emigration by unskilled Indian laborers to overseas colonies. In 1930, under pressure from Indian nationalists, the Government of India banned all unskilled labor migration to Malaya for a brief period. The Government of India argued that this was done to protect the interests of the Indian laborers in Malaya as the government had received reports from Malaya that, due to the economic depression, there was a significant fall in the standard of living of Indian laborers in the country. In these conditions, the only movement of unskilled laborers the Government of India was prepared to allow was assisted migration for those whose families were already in Malaya. Furthermore, from the early 1930s, the Government of India began signaling to Malaya that it would not be able to give any assurances with regard to future Indian labor migration. In particular, Malaya would no longer be exempted from Rule 23 of Indian Emigration Rules, which required one male labor migrant to be married and accompanied by his wife for every five single men migrating.[27] Again, in the May 16, 1934, meeting of the Indian Immigration Committee (IIC) of Malaya, it was highlighted by the chairman of the IIC that the Government of India had pressed for further changes in the emigration rules for unskilled labor to Malaya; the previous system under which only informal consent of the village headman was required was no longer deemed adequate.[28] Coolies now needed a documentary permit from the village headman to allow migration. The IIC was highly critical of this amendment, claiming that it would "unnecessarily" complicate the recruitment process. In response, the IIC proposed that the Government of Malaya write to the Government of India to inform them that planters in Malaya were maintaining the minimum wage for coolies on their estates and that as economic conditions were improving, those coolies who had returned to India were now contacting friends and authorities enquiring about when they could again migrate to Malaya. Being concerned about their future ability to recruit new coolies, the IIC was desperate to get back those coolies who had repatriated to India during the depression years. Although this issue was briefly addressed, the Government of India's reluctance to allow the emigration of coolies to Malaya continued until 1938, when they completely banned assisted emigration of unskilled labor. The main issues of debate between the IIC and the Government of India during this period were minimum wage and sex ratio. Rule 23 of the Emigration Rules regarding sex ratio was finally imposed on Malaya in 1936.[29]

The anti-colonial movement in India initially aimed for moderate reforms focused on alleviating poverty and socioeconomic ills of the colonial regime. The issue of Indian emigrants in overseas colonies of the Empire was not initially a priority for Indian nationalists, and barely featured amongst nationalist concerns until the early twentieth century. However, with M. K. Gandhi's involvement in the issues of Indians in South Africa and eventually in other colonies, a focus on the situation of labor migrants became a strategic means for nationalists to question the moral obligation of the colonial power toward its subjects. Thus, by the first decade of the twentieth century, the Government of India faced extreme opposition from growing anti-colonial public opinion centering on the abuses of the indenture system and the grievances of overseas Indian laborers.[30] As a result, the Government of India became anxious to emphasize its legitimate position as a paternalistic colonizer and tried to appear determined to secure fair treatment for overseas Indian laborers. Such efforts to restore legitimacy came at the cost of the interests of colonial planters and governments in other colonies.

TENSIONS AMONGST PLANTERS IN MALAYA

During the early twentieth century, as Indian nationalism within the country and around the world increasingly focused its protests against the indentured labor system, planters and colonial administrators in Malaya began experimenting with the *kangany* system. Significant numbers of planters wished to retain the indenture system, however, and voiced their concerns through various channels.[31] During debates in the Legislative Council of Malaya around the Labor Recruitment and Supply Bill of 1902, Mr Vermont, a planter of the Wellesley Province of British Malaya and a member of the Council, told the Council that he had personally experienced grave failures in recruiting coolies through the *kangany* system, and urged the Council to aid the planters to recruit more efficiently. In response, the Governor, presiding over the Council meeting, encouraged Mr Vermont to learn how to solve recruitment issues from the planters of the Pacific island of New Caledonia, where British coffee plantations had faced similar problems since the 1890s. In reply, Mr Vermont harped on the fact that "planters in Caledonia are billionaires" and that he was not.[32] *The Straits Times* published this debate soon after the Council meeting. Mr Carey, a planter from Selangor, in a letter responding to the debate in *The Straits Times*, argued that Mr Vermont's pessimistic remarks with regard to labor supply were unjustified as they were merely "his personal experience with coolie recruitment for his own estate in Province Wellesley." Mr Carey further claimed that he had experienced no problems in recruiting a good number of coolies from India through the *kangany* system and that this was the general experience of planters in Selangor. He added, "I see no sign of Tamil labor famine or any indication or fears to be expected in any given term of years."[33]

Mr Carey's response to the Council debate invited a longer discussion on the topic by other planters, amongst which the letter from Mr Gordon Brown (planter at Sungei Krudda estate, Perak) to the Editor of *The Straits Times* clearly reflects that there were a plurality of interests and opinions, resulting in brewing tensions between planters. In his letter, Mr Gordon Brown wrote:

Sir, I read with great interest your leading article on the cooly [*sic*] question on November 2nd. I noted you considered Mr. Vermont's remarks pessimistic, for Mr. Carey asserts that there is no difficulty in recruiting coolies for Selangor. Writing from Perak I find it most difficult to recruit coolies. I unfortunately have not got any of the well-fed, exhibition kanganies to send to India as a walking advertisement and so I have to deal with the professional recruiter. I have been trying to get sixty coolies since last January, I have only succeeded in procuring twenty-nine; though I took a trip over to India myself to facilitate matters.

I find my requirements are best suited with indentured coolies but I would be glad to get any species to go on with. I believe there is just now an actual stoppage of shipments of any coolies other than kanganies; these gentry should shortly be in great demand. I gave the kangany system a trial a few months ago but the selected individual has neither returned nor been heard of since. It is aggravating for us who feel the pinch so badly here, to learn that Mr. Carey sees no signs of a Tamil labor famine as Selangor is well off.[34]

Thus, planters who were not well-off like Mr Carey had more at stake if the colonial government refused to support their labor needs. Realizing this, the planters became all the more interested in anchoring the Indian labor force in Malaya, for which labor reproduction using Indian coolie women became absolutely essential. Moreover, with the Montague Chelmsford

Reforms of 1918[35] the colonial Government of India became visibly amenable to pressures from the Indian National Congress and this served as a clear signal to the Government of Malaya that the Government of India could not, or would not, continue to favor Malaya at the cost of the Indian people. In the 1920s, following the enactment of the Indian Emigration Act, 1922,[36] the governments of India and Malaya had an open disagreement regarding labor policies. In fact, there arose a series of debates in India as to whether emigration of Indian unskilled labor to Malaya should be allowed at all after March 1923. Subsequently, the Government of Malaya's anxiety regarding the regular flow of Indian labor to Malaya was expressed in the correspondence between the two governments. Planters and recruiters from Malaya began to lobby, making anxious pleas along with public comments through various channels in support of an uninterrupted labor supply from India. For instance, a recruiter from Malaya, in his letter to the Editor of *The Straits Times* in 1922, expressed his and the planter community's discontent by stating that the 1922 Act was "extremely unfavorable for recruiting" and that "the PAM rightly stigmatized the Act as sinister." Appealing for the unrestricted immigration of unskilled Indian laborers into Malaya, he even argued that such migration was not only advantageous for Malaya but brought advantages to the Indian laborers and India too and hence should be allowed to continue.[37] Finally, in 1923, Malaya (inclusive of FMS, Unfederated Malay States [UFMS], and SS) came under the Act's stipulations. Although Indian emigration to Malaya was not completely banned, the Government of Malaya was forced to amend the prevalent Labor Code in Malaya in line with the Act in order to be assured of labor supply from India.

ADDRESSING LABOR CONCERNS THROUGH PLANNED GENDERED LABOR RECRUITMENT

Given the labor supply insecurities arising from the aforementioned socioeconomic and political factors, the eagerness of planters to secure a locally settled pool of Indian laborers came as no surprise. Planters, from the early 1900s, began to encourage recruitment of coolie women as laborers and by 1910 there was clear collaboration between colonial planters and colonial administrators in Malaya to ensure increased immigration of working-class

Indian women.[38] As mentioned earlier, such gendered labor policies were justified by the colonial Government of Malaya's interest in providing a more balanced sex ratio in the plantation colonies to improve the quality of social life amongst labor-class Indians. This policy enabled the Government of Malaya to respond positively to pressure from Indian nationalists and the colonial Government of India, whilst also moving to end Malaya's dependence upon India for labor.

The census reports during 1901–1931 clearly record the growth of colonial interest in encouraging Indian women's migration.[39] G. T. Hare, the superintendent of the 1901 census for British Malaya, reported in the 1901 census that the increase in Tamil females had been "most remarkable" in the years between 1892 and 1901, and that the 1901 census recorded an approximate increase of 231 percent since the last census. Hare, expressing a positive view of Tamil women's migration to Malaya, remarked, "It is hoped that the Tamil female population and immigration will improve in the future years as Tamil females are adapt [sic] to agricultural work and have no difficulty in getting employment in Malaya. The importation of Tamil families should therefore be encouraged as much as possible...."[40]

Migration of coolie women was also promoted by the Labor Department of FMS, which asserted that Indian coolie women made an excellent source of labor. In 1910, C. W. Parr, Commissioner for Labor in FMS, in his report of the Commission Appointed to Enquire into the Conditions of Indentured Labor in the Federated Malay States, stated, "Steps should be taken to encourage the immigration of women .... employers should be encouraged to import as many women as possible. Women are said to work well and to make excellent tappers...."[41]

The need for female labor became so crucial for the colonial enterprise that *kanganies* were regularly given infrastructural aid to ensure that they recruited more single female coolies by being paid extra for every woman they recruited. The Superintendent of Indian Immigration at SS and FMS, L. H. Clayton, noted in his annual report of 1908, "Recruiting allowance for a male coolie recruited by a kangany was $3.00 whereas for a woman coolie it was $3.50."[42] It is telling that even though women were paid lower wages than men as workers, the planters paid more to recruit them. This hints at how crucial coolie women had become for the survival and success of the rubber estates in Malaya.

Three years later in 1911, A. M. Putney, the superintendent of the 1911 census for British Malaya, in his review report of the 1911 census, emphasized the need to increase the number of women migrating to Malaya. He insisted, "The sex ratio disparity amongst the immigrant communities were disconcerting for the Government of Malaya."[43] He even advised administrators and planters to focus specifically on improving the sex ratio of coolie-class Indians. In the same spirit, J. E. Nathan, the superintendent of the 1921 census of British Malaya, in his report on the 1921 census observed: "Both planting community and the government have long recognized the desirability of lessening the disparity between the sexes among estate-laborers and coolies recruited from India and they are being encouraged to bring their wives and families to FMS."[44]

From 1928 to 1930, the rubber industry in Malaya experienced a major slump and various studies suggest that most laborers tended to return to India during such slump periods. Hence, the 1931 census can be used as a litmus test to judge the success of colonial initiatives with regard to anchoring the Indian estate labor population in Malaya. Superintendent C. A. Vlieland, in his report on the 1931 census, argued, however, that the popular idea that there was a marked exodus of Indian Tamil labor from Malaya during slump years was a myth caused by "overestimation." He explained that the estate population of Tamils remained more or less the same compared to pre-slump years and that the estimated decrease was only 1.86 percent. He further hinted that the exodus of Tamils of other classes and of Ceylon Tamils could have been misinterpreted as including Tamil estate laborers too.[45] Vlieland's arguments are supported by vagrancy reports of FMS during 1930–1935, which suggest that many Indian coolies, particularly Indian coolie families were not allowed to leave Malaya during the slump period. Rather, they were left to their own devices or locked up in vagrant asylums. Arguably, planters may have collaborated with administrators in Malaya to keep coolie families in the country in anticipation of a market recovery, in order to avoid increased recruitment costs during the recovery.[46]

The censuses from 1911 to 1931 clearly show a constant improvement of the Indian Tamil coolie sex ratio. The total percentage of Indian women coolies on estates rose from 23 percent in 1901 to 35 percent in 1921 and over 39 percent in 1931 (see Table 1.1). Nonetheless, throughout the colonial history in Malaya, there remained a constant sex ratio imbalance amongst Indians. But to make

Table 1.1 Indian male-to-female ratio on FMS rubber estates (1911–1931)

Year	Indian Male-to-Female Ratio
1911	3:1
1921	1.8:1
1931	1.5:1

Source: Compiled and calculated from: *The 1911 Census of British Malaya; The 1921 Census of British Malaya;* and *The 1931 Census of British Malaya.*

a fair assessment of the situation it needs to be acknowledged that sex ratio imbalance was a marked problem amongst all immigrant communities, especially amongst estate populations, and when compared to other groups, the sex ratio of the Indian community was the most balanced. This suggests that Indian nationalist pressure on the issue was effective in producing significant policy responses.

COOLIE WOMEN AND CALLS FROM THE EMPIRE'S RUBBER GARDEN

Most studies of coolie labor migration, whether on the indenture or the *kangany* system, not only focus on male migration, but also over-generalize the recruitment and migration process as one characterized by kidnapping and fraudulent recruitment of laborers.[47] In reality, for many laborers, migration was seen as a positive alternative to unemployment, hunger, family problems, and caste prejudices in their homeland. Whilst there were instances when coolies were indeed duped and kidnapped by recruiters, the fact remains that there were many others who willingly and consciously chose to migrate hoping that the new host society would offer better employment conditions and prospects than what they were leaving behind.

Coolie women have been widely portrayed in colonial and nationalist discourses either as appendages to their coolie husbands who followed their men, or as victims of kidnapping or false promises by recruiters. Neither of these depictions does justice to the variety of reasons motivating coolie women to migrate or the spectrum of their experiences of migration. Some women migrated alone, some as contractual wives, and some as coolie wives. Their personal situations and motivations could vary greatly: some wished to escape family quarrels, some were widows mistreated by relatives and society, some were involved in prostitution. Such stories seldom made it to the archives, primarily because recruiters sought to hide such facts about their recruits' background during the coolie registration process at the ports of disembarkation, as, due to initiatives of the colonial Government of India, the Protectors of Emigrants might prevent such women from migrating and if they were found to be eloping, then they would be sent back to their families.

Colonial discourses represented coolie women as appendages to their men for two reasons. First, to avoid responsibility for allowing the supposed kidnapping or fraudulent recruitment of women and, second, to justify paying coolie women lower wages than coolie men (see Chapter 2) as they were presumed to be married to wage-earning coolie men. Indian nationalists, on the other hand, seeking to emphasize the victimhood of coolie women at the hands of the colonial power, always presented coolie women as victims of fraudulent lures and kidnapping by labor recruiters. Scholars of Indian and Malayan history who focus only on this coercion theory of recruitment effectively accept the erasure of the agency of coolie women propagated by both colonialists and anti-colonialists. They fail to recognize that, for many coolie women, migration to Malaya was a conscious decision viewed as a positive alternative, sometimes the only alternative, to adverse conditions at home which might range from hunger to abusive or unhappy marriages or a disgraced life as a *devadasi*[48] or a widow in a caste-prejudiced society. As Shobna Nijhawan establishes in her recent study of Indian women nationalists and the politicization of indentured labor issues, Indian women nationalists such as Nandrani Nehru and Savitri Devi argued that all coolie women recruited from India for the plantation colonies were victims of deceit and fraud. In examining cases of coolie women who escaped home out of choice, Nijhawan proves that these nationalist assumptions were highly problematic,[49] disregarding that many women chose to voluntarily migrate to escape socioeconomic conditions.

In fact, economic conditions in India, particularly in famine-ridden Madras, and the constant social problems arising from the caste and gender structures of Indian society under British rule, seemed to favor the planters by creating ample reasons for migrants to leave. Women of different age, caste, class, marital status, and geographical location migrated for a broad range of different reasons, and their life situation also influenced their experiences during and after migration to Malaya. Moreover, each coolie woman, whether migrating as wife, mistress, or single woman, responded in unique ways to the complex situations and relations in which she found herself. Thus, categorizing all these migrant women as "dependents" accompanying male relatives is clearly not in accord with the evidence of a broad range of migrants and situations.

Push factors such as famine or abusive social systems are insufficient to account for the varied reasons for which many coolie women, especially single women, migrated to Malaya. While some coolie women migrated as "coolie wives" (either as genuine wives or as contractual wives to migrating coolie men: a status discussed later), there were many others who migrated alone to escape abusive marriages, family quarrels, or lives as widows or prostitutes. Abbe Dubois, a French missionary in Tamil Nadu in the late eighteenth century, opined that the position of women in south Indian society was no better than that of slaves, who were expected to satisfy the physical needs and desires of men. He further noted that during the colonial period, it was a regular scene to witness Tamil women being beaten by their husbands and in-laws, and if ever she managed to escape to her father's house, she would be sent back to accept the marital authority of her husband over her. Dubois also opined that being a widow without a son was the worst possible situation for women. Due to the prevalence of child marriages, many young girls were married off to elderly men, and as a result they would become widows at a very young age. If they had not borne a child by then, they were looked down upon and treated with "scorn."[50] While Dubois writes about the social position of women in the eighteenth century, various scholars have presented similar views of women's situation in nineteenth- and twentieth-century southern India. For instance, the social historian P. Subramanian notes that the position of women during the nineteenth and twentieth centuries in south Indian society was more deplorable than that in the rest of India. He argues that this was due to strict adherence to the caste system, which further deteriorated with the Mughal invasions. Subramaniam claims that, to protect their culture from outside influences,

Tamils emphasized their cultural uniqueness through customs such as sati and practices of caste distinction. He insists that the status of a woman after her marriage was just like that of a Shudra in the caste-divided society, having no rights but only duties toward men.[51] Although these generalizations may well be exaggerated depictions of the situations of colonized women of a type frequent in colonial narratives, nevertheless, they were based, to some degree, in reality. It was true that there were a large number of widows and *devadasi*s in Madras during the late nineteenth century. The Census of Madras Presidency of 1891, a period well before migration to Malaya began, records around 20 percent of the total population in Madras as widows.[52] Such social conditions seem to have changed little for women in Madras up until the 1930s. For instance, the *Manifesto of Madras Devadasis* in 1927 reported that there were 20,000 *devadasi*s in Madras alone.[53] The fact that widows and *devadasi*s were not treated well in Indian society remains unquestioned; such issues still arise today. It seems probable that for widows and *devadasi*s in Madras, the need for labor in Malaya offered the hope of a better life free of the restrictive customs of Tamil Nadu.

Concurrently, during the 1920s and 1930s, social movements in south India sought to "emancipate" the "backward castes," and issues around women featured as popular concerns for these movements. The Self-Respect Movement became one of the most popular amongst south Indian lower castes, especially Tamils. Launched in 1925 by E. V. Ramasamy, better known as Periyar, the movement encouraged members of the socially and economically "lower" castes of south India, especially women, to move beyond the caste identities and cultural boxes in which they were placed by Brahmins through the exploitative caste system. Periyar, while focusing his movement amongst the non-Brahmin and lower castes of India, propagated female education, widow remarriage, and women's right to inherit property. He even propagated the idea of women's right to desert a relation and their marriage if they were not happy with it, and also promoted the idea that women had the right to "birth control" (by removing their uterus) and the right to decide whether they wanted to play a reproductive role at all.[54]

The popularity of the Self-Respect Movement and its ideals amongst the lower-caste masses suggest that women of these castes were likely to have been influenced by ideas of being able to assert their rights and control their lives and marriages. Periyar's movement focused on the districts of Madura,

Tanjore, Trichinopoly, Arcot, Salem, Chingelput, and Coimbatore, amongst others, which were the districts wherein the majority of the lower-caste masses resided.[55] Not coincidentally, these were also amongst the most popular districts for recruitment of coolies for Malaya, making the conjecture that some migrant coolie women were influenced by the ideals of this movement not unlikely.

While exact figures are unavailable in the archives, the eventual and considerable increase in the number of single coolie women and coolie families migrating to Malaya led to the appointment, by the colonial Government of Malaya, of lady inspectors on board ships, to chaperone Indian coolie women migrating alone across the *kala pani* or "dark waters." In 1925, Mr Mukarrains, the Honorary Commissioner for the Depressed Classes in Straits Settlement and Federated Malay States, highlighted in his *Report on the Traffic between South Indian and Malayan Ports* the importance of the regular appointment of "lady inspectors," as no woman from India was keen to travel overseas without a "leader." He further acknowledged that throughout 1925, lady inspectors were seen on board ships from south India to Malaya to help and guard the women passengers travelling alone. They were appointed by the Department of Immigration and the salary was 200 rupees per month.[56] Although neither census nor migration records are detailed enough to inform us how many single women migrated to Malaya from south India, these appointments confirm the significant numbers of such women migrating during the 1920s and 1930s. Another indication of the increase in single women migrants is that the Protectors of Emigrants at the ports of Negapatnam and Madras (Avadi) often detained single coolie women, who were brought to the ports close to the ensuing shipment date, and held them until the next shipment. This was done to ensure that if or when the relatives of such women came in search of these women, the concerned women could be returned.[57] This effort by the colonial Government of India clearly came as a result of the increased politicization of the coolie recruitment issue by Indian nationalists in order to question the moral obligation of the colonial power toward its subjects. Nonetheless, the fact that there were sufficient single coolie women migrating to justify such measures suggests that many women were deploying situational agency to seek better lives than those they enjoyed in south India. There was, of course, no guarantee that by escaping the adversities at home, coolie women would necessarily find better socioeconomic conditions in Malaya, but this study emphasizes that by making the effort to better their situation, these women demonstrated the situational agency which colonial and anti-colonial discourses denied them, even if such fleeting agency might only lead to escaping one situation of oppression before being threatened by another.

Also relevant to the independence of coolie women was the fact that not all women who were enlisted as "married" coolie women accompanying their coolie husbands were in reality married to them, or married at all. Historian Frank Heidemann, in his study of the *kangany* system of recruitment for Malaya and Ceylon, argues that *kanganies* had considerable influence on the social relations of coolies, as they used to create alliances between coolie men and coolie women to manage the shortage of the latter on Malayan estates.[58] When recruiting coolies, Heidemann explains, *kanganies* often "connived them" to become "coolie husband and wife" in front of the immigration officers, who thereafter would allow them to live in such intimate arrangements "as regular as any other union." Such contractual marriages were known as *cert-k-kolu-tal* (joining together in a play).[59] The actual number of married couples migrating is questionable, then, since the term "married" in migration records could have a variety of meanings in real life. *Kanganies* made use of the contractual marriage system to increase the number of coolie women migrating, since they were paid extra by planters for recruiting women.[60] Moreover, such marriages were again reflective of the coolie women's exercise of choice in agreeing to the arrangement suggested by recruiters. These conditions could be restrictive of autonomy but did not extinguish it altogether. For women who had previously been abused wives or widows, such arrangements may have been an opportunity to seize life afresh. Such unions, then, were episodes of autonomy, wherein coolie women were able to exercise some control over their lives and those of others. Examples of such cases are discussed in details in Chapter 4, which explores how such port marriages influenced the later lives of coolie men and women in Malaya.

Interestingly, the Labor Commission (composed of Mr N. E. Marjoribanks, Mr Khan Bahadur, and A. K. G. Ahmed Tamby Marakkayar) appointed by the Government of Madras (1916) to visit the Malay Peninsula to review the condition of Indian labor reported that most south Indian workers coming into Malaya usually did not bring their womenfolk from India, but developed contract alliances locally.[61] They also reported that while most women coolie migrants to Malaya were married women accompanied by their husbands, some were "no doubt prostitutes."[62] In fact, as early as 1907, while registering a government order in colonial India regarding Indian migration to Ceylon and Malaya, it was claimed, "No Tamil women can go to the Federated States of Malaya and return with a rag of reputation left."[63] Thus, in the absence of marriage registration norms in India, the marriage of coolie couples migrating to Malaya was questionable from the start.

Further, the women who migrated as "coolie wives" were not limited to being merely domestic partners. Rather, they were made aware that they were being recruited as coolies, to work on estates alongside the men. Under pressure from Indian nationalists, the colonial regime made considerable efforts to ensure that coolie recruitment was a fair process, making it mandatory that coolie men and women, whether migrating alone or as couples, proved their knowledge about their ensuing employment, expected tasks, and wages, when Protectors of Emigrants interviewed them at the ports.[64] So, while some duping and bribery may have persisted, women migrating as coolie wives were generally made aware of the socioeconomic role that they would play upon arrival.

(RE)CONCEIVING INDIAN COOLIE WOMEN'S MIGRATION HISTORY

This chapter has shown that contrary to stereotypes, neither were all coolies male nor were coolie women always wives or dependents of their male relatives. Rather, it highlights that female coolies had a range of interests and experiences in the recruitment and migration process. Instances of women laborers consciously choosing to migrate coexisted with instances of women being kidnapped or tricked into migration. This variety in experiences of coolies in the recruitment and migration process also influenced their lives and social position in estate society on arrival. Though a coolie woman's choice to migrate was often made under extreme social or economic conditions, the fact that many coolie women exhibited a reasonable conscious act of decision-making cannot be discounted.

2

"TAPPING" RESOURCES

(RE)FIGURING THE LABOR OF COOLIE
WOMEN ON ESTATES

We tapped, weeded and made rubber. We made this land the *rubber king*!
But it is we who are forgotten.

—Pachaimmal,
former coolie woman on Sungai Buaya estate, 2011[1]

This is how Pachaimmal chooses to remember the contribution she and other
coolie women made to the rubber industry in British Malaya. Sharing the
pain of anonymity and lack of acknowledgment, Pachaimmal's words serve
as a reminder of the experiences and crucial role of coolie women as laborers
on rubber estates. Even a cursory glance at relevant administrative reports
dealing with Indian labor in Malaya, including the annual reports of the Labor
Department of the Malayan government,[2] show that female coolies were
counted and recorded as individuals whom the planters employed as laborers
in their own right and not as parts of family units. Every coolie woman
featured individually on estate payrolls with their own wages according to the
labor they produced for the estates. But this crucial aspect of coolie women's
identity usually remains silenced in both colonial and Indian nationalist
discourses concerning estate labor in British Malaya. Rather, both planters'
memoirs and Indian nationalist literature, which have become primary
sources for understanding coolie societies, highlighted only the victimhood
of coolie women, whether in relation to abuse by coolie men or capitalist and
colonial exploitation. While administrative records were accessed primarily by
government officials, memoirs and other colonial literature, such as newspaper

articles as well as nationalist literature, were accessible to the public, making them much more influential on public imaginations. Undeniably, these depictions portrayed certain realities of estate life, but in leaving out the agency of coolie women, they also left out many shades of these women's experiences and many dimensions of their identities.

Before progressing, it will be worthwhile to gauge a few examples of the representation of coolie women in popular colonial and nationalist discourses concerning British Malaya. Planters or plantation staff, in their memoirs and novels, often portrayed coolie women as dehumanized objects and, in other instances, described them as victims of coolie men or *kanganie*s, who, according to the planters, treated coolie women ruthlessly.[3] These narratives conveniently left out the role of planters in abusing and exploiting coolie women, but they also left out any explicit discussion about the importance of the active role of coolie women as laborers on estates.[4] In his narrative, Pierre Boulle, a technician on rubber plantations in Malaya, 1936–1939, recorded the crude and verbally abusive behavior of a *kangany* towards a coolie woman under his supervision, "The *kangani* shouted 'Whore!' ... Munniammah bowed her head, covered with confusion and encumbered by her tools and her bag which hampered her movements.... The *kangani* called her a clumsy sow and once again a whore...."[5] Another planter, Leopold Ainsworth, in his memoir expressed his disgust at the appearance of the coolie women laboring on his estate, describing them as "smelly, sweaty" and "uncivilized." He goes on to give a dehumanizing description of such women as "drab, musty-smelling, human weeding machines."[6] It is these readily available but dehumanized and sexualized depictions of coolie women that tend to appear in academic studies, both past and contemporary, rather than the view of women as independent workers and vital economic actors that can be fleetingly glimpsed through such descriptions.[7]

Indian nationalists too, in order to serve their political interests and goals, chose to depict coolie women as frequently abused victims of planters and the colonial administration. Scholars like Sobhna Nijhawan, Madhavi Kale, Ashwani Tambe, Brij Lal, John Kelly, Ashrufa Faruqee, and Gail R. Pool have closely analyzed the politicization, by Indian nationalists, of European planters' abuse of Indian coolie women in Fiji, Mauritius, and British Guyana.[8] These studies have explored how such depictions of coolie women became instrumental in shaping not only the national movement of India but also the salient conceptions of coolie women in plantation colonies.[9] While these studies are invaluable in helping us understand the suffering of the coolie women and the politicization of such experiences, there remains much scope to explore other aspects of the coolie women's lives, roles, and experiences on the estates.

Rarely have scholars of Indian labor history, particularly in Malaya, addressed how the heavily biased representations of coolie women, as "dependents," secondary laborers, or victims in both colonial and nationalist discourses, may have influenced their assessment of coolie women's roles and experiences in Malaya.[10] I suggest that scholarly views to date have been limited as a result of insufficiently critical readings of terms like "victim," "dependent," and "primary" and "secondary" laborers, which appear in planters' memoirs, newspapers, nationalist literature, and administrative records: all literature serving specific agendas which were usually not those of coolie women. Many scholars have failed to acknowledge that these terms do not necessarily have fixed definitions and have often been used differently in different contexts by administrators, planters, or nationalist writers. In other words, these terms have been situational in their definitions. Uncritical acceptance of such terms leads to an understanding of identities as fixed categories rather than products of specific relations that can easily change depending on the situations in which they are found. A more critical reading can bring out the nuances hidden in definitions of dependence, dependents, and secondary laborers. Therefore, in considering the archival records, this study focuses on the importance of assessing who was using certain terms or phrases and in what contexts. In so doing, it exposes presences and silences in the archives that can reveal aspects of coolie women's lives, labor, and engagement with estates which less critical readings leave occluded.

Studying the myriad contributions and experiences of coolie women as individual laborers on estates not only allows us to (re)figure coolie women in colonial history, but also allows us to capture many nuances of colonial labor history that otherwise remain hidden. In addressing the aforementioned themes, this chapter weaves a tapestry of intriguing case studies to shed light on the diverse contributions and experiences of coolie women as laborers on estates. Whilst each case study is unique, all reveal ways in which coolie women understood their roles and rights as laborers: an understanding on which they based their engagement with various actors and institutions within estate society.

The chapter first explores the multiple roles of coolie women on rubber estates and how they have been recorded. In the light of this investigation, it goes on to demonstrate that categories such as "independent" or "dependent" are rarely self-evident or fixed. Rather, it shows how such categories are situational, maneuverable, and remain in a state of fluidity. Finally, it examines the attempts of coolie women to negotiate their rights as laborers, both individually and collectively, with the various authorities on the estates on which they worked. In the process, it shows how women's active participation in the labor force enabled them to gain knowledge about their roles and rights, which they then deployed to make demands, maneuver for position, and negotiate their interests.

PRODUCING AND REPRODUCING LABOR

Before presenting a detailed analysis of the ways conceptions of the dependency of coolie women were deployed in the discourses of colonialists and Indian nationalists, I first describe what these discourses tend to leave out: the actual work in which coolie women engaged. In this section, I show how coolie women were valued for their roles as laborers as well as for their role in reproducing the labor force by planters and colonial administrators alike.

PRODUCING LABOR

Coolie women in Malaya engaged in all types of tasks on the estates and were not restricted to any particular job.[11] Both coolie men and women engaged in all segments of the rubber production process: from weeding and tapping to creping rubber in factories. There is no evidence of any significant gendered division of labor. However, while the work on the rubber estates of Malaya was not gender-exclusive, pay remained gendered.

To understand the lives of plantation workers, it is necessary to understand the rubber production process. As noted in Chapter 1, rubber production depended heavily on a constant labor supply. The initial phase of production required thorough clearing of jungle or undergrowth from the land. After the rubber seeds or saplings were planted, a constant and careful process of oversight followed which required regular and consistent weeding and fertilizing of the immature rubber plants. Rubber trees take approximately six–seven years to mature and must have a trunk diameter of at least 6 inches before they can be tapped for latex: the liquid milk from which industrial rubber is manufactured. During these six–seven years, weeding and fertilizing were the main tasks on a rubber estate. Upon maturation of the trees, rubber estates required a complex number of simultaneous tasks—weeding, tapping, and factory work. While weeding does not necessarily require much skill, tapping does. Tapping is the process through which latex is harvested by carefully slicing a groove into the bark of the tree in a downward spiraling pattern (see Figure 2.1). These slices have to be carefully made at a depth of a quarter inch using a hooked knife to peel back the bark, at the same time being mindful not to go too deep to ensure the core of the tree is not harmed. Usually only one side of the tree is tapped at a time to allow the opposite side to heal, rendering it ready to be tapped in the next iteration. Tapping skill is also crucial in terms of the amount of latex that can be drawn from each tapping. If tapping is done carefully and with skill, a tapped panel can yield latex for up to five hours. Thus, upon maturation of rubber trees, tapping became one of the most crucial and prized jobs on the estates. Once rubber was successfully tapped, the liquid rubber was quickly transported to factory shops (Figure 2.2) on the estates to manufacture rubber sheets (Figure 2.3) from the liquid latex by passing the liquid through various acids and thereafter passing them through rollers and finally smoking them into sheets. These rubber sheets would then be sold in the world market.

I now turn to coolie women's place in these various tasks on rubber estates.

Weeding

Most studies of colonial rubber estates in Malaya erroneously record coolie women as casual laborers engaged primarily in weeding activities. The impression is often given that coolie women were secondary laborers and that weeding was relatively less important than other estate work. In reality,

TAPPING A RUBBER TREE,
MALAYA

Figure 2.1 Indian coolie woman tapping a rubber tree in Malaya, 1900
Source: Lim Kheng Chye Collection, courtesy of National Archives of Singapore.

weeding was as crucial as tapping on rubber estates, especially during the months with heavy rainfall and particularly when rubber plants were young.[12] Weeding ensured the survival of young rubber plants as weeds frequently competed with them for nutrients from the soil and interfered with the plant's root system.[13] In 1906, the Director of Agriculture of FMS reported

Figure 2.2 Rubber tappers carrying pails of latex from estate to factory in Malaya, 1900

Source: Lim Kheng Chye Collection, courtesy of National Archives of Singapore.

that weeding costs during the rubber planting and growing years were the most important and most expensive labor costs on estates, amounting to an expenditure of at least two British Malaya dollars (hereafter dollars) per month per acre.[14] Even after reaching maturity, rubber trees required daily weeding to ensure healthy growth, which in turn ensured quality rubber milk

Figure 2.3 Coolies working in a rubber factory, 1900

Source: Ministry of Information and the Arts Collection, courtesy of National Archives of Singapore.

production. Furthermore, as rubber plantation historian Colin Barlow notes, on some estates the intensity of weeding became more important, depending on the climate, and the chances of disease or infection of the immature rubber seedlings. Barlow also notes that the initial phase of weeding involved heavy tasks of clearing jungle, which were entrusted to coolie men, and lighter tasks of fertilization and maintaining the health of newly planted rubber saplings, which were given to women.[15] While this was the case in Malaya in the initial phases, visible gendered differences in weeding tasks disappeared after the initial clearance. Consequently, weeding jobs were not exclusive to coolie women in Malaya: both men and women were enlisted as weeders on estates. Upon maturation of rubber trees, however, the wages offered for weeding tasks were lower than those for tapping tasks. Hence, coolies, both women and men, often worked double shifts as tappers in the morning and weeders in the afternoon.[16] While women and men were expected to complete the same amount of weeding per day, gendered pay structures resulted in coolie women being paid less than male coolies for the same jobs (see Table 2.1).

Table 2.1 Daily wages (in cents) of Indian weeders on FMS rubber estates (1918–1936)

	Perak		Selangor		Negri Sembilan		Pahang	
Year	Men	Women	Men	Women	Men	Women	Men	Women
1918	For men: 27–30; For women: 20–25							
1925	45	35	35–40	30–35	35—40	30–35	45–50	40–45
1926	40–50	30–35	40–50	30–40	40–50	30–40	50–55	45–50
1927	40–50	30–45	40–45	30–40	40–50	30–40	55–60	45–50
1928	40–50	30–45	40–45	30–40	40–50	30–40	50–65	40–50
1929	50–65	40–50	50–55	40–45	50–55	40–45	50–65	40–50
1930	40	32–40	40	32–40	40	32–40	40	32–40
1931	30–35	25–30	30–35	25–30	30–35	27–32	35–47	30–37
1932	25–30	22–25	25–40	22–32	25–30	22–25	28–47	24–37
1933	32	26	28–30	24–25	28–35	25–30	37	30
1934	35–40	28–32	28–40	28–32	30–40	28–32	42–55	32–40
1935	35–40	28–32	35–45	28–35	39–40	28–32	40–50	32–40
1936	40	32	40	32	40	32	40–60	32–40

Source: Compiled from: AN 1957/0187600: *Annual Labor Department Reports of FMS* (reports from years 1912 to 1921); India Office Records (IOR) L/E/7/1341: *Annual Report of the Labor Department*, FMS (all years from 1922 to 1927); IOR L/E/7/1532: *Annual Report of the Labor Department*, FMS (all years from 1928 to 1929); IOR L/PJ/8/258–259: *Annual Report of the Labor Department, FMS* (all years from 1930 to 1936).

Note: Reports from years 1912–1914, 1919, and 1920–1924 did not record wage details for weeders.

Tapping

Tapping was one task on the estates that offered coolie women occasional opportunities to achieve equal pay with coolie men. From time to time, some estate managers tried to incentivize tapping and increase rubber production by paying the tappers according to the amount of rubber they tapped rather than a fixed daily wage.[17] On estates operating such piecework systems of payment, coolie women could compete with coolie men and obtain equal or greater pay depending on their productivity.[18] While the majority of estates paid coolies flat gender-based daily wages for tapping 250–300 trees per day (see Table 2.2), the Agent of the Government of India in Malaya noted, in 1928, that many estates had begun experimenting with this new system.[19]

Payment by results incentivized the increase in rubber-tapping and thus appeared rational from the planters' perspective, but the available records

Table 2.2 Daily wages (in cents) for rubber-tapping on rubber estates according to estate locations in FMS

Year	Perak Men	Perak Women	Selangor Men	Selangor Women	Negri Sembilan Men	Negri Sembilan Women	Pahang Men	Pahang Women
1912–1914*	27–50							
1918	33–35							
1919	40–50							
1924	40–50	30–40	35–40	25–35	35–42	30–40	45–50	35–45
1925	45		40–45		45–50		50–65	
1926	45–50	35–35	40–50	35–50	45–50	45–50	50–60	50–60
1927	45–55	35–50	45–52	40–50	45–50	45–50	50–60	50–60
1928	45–55	35–50	45–52	40–50	45–50	45–50	50–65	50–65
1929	50–55	40–45	50–80	40–60	55–70	45–50	50–70	50–65
1930	45–45	32–40	45–50	45–50	45–50	45–50	50–60	50–60
1931	30–40	27–40	30–40	27–40	35–45	45–50	30–40	30–37
1932	26–40	24–32	26–40	24–32	27–40	24–32	30–47	26–37
1933	32	27	28–32	24–30	30–35	25–30	40	30
1934	35–40	28–35	35–40	28–32	30–40	28–32	40–64	35–54
1935	35–40	28–32	35–45	28–40	35–42	28–32	40–60	32–57
1936	40	32	40	32	45–45	32–45	45–50	33–44

Source: Compiled from: AN 1957/0187600: *Annual Labor Department Reports of FMS* (reports from years 1912–1921); IOR L/E/7/1341: *Annual Report of the Labor Department, FMS* (all years from 1922 to 1927); IOR L/E/7/1532: *Annual Report of the Labor Department, FMS* (all years from 1928 to 1929); IOR L/PJ/8/258–259: *Annual Report of the Labor Department, FMS* (all years from 1930 to 1936).

Note: *For these years no separate data was recorded for different regions or sex-based wages in the available records

in archives suggest that such non-gendered pay structures were not always appreciated by coolie men. In 1929, H. C. Bathurst, the Director of the Labor Department in the annual report stated that Indian coolie men at a rubber estate in Selangor, which had recently introduced the piecework wage system, had gone on strike as they resented female tappers earning equal wages.[20] In his report, Bathurst reported that, on the introduction of the piecework system, the coolie men became "jealous" and felt "threatened," fearing they would lose their economic privileges if coolie women earned more than them. It is important to note here that Bathurst observed that the economic privileges of coolie men were at stake, but in no way did he suggest that coolie women were necessarily "dependent" on men.[21] The file ends with a note suggesting that the strike was settled by the Labor Department officials, but does not explain how it was settled.

The system of payment by results provoked opposition from coolies not only due to the implications for gendered pay differentials, but also because rubber yields depended on the season, soil condition, and atmospheric conditions, and coolies thus found it unjust to expect them to produce consistent quantities of rubber.[22] In 1935, for example, both coolie men and women went on strike on the Sendayan estate at Negri Sembilan, when the manager introduced the piecework system. The coolies finally called off the strike when the manager reintroduced the old pay system.[23] Nonetheless, whether daily wage system or piecework wage system, tapping was undoubtedly a crucial task for the plantation industry and coolie women were widely engaged in tapping work on estates.

Factory Work

The numbers of coolies working in factories, both male and female, were far less than those working on estates as weeders and tappers. While factory wages were higher than agricultural wages, coolie women in factories seldom had the opportunity to earn the same wage as their male counterparts (see Table 2.3) as the payments were mostly in the form of daily wages rather than piecework.[24] Some records have even suggested that coolie women and men who worked as tappers earned more than workers in estate factories.[25] However, this remains a debatable observation, as the annual Labor Department reports published by the Government of Malaya throughout 1910–1940s reported that coolies working in the rubber factories were paid more than tappers.[26]

Based on the calculation of gender ratios from Tables 2.1, 2.2, and 2.3, the intriguing fact emerges that from 1924 to 1929, the gender wage gaps for weeders, tappers, and factory workers decreased. Nonetheless, it is important to note that the wage ratios between men and women always favored men, and that certain jobs—particularly factory jobs—were sex-typed for men, thereby affecting the bargaining power of coolie women in those sectors. Moreover, as soon as economic depression set in between 1929 and 1936, gender wage gaps increased, and the worst hit sector, with increased gendered wage ratio

Table 2.3 Daily wages (in cents) of factory and store coolies on FMS rubber estates

	Perak		Selangor		Negri Sembilan		Pahang	
Year	Men	Women	Men	Women	Men	Women	Men	Women
1924*	40–60		35–60		35–60		45–60	
1925	50–$1		40–55		60		55–65	
1926	50–80		50–60		60–65		65–75	
1927	50–80		50–60		60–65		65–75	
1928	50–80		50–60		60–65		60–65	
1929	50–80		50–75		55–80		60–65	
1930	45–50		40–50		40–48		50–60	
1931	35–50	35–50	35–50	35–50	35–50	35–50	35–50	35–50
1932	35–50	35–50	35–50	35–50	35–50	35–50	35–50	35–50
1933	35–40	30	37–50	32–45	40–55	–	47–60	37
1934	40–45	32	40–50	30–35	42	32	45–65	–
1935	40–50	30–35	40–50	32–40	40–50	32–35	45–65	32–35
1936	45–50	32–36	40–50	32	45–55	35–45	47–60	40

Source: Compiled from: AN 1957/0187600: *Annual Labor Department Reports of FMS* (reports from years 1912–1921); IOR L/E/7/1341: *Annual Report of the Labor Department, FMS* (all years from 1922 to 1927); IOR L/E/7/1532: *Annual Report of the Labor Department, FMS* (all years from 1928 to 1929); IOR L/PJ/8/258–259: *Annual Report of the Labor Department, FMS* (all years from 1930 to 1936).

Note: *No separate data was available in the archives for male and female wages.

gaps, was the factory sector, revealing that coolie women were the most disadvantaged as factory workers in economically volatile periods. These figures reinforce the idea that planters and managers often treated women laborers as easily dispensable labor sources, also showing that it would have been increasingly difficult for coolie women to be "single" during a period of economic depression, especially if they had to run households alone. Therefore, the pay structure was built to provide some cushioning for coolie men who were seen as primary workers and wage earners for a household against hard times, whilst providing no such support for female workers, an issue which will be further discussed later and in the following chapters. This categorization of men as primary and women as secondary workers disadvantaged coolie women during periods of economic difficulty as planters perceived them primarily as dependents of their male relatives, and used that argument to institute massive wage cuts and labor dismissals.

Comparing gendered wage ratios in Malaya to those in other colonial plantation societies, we find that in Jamaica, coolie women were paid approximately 50 percent of coolie men's wages;[27] in Fiji, women were paid less than half of coolie men's earnings, because most of the tasks women were assigned to were categorized as less laborious;[28] and in Sri Lankan tea estates, women were paid significantly less than men in an industry overwhelmingly dependent upon female labor, because planters insisted that women's work was inferior and easily replaceable on the estates.[29] Thus, coolie women in other colonial plantations experienced greater socioeconomic marginalization than coolie women in Malaya, making them even more dependent upon male economic support. It must be assumed that if Malayan planters could have retained female labor whilst paying the lower rates characteristic of other plantation colonies, they would have done so, suggesting that coolie women in Malaya were able to use the planters' constant fear of labor shortages, resulting from British Malaya's late entry into the Indian labor market, to negotiate better pay for themselves.

REPRODUCING LABOR

Coolie women were valuable for plantations not only for their labor, but also for their wombs. They were relied upon for the local *reproduction of labor* to guarantee a future labor source for the estates. The colonial plantation authorities thus expected coolies to continually produce labor for the estate economy, in both "public" and "private" spaces. Coolie women's reproductive work, then, was not solely a part of the coolie domestic economy; rather, it formed a crucial part of the colonial plantation system and its future. Planters' reliance on both the manual labor and the reproductive labor of coolie women in Malaya was no anomaly. As Piya Chatterjee, Janaki Nair, Jennifer Morgan, and others have shown, plantations across the colonial world regarded women laborers especially as labor reproducers for plantation societies.[30]

Recording coolie women's reproductive labor not only allows appreciation of how coolie women's work and bodies were inseparable from the colonial estate economies, but also highlights the interconnectivity of the two spaces and reaffirms the claims of feminist scholars that normative ideals of analyzing public and private spheres as isolated spaces are unattainable and unnecessary.[31]

While labor reproduction was as crucial as manual labor to the planters, it was *not* recognized as paid work. Nonetheless, as this form of "work" remained crucial for the planters and the future economy of the estate, reproduction by coolie women was promoted and supported by the estate administrators through other means.

Planters usually paid maternity allowances to pregnant coolie women on their estates, one month before and one month after their confinement period.[32] The allowances usually amounted to two-sixth of the concerned coolie women's average earnings in the previous six months for the first child, and for subsequent childbirths two-eleventh of the average earnings of the previous eleven months' earnings. It was often reported by officials that coolie women rarely benefitted from such allowances as coolie men frequently took the money from their wives and spent it on alcohol.[33]

Estates that paid laborers by results paid pregnant coolie women an exceptional extra percentage, which was calculated on their daily-result-based income. It is important to remember that, as these estates paid according to daily results, there were no gender-based wage differences. Estate and Labor Department authorities often noted that other laborers, particularly the male relatives of the pregnant coolie women, would give extra latex to the latter to allow them to benefit from a greater extra payment.[34] Presumably, the concerned woman and those who contributed toward her extra latex later shared the rewards. This provides an interesting glimpse of the ways coolies used awareness of their rights to collaboratively maximize their earning opportunities. Such complex collaboration between male and female coolies suggests that the image of the coolie husband irresponsibly drinking his wife's maternity allowance was far from being the full picture.

Planters were not the only ones supporting reproduction of labor. The Planters' Association of Malaya, together with the Labor Department, devised special supervisory rules for planters to ensure pregnant coolie women were not overworked and avoided miscarriages, and there were also medical initiatives to improve maternal health and childbirth processes on estates. Furthermore, managers of estates without sufficient medical facilities and midwives were allowed to send their pregnant coolie women to the nearest district or general hospitals.[35] The Labor Laws in Malaya allowed pregnant coolie women to abstain from work for one month before and after confinement. The interest of the colonial administration in the health of coolie women can be traced not only to their desire for a sustainable labor force, but also to their anxiety about accusations from the colonial Government of India, which regularly blamed the Government of Malaya for the unsatisfactory sex ratio among Indian coolies, which was often argued to be contributing toward high social crime and mortality rates among Indian coolies.

While the planters encouraged coolie women to reproduce labor, they did not want the women's mothering concerns to become an obstacle to their return to full-time estate work. By the 1910s, with more labor being locally reproduced, the planters were forced to set up *line crèches* to relieve coolie mothers of responsibility for their children during work hours.[36] By 1929, there were reports of an insufficiency of line crèches in some parts of FMS. The annual reports of the Agent of the Government of India in Malaya continually reported that the conditions of childcare in the line crèches were pathetic and hence coolie women were often forced to look for other alternatives, such as leaving younger children with relatively older children on estate lines.[37] Pachaimmal's recollections of line crèches on her estate add weight to such reports. In one of her interviews with me, Pachaimmal recollected that her mother would leave her at a pathetic line crèche on the Sungai Buaya estate until her mother finished tapping.[38]

Once again anxious about what Indian nationalists would do if they became aware of the conditions of the crèches, the Labor Department of Malaya made attempts to address this situation. They recommended all planters to provide crèches on all estates with ten or more coolie children under the age of three, or all estates with fifty or more female laborers. Each line crèche was to employ at least one *ayah* and supply free food, that is, milk, *kanji*, and rice for the infants.[39] The *ayah*s employed in these crèches were older coolie women who were no longer physically fit for strenuous work on the estates.[40] It is important to note that these arrangements did not necessarily demand added expenses from the planters or the government. Most planters in the 1920s and 1930s maintained estate-toddy shops to sell toddy to their coolies. The profits from these sales (which were substantial) were used to sponsor the maintenance of the crèches, provisions for food for children, and pay wages to the *ayah*s.[41] Therefore, the coolies paid for the "benefits" they got on estates.

Thus, be it hard labor or reproductive labor or labor of care, coolie women performed a central role in various capacities for the colonial estates, and as the aforesaid discussion shows, the gendered wage differences and gendered bonus eligibility indeed placed coolie women at an economic disadvantage compared to coolie men, which reflected their designated status as "secondary laborers" on the estates, despite the centrality of their work.

ASSESSING "DEPENDENCE" AND "DEPENDENT" IMAGES OF COOLIE WOMEN

Based on the aforesaid descriptions, it is now possible to better assess and re-figure coolie women's role in the history of colonial estates of Malaya. This also requires a careful assessment of who created the image of coolie women as dependent upon coolie men and in what circumstances the categorization and imagining of coolie women as "dependents" were produced.

The fact that coolie women had their names listed on payrolls as separate labor units undeniably pointed toward a degree of economic independence. The incentives provided by Malayan planters to labor recruiters in India to recruit coolie women also proves that, at the point of migration, coolie women were valued in their own right for their capacities as individual bodies of labor by planters and recruiters.[42] As historian Marina Carter has shown, the listing of Indian coolie women as independent and separate labor units having access to their own pay was crucial, both in regard to their position in estate societies and their awareness of their labor rights. Carter shows how coolie women in Mauritius, when compared to the coolie women in other colonial estates, were the most vulnerable, as they were strictly imported as wives or daughters and not as workers. The lack of contracts denied them any individual recognition on migration records and not being listed as separate labor units made them much more vulnerable to exploitation and abuses than coolie women in other colonies.[43] Therefore, being counted as independent labor units enabled coolie women to earn individual wages, which also shaped their ability to "know" and negotiate their rights and situations as laborers.

Not only recruiters and planters, but also government administrators, in their respective records of recruitment contracts and migration records, considered coolie women as independent migrants and units of labor. In particular, the political concerns of the Government of India and the Government of Malaya with the sex ratio of Indian coolies in Malaya, and their consequent push to increase the number of coolie women recruited for Malayan plantations, ensured that coolie women figured as an independent category of migrants and laborers who were counted as individuals in the female labor migration category, irrespective of their relation with or dependence on male coolies.[44] Hence, in the records of migration taken at the embarkation point in India and the disembarkation point in Malaya, immigration officers counted the number of male and female laborers separately. Furthermore, while the immigration officers validated marriages at the port of embarkation, they did not record such marriages or the economic dynamics of coolie households, maintaining an official focus on the individual laborer: male or female.[45]

Once landed in Malaya, however, the language used for enumerating and recording coolie women's labor became far more complex. While government officials from the Labor Department in Malaya and the Agent of the Government of India in Malaya continued listing coolie women independently as female labor units and wage earners,[46] planters actively censored references to coolie women as independent laborers. Arguably, this was to justify gendered pay structures for coolies and to deny coolie women bonuses and rations. This denial allowed planters to assign the same tasks to coolie men and women but saved them the cost of paying them equally. Planters often argued that, as most coolie women were wives of coolie men, their wages were supplemental to the household and that one bonus and ration for the family was enough.[47] Nevertheless, planters continued to record coolie women separately on the payrolls, which hints that coolie women continued to be valued as independent units of labor despite the planters' refusal of explicit recognition. Thus, planters deployed patriarchal presumptions regarding gender roles in a household economy to serve their own economic interests.

Such representation of coolie women also helped planters justify the large-scale dismissal of coolie women during slump years.[48] Slumps affected the rubber economy badly, and the planters often found it economically difficult to maintain the full strength of labor forces on estates. Nonetheless, the planters were careful not to let go of their labor resources completely since that would have led to repatriation of their coolies to India, which, in turn, would have required them to pay for further labor recruitment when the rubber industry had stabilized. Under such circumstances, the use of the term "dependents" and the dichotomous categorization of workers into primary and secondary labor proved useful to the planters. Claiming that coolie women were supplemental earners to the coolie household and were only secondary laborers on the estates, the planters kept coolie men (particularly those with families on estates) employed, while either dismissing coolie women or massively reducing their wages. This allowed planters to reduce employment but simultaneously allowed them to keep coolie families on the estate, thus ensuring a sufficient labor force once the rubber industry recovered.[49]

Interestingly, the slump period was the *only* time that colonial administrative officials from the Labor Department in Malaya and the Agent of the Government of India in Malaya used the term "dependents" to describe coolie women in their reports. The primary reason behind this was because most coolie women lost their laboring and earning opportunities, and even those who were retained on the estates had to work for massively reduced wages, which reduced them to near-complete economic dependence on male members of the household.[50]

Thus, the administrative categorization of coolie women as independent or dependent bodies or units of labor was significantly different from the representation of coolie women by the planters. While administrative records understood dependence and independence as fluid categories determined in relation to an individual's capacity to labor and earn, planters used more rigid definitions, with coolie women *always* classified as dependent, thus justifying a gender-based pay and benefits structure, which resulted in women receiving less pay for equal work.

While administrators and planters constructed their economic, political, and gender-based definitions of dependence and independence, coolies navigated their own understanding and engagement with such terms within families wherein coolie men and women depended on each other for survival. In typical coolie families, coolie men earned more and contributed more to the household income, but coolie women still made a substantial and essential contribution, amounting to about 40 percent of the total household income.[51] Such figures suggest that without the earnings of coolie women, coolie households would not have been sustainable. Coolie men and women, therefore, were mutually dependent. The accounts given earlier of collaboration between male and female coolies around piecework and maternity allowances strengthen the picture of fluid relationships of cooperative interdependence between men and women coolies. Hence, the planter categorization of coolie women, as always dependent upon independent men, presented a distorted picture of the reality which served their own interests.

These revelations push us to not only *re-figure* the coolie women as laborers whose work was of equal significance to that of coolie men, but also allows us to appreciate that the categorization of women as dependents or as secondary laborers on colonial estates was more influenced by capitalistic considerations of profit than by actual gendered capacities for labor. By illuminating the fluidity and changeability of such categories and identities, we reveal that they are not fixed and essential, but situational and relational. As Donald Reid has shown, our language constructs categories, which we often use to describe concepts but these concepts do not always reflect all possible realities of the identity to which they refer.[52] On a similar note, William Sewell has boldly called for the elimination of dichotomies that inform our understanding and assessment of work and labor. Sewell insists that assessments of labor histories should be based on how various identities were constructed in relation to power and scarcity.[53]

COOLIE WOMEN, LABOR STRIKES, AND RIOTS

Coolie women not only performed hard labor and reproductive labor for estate economies, but also simultaneously performed an essential political function in the arena of labor politics alongside coolie men. Undeniably, the visual presence of coolie men in the process of proletarianization of estate labor was greater than that of coolie women, primarily because of their greater numbers. Nevertheless, coolie men regularly depended upon their female fellow workers in their active engagement in labor politics on estates. At times, coolie women actively engaged in striking and rioting, whilst at other times, the particular grievances of female coolies were central to political mobilization and complaints against estate authorities. Therefore, in labor politics as in work, coolie men and women were not always related through hierarchical constructs, nor were they parallel or separate labor groups on estates; rather, they were interdependent. As Joan Scott in her seminal study of the place of women in the making of the English working class has shown, "the feminine was always a central figure in representation of working-class politics."[54]

In 1937, all Hindu Tamil coolies, men and women, at Batu Caves estate went on strike because they did not receive their "Diwali" advances. Such collaborative efforts appear to have emerged from the evidently shared interests and shared suffering amongst coolie men and women. These instances also provide sufficient grounds to reject the presumption that coolie women were dependents and, thus, apolitical figures in colonial estates.[55]

There were also incidents wherein coolie women participated in labor politics, but as implicit partners: that is, coolie men took up the suffering or abuse of women coolies to demand compensation from estate authorities. Most frequent complaints included assaults on and sexual abuse of coolie women by those in authority on estates. In such cases, the coolie women's cause became a defining feature of labor activism in more organized forms. On February 17, 1913, Murugan, alias Periasamy, an estate coolie from Tremelbye estate in Kuala Lumpur, sent a letter, said to have been written through an estate letter writer,[56] to the Labor Controller highlighting the "great deal of immorality" that was being perpetrated by overseers and planters on the estates against coolie women. Murugan, in his letter, complained:

The officer in Klang Indian Immigration Department used to go to the Estates for picnic or pleasure trip at times. When, the Managers of Estates as a rule, used to treat him as a new guest with all possible delicacies and at last used to supply him with a selected woman from the gang of coolies he got in his Estate for the night, and sometimes, he fills his pocket with currency notes; thus the Manager of Estate earns a thick friendship with Indian Immigration Officer. Now the Manager of Estate has best friendliness towards the Indian Immigration Officer, he begins to maltreat his coolies in several ways; some in womanising and others in cutting down the wages of the coolies to show more profit to their head office than their predecessor.[57]

Murugan did not limit his complaints to the estate managers. In his letter, he thoroughly described the wickedness of other estate authorities like the assistants, conductors, and office clerks who "openly called the good-looking female coolies to their respective quarters for the night, if they are bachelors."[58] He further added, when a coolie couple gave their notice to the planters to quit the estate, usually "the husband's notice was duly accepted and carried out (paid and sent out at the expiry of the month) leaving the wife in the estate if the woman was handsome and young."[59]

In his letter, Murugan complained that such immoral practices by planters and other estate authorities had turned hundreds of young Tamil coolie women into wandering prostitutes who moved from estate to estate and were kept by the managers, conductors, and clerks as concubines. Murugan even insisted that there should be some legislation to make "such people who wish to take a woman from cooly gang as a wife can do so under the proper registered marriage system" as this according to him would help repress immorality.[60]

Murugan's letter also included brief complaints from coolies regarding the wages they were paid, but the primary focus of the letter was on the sexual abuse and exploitation of coolie women on the estate. Upon receiving this letter, there was a flurry of notes exchanged between the Undersecretary of FMS and the Labor Department to examine the claims in the letter and the identity of the writer. In the meantime, Murugan's letter attracted media attention in India where it was published in the daily newspaper *Bengalee* and later reproduced in other leading dailies. Anxious to close the case quickly before Indian nationalists capitalized on the issue, the Government of India and the Government of Malaya urged the Labor Department of Malaya to investigate the case. Upon investigation, the Controller of Labor in Malaya, J. Aldworth, claimed that the letter was of no importance as the identity of the writer was questionable and that almost all of the accusations were false.[61] Whether Murugan's accusations were false or not, the author of the letter evidently tried to strategically deploy coolie women's experiences and concerns to support a larger political agenda against plantation authorities.

In 1929, another similar case was reported. An estate manager of a rubber estate in Perak had allegedly "ravished" one of his female coolies. Consequently, she complained to the agents of the Labor Department of Malaya and the Agent of the Government of India (during their regular visits to the estates). Eventually, the coolies of the estate, with the help of the Labor Department agents and the Agent of the Government of India in Malaya, collectively reported the case to the local magistrate, which led to the estate manager being tried in court. While the result of the case is not known, the efforts of the coolies to seek redress and the mobilizing role of the coolie woman's experience are noteworthy.[62]

In 1941, Indian estate laborers organized one of the most prominent Indian labor strikes in Malaya. Amongst many grievances it addressed, the issue of coolie women's honor and security on estates was at the forefront. In fact, Murugan's demands seem to be echoed in the demands made in the Klang strikes of 1941, wherein Indian laborers demanded "the Europeans and black Europeans to cease abusing, molesting and harassing Indian coolie women."[63] Coolie women in such cases thus engaged in labor politics not necessarily as dependents, but as active agents alongside coolie men by offering a consistent backdrop of gendered resistance to the estate system, which formed a basis for organized labor movements, strikes, and riots. Despite the implicit paternalistic ideology in such strikes, wherein coolie men appeared to champion the cause of their female fellow coolies, the nature of the protests reveals that coolie women were actively participating in bringing forth such complaints.

Whilst coolie women's experiences of vulnerability in these instances are perceived through a gendered morality of protection, it is clear that women and their grievances played a significant role in the development of estate labor movements. Thus, even though the coolie women might have been visually small in number, their vulnerabilities, voices, and issues were anything but small, becoming the grounds for labor activism and proletarianization. As Judith Butler in her recent study has shown, vulnerability offers a path to forming resistance.[64] Thus, the vulnerabilities of coolie women gave coolie men a political channel to launch labor movements. It can be argued that while there were often times when coolie women depended on coolie men economically, coolie men frequently depended on coolie women politically as a source of "voice." Moreover, during strikes and riots, coolie men and women stood, and sometimes fought, together. Such interdependence exposes the cracks in the seemingly formidable and divisive walls of patriarchy, thereby demonstrating the arbitrariness of gendered labels of "independent" men and "dependent" women.

COOLIE WOMEN AND NEGOTIATIONS WITH ESTATE HIERARCHIES

Before progressing further, it is important to lay out the hierarchies in a rubber estate, as this will help one understand the various power dynamics within which coolie women on the estates had constantly to negotiate (see Figure 2.4). At the top of the hierarchy was the Manager, who at times was aided by an Assistant Manager. Next were a group of conductors or overseers who supervised the everyday weeding, tapping, and factory work on the estates. Below the conductors were the group leaders, or *kanganies*, senior coolies who at times served as labor recruiters in India. Figure 2.5 offers a glimpse of a *kangany* along with other estate overseers supervising the work of an Indian coolie woman on an estate. Understanding this hierarchy allows us to reflect on the various layers of subjugation and everyday violence that coolie women had to negotiate.

Coolie women's experiences as laborers and their vulnerability as women not only created opportunities to proletarianize the coolie community, but also offered them the opportunity to engage and negotiate individually with

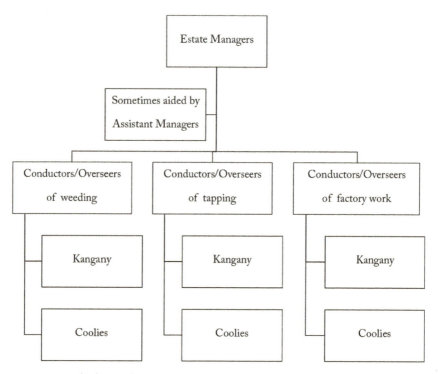

Figure 2.4 The hierarchy on rubber estates
Source: Author.

Figure 2.5 "Five people among rubber trees"—Indian coolie woman and her estate overseers
Source: Frank and Frances Carpenter Collection (Library of Congress), https://www.loc.gov/item/98514879/.

estate authorities. Importantly, these negotiations usually remained hidden in the everyday rather than assuming the theatrical elements of an "event." As James Scott, in his seminal work, *Weapons of the Weak*, noted, rebellions and revolutions from oppressed communities "are few and far between," but there are equally eventful and important everyday forms of struggle and resistance initiated by the "powerless" to defend their interests by the best possible means available to them.[65]

Coolie women's engagement with estate authorities regarding their labor rights extended from complaints against estate authorities to non-compliance with orders and making demands for better treatment. These forms of defiance and negotiations were met with a variety of responses: most were suppressed, some achieved modest results, while others were met with violent retaliation from the authorities. Irrespective of the results of such initiatives, the fact that coolie women were aware of their position in the estates as laborers and actively engaged with the authorities is a telling example of their agency, however implicit and fleeting it may be.

The most frequent complaints coolie women brought against estate authorities were regarding physical assaults inflicted on them by estate officials.[66] These were not the only complaints, however. Sometimes complaints of assaults were made together with other complaints, for example, of the non-payment of appropriate wages. On December 5, 1909, Angama, a coolie woman on an estate near Parit Buntar in Perak, reported multiple attacks and abuses against her by her Indian estate overseer, Meyappa Chetty, and his *kangany*, Maruthamuthu. The two men were eventually charged under Section 323 of the Malayan Penal Code for voluntarily causing physical hurt to Angama. During the five full days of the hearing, the court was reportedly crowded with an unusually large gathering who watched the proceedings with considerable interest.[67]

In her witness, Angama reported that while she possessed employment papers, which stated she was a free coolie,[68] she had been treated like an indentured coolie and forced by overseers Maruthamuthu and Meyappa Chetty to work as an indentured coolie. Fearing that she might complain to the police or other government authorities, the accused even restricted her mobility by not allowing her out of the estate. It was only after the estate was sold to another owner that Angama went to the police at Parit Buntar to register her complaints against the former estate overseers. In her deposition, Angama accused the two men of the following:

1. They worked and treated her like an indentured coolie, while she was an approved free coolie.
2. They paid her ten cents less than she was entitled to and when she complained, Meyappa Chetty slapped her on her face.
3. When she asked for leave from work on account of being sick, she was report-edly assaulted and kicked by Maruthamuthu. She further stated that while Maruthamuthu beat her several times on her "tender, private parts" with a

rattan, two other women from the estate—Periya Sinamma and Sinna Sinna-mama—held her hands.[69]

Amongst all three complaints, the last one merits serious attention. The fact that other women on the estate participated in the physical abuse of Angama hints that coolie women could face violence and abuse even from other women. As there were no discussions about the identity of the two women involved, there is no way to determine whether this hierarchical relation was due to age, caste, class, or situational issues. It is possible that these women were Angama's fellow coolies who, by supporting the men in power, hoped to enjoy some privilege vis-à-vis other coolies. Another possibility is that they could have been female relations of the perpetrators.

While the case was being heard, A. S. Haynes, the Assistant Superintendent of immigrants, was sent to the estate by the magistrate to investigate further. Upon investigation, Haynes testified that on his visit to the estate, thirty-two coolie men and eight coolie women voluntarily registered similar complaints against both *kangany* Maruthamuthu and overseer Meyappa Chetty. Based on this evidence, the magistrate, H. H. Raja Chulan, sentenced Marthamuthu to a fine of 200 dollars and Meyappa Chetty to a fine of 100 dollars.[70] By the conclusion of Agama's case, five similar cases had been lodged against Meyappa Chetty and Maruthamuthu by her fellow coolies and were scheduled to be tried in court.[71] Angama's case thus serves as a crucial example of how a coolie woman's *episodic* and individualistic effort to seek justice for herself offered fellow coolies, not all of them women, situational access to channels through which to redress their grievances against common offenders. At the same time, the case demonstrates the limits of what the colonial legal framework allowed to be challenged, for whilst the Indian offenders were indeed punished, the plantation system which allowed and incentivized such behavior was never questioned.

Archival records also provide testimony of coolie women standing up individually for various other labor-rights-related issues. On January 5, 1923, a seven-months-pregnant coolie woman lodged a complaint against a European estate manager at the local magistrate's office in FMS. She accused the manager of hitting her nineteen times with a rattan. In her witness, she stated that the manager and the overseer had ordered her to weed while it was raining. But, upon receiving these orders, she had insisted that as she was pregnant, by the labor laws, she should be exempted from such physically challenging tasks as weeding. Enraged by her refusal to weed, the manager took recourse to physical abuse. While no further discussion or report about this case is found in the archives, the available details provide enough ground to correct the perception of coolie women as subservient and passive victims. Rather, it shows how coolie women were aware of the "rights" guaranteed to them through the labor laws and used this consciousness to resist exploitation by estate authorities.[72] In this instance, the coolie woman understood the rights her situation of pregnancy afforded her and used that knowledge to engage with the estate authority. The case demonstrates that coolie women were able to *read* their value to the estates, not only as labor producers but also as labor reproducers: a value on which they could capitalize to obtain fleeting and situational breaks in long periods of suppression. Such cases show that while coolie women were regularly exploited and oppressed, they did not necessarily give in to oppression without negotiation or challenge.

Coolie women even tried to make estate authority accountable for the personal losses they suffered while working on the estates. The 1939 case of *Narasamah vs Cicely Rubber Estates* offers a rare glimpse into such initiatives by coolie women.[73] Narasamah, a coolie woman, was struck by lightning while working on Cicely Rubber estate at Teluk Anson, Perak, and the lightning killed her. Following Narasamah's death, two women from the same estate, Appahmah and Kanammah, who had witnessed the tragic incident, approached C. Forsyth, the Assistant Controller of Labor, and successfully registered a legal case against the estate company and the estate manager to demand workman's compensation for Narasamah's death. They also demanded money for the maintenance of the deceased's children, because the deceased was raising the children alone. The Supreme Court dismissed the case with the argument that Narasamah was not exposed to any abnormal or excessive conditions due to her employment and that anyone under similar circumstance would have suffered the same.[74] Although Appahmah and Kanamah had failed in achieving their desired goal, their intent and efforts to redress injustice and claim certain labor rights against the estate authority are noteworthy. Irrespective of how inconsequential the daily strategies of coolie women in such cases might have seemed, they offer evidence of the fleeting agency of coolie women through which they made conscious efforts to address their needs, demands, and grievances and tried to navigate the terrains of various power structures, seeking the best outcomes for themselves or those they cared about, such as Narasamah's children. They did not passively accept the status of victim, but strove to exert agency wherever opportunities were afforded. Such cases reveal the limitations in focusing on results instead of intent while analyzing everyday resistance.

All these cases show how coolie women registered their distress at their workplace and their desire and efforts to overcome obstacles and relieve hardships. It is evident that they acted consciously and turned subjugation, exploitation, and even tragedy into action. In their oppressed plights, they did not shy away from the chance to negotiate their rights while being aware of the dangers such negotiations could provoke. Rather, they showed courage in exploring what such engagements could bring to them. It is clear from these cases that coolie women took their chances in negotiations, as there was no fixed or obvious outcome of such engagements. It is this "self-image," self-identification, and self-determination with which we as historians must engage. In the process of examining the evidence, we reveal telling signs of how coolie women's labor experiences conditioned and influenced their hopes, dreams, collaborations, and expectations from the workspace.

REMEMBERING COOLIE WOMEN'S "IDENTITIES" AND CONTRIBUTIONS ON ESTATES

This chapter has explored coolie women's engagements with labor structure, fellow laborers, and authorities on estates, showing how coolie women crossed and transfigured various categories and identities through their everyday engagements. In the process, it has demonstrated the importance of critically analyzing terms used to describe work and labor in gender histories. A close reading of how coolie women were recorded in various official correspondences, administrative and plantation records allow us to foreground the politics behind the dynamics of category production, showing how and why certain individuals were assigned to certain categories by different actors. The chapter reveals that who fitted in what category was not self-evident and that not only did different actors take different views, but these views were situated, tending to serve the interests of the actors in question. Importantly, therefore, the chapter makes visible how constructions of categories and identities became modes of organizing social, racial, and class relations and, thus, became sites of proliferating and competing discourses in colonial politics.

The chapter, then, provides a ground on which we need to reorient our understanding of identities and categories in labor history by exploring how such categories and identities were created and whose interests these served in different contexts. In so doing, the chapter shows how categories and identities associated with various roles and experiences cannot be understood within a fixed hierarchy of positions or identities. Rather, these can be best perceived as flickering relations and fleeting situations. Planters, officials, male and female coolies—all assumed certain positions from which they actively engaged with the discourses of plantation and Empire.[75] Hence, there is a need to de-categorize and de-fragment our understanding concerning the labor roles and experiences of coolie women. Placing the coolie women's active labor participation, their self-identification and fleeting moments of resistance at center stage, the chapter enables us to move beyond the colonial and nationalist figuring of coolie women as marginalized and dependent laborers, to present a more rounded picture of women as productive workers, family breadwinners, cooperative strategists, and active agents in forms of resistance ranging from legal challenges to riots.

Together, the case studies in this chapter concerning women's labor, their participation in labor politics, and engagements with the estate authorities, question the simplistic representation of coolie women as dependents and secondary workers on colonial estates. These representations are, at best, partial truths which served the interests of planters. They disregard the textured realities of estate life, that is, that the oppression, abuse, and exploitation of coolie women existed side by side with coolie women's contribution to the plantation industry and their initiatives to overcome or at least mitigate various challenges of life on estates. Coolie women could be victims, but they were never *merely* victims: rather, they were agents of both labor and labor politics in Malaya. Perhaps they were not always conscious of *making* history, but they were arguably more conscious than we often presume. The evidence presented in this chapter shows that many coolie women had clear understanding of their roles and rights as laborers in different contexts and used this knowledge to create their own narratives in negotiation with estate authorities.

Having established the agency of coolie women in this chapter, the next chapter goes on to further examine the mutual dependence of coolie men and women while exploring ways in which coolie families sought to increase household income by using their domestic space in various entrepreneurial ways.

3

MANAGING "PARTNERSHIPS"

DOMESTICITY AND ENTREPRENEURIAL ENDEAVORS

As we passed by one of the Indian coolie lines I had another shock, for I saw a young Tamil woman tied by her long hair to one of the uprights of their house and being beaten with a stout cane, while she uttered the most blood-curdling yells and moans as each cut of the cane made its great weal on her soft skin. Sick and appalled at the sight, I made haste to set about the man using the cane, but my friend grabbed me and held me back, assuring me that it was the custom amongst the Tamils and all Orientals to beat their womenfolk when they had done wrong, and that any interference on my part would be resented by both the man and his wife and would be likely to cause great trouble.[1]

—Leopold Ainsworth,
British planter in British Malaya (1933)

It is with these lines that the author Leopold Ainsworth, a European planter in British Malaya in the 1930s, described his first impressions of Indian coolies and their intimate relations on the estate of which he had recently become the manager. In the process, he also creates a generalized and yet vivid impression of the everyday intimacies of coolie couples for his readers. Such records were not unique to British Malaya. Colonial plantations across the British Empire, which employed Indian immigrant coolies, have dutifully recorded cases of spousal or domestic violence occurring in coolie lines—whether in planters' memoirs, local criminal records, or even in parliamentary discussions concerning coolies. For instance, in 1902, following a rise in violent "domestic" incidents amongst coolies on plantations in Fiji, the local Immigration Department was moved by the Colonial Office in Britain to investigate the quality of social life for the indentured laborers in Fiji. W. E. Russell, one of the Immigration Inspectors, argued, apparently based on his findings, that each congregation of Indian coolies in Fiji was "a veritable hotbed of murder."[2] Similarly, a Colonial Office Commission sent to British Guiana in 1871 to study the condition of Indian laborers there asserted that Indian men killed their partners at a rate "142 times greater than in India's provinces."[3]

In their attempts to explain violence in coolie lines across the British Empire, colonial administrators frequently resorted to racist stereotypes, which depicted coolie women as victims of irresponsible and violent coolie men. The coolie "houses" and households in colonial administrative records have been showcased as troubled and chaotic spaces,[4] regularly disturbed by physical abuse and even murder of coolie women by their men. In such simplistic depictions of spectacular "events" of violence, all coolie women tended to become homogenized into a single category of "passive victims" and likewise all coolie men were stereotyped as potential perpetrators of violence against their wives. In deploying such stereotypes, colonial records have often played with the idea that such violent episodes resulted from the fact that Indian coolie men who were away from the motherland had lost their "power" or hold on the bodies of their women. In certain cases, women were undeniably victims of "domestic" violence in coolie lines, but the narratives set forward by colonial administrative reports and memoirs presented such cases as routine rather than exceptional.

Few scholars seem to realize that the historical basis for such generalized claims is shaky; fewer openly recognize that such a misreading of the past poses a threat of constructing "given" categories within which contemporary multicultural societies continue to frame culprits. Most scholarly works on coolie lives in colonial contexts tend to implicitly accept the colonial stereotypes of coolie men and women and to accept that domestic and sexual violence had been a part of everyday life in coolie lines without probing into the complexities involved in such violence.[5] A more careful look at the records, and the creation of a dialogue between presences and absences in the archives,[6] reveal that while such violent incidents did occur from time to time, they were not necessarily "domestic" violence and that the violence of the Empire and an exploitative plantation economy played a role in such incidents. As discussed in Chapter 2, colonial archives often obscure the fact that coolie women were laborers in their own right, despite the fact that their low wages made it difficult for them to survive on their own. However, while women as independent laborers have been categorically excluded from most archives, in cases of domestic violence we find colonial archives meticulously recording their victimhood, thereby giving coolie women some legitimacy as subjects of colonial plantation societies. The question at stake is: were such representations of coolie "domestic" relations and coolie households based on inherent and ineradicable violent coolie traits, as colonial administrators and planters suggested, or did it result from the failure of colonial infrastructures and officials to address underlying socioeconomic issues?

In most plantation economies, planters, managers, and overseers violently punished their workers. How is coolie "domestic" violence placed in relation to workspace-related violence wherein supervisors perpetrated various kinds of violence toward coolie women? If "domestic" violence by Indian men was so common, what caused them to commit such crimes? Was the scene of the violence always a "domestic" space? What did "domesticity" mean for plantation coolie households? Investigating the ways in which the image of victimized coolie women in violent coolie households was popularized, this chapter goes on to ask the deeper question which colonial and nationalist discourses as well as some recent studies have all avoided: to what extent were these purely cases of domestic violence, and to what extent was such eventful visible violence caused by a more routine but less visible form of violence generated by the Empire and an exploitative plantation economy?

Addressing the aforesaid questions, the chapter also reveals how coolie women and couples negotiated such insidious projections of colonial governance. First, the chapter elucidates the various roles coolie men and women assumed in coolie households, challenging stereotypical conceptions of coolie men as violent and coolie women as passive victims. Second, the chapter explores the socioeconomic nature of the spaces wherein the violence took place, questioning the categorization of coolie houses as purely domestic spaces and going on to question the extent to which the violence that sometimes took place within them was marital and to what extent it had other causes, such as financial disputes. Third, the case studies provide deeper insights into the responsibility of colonial society in such cases, showing that the plantation system and the colonial administration appear to be inseparable from the violence that occurred between coolie couples on the estates. In the process of uncovering these aspects of coolie life and death, the case studies in this chapter reveal how crude stereotypes of coolie households disregard the diverse realities and relations in which coolie men and women actually engaged within the space of their households within the colonial setting. An important caveat: this study in no way denies that Indian coolie men were occasionally violent, nor does it justify such violence in any way; rather, this section seeks to understand how stereotypical images of coolies obscured certain causal aspects of this violence and occluded the complex realities of coolie domesticities.

At this point, it is crucial to introduce the concept of "everyday violence" as opposed to "eventful violence." I borrow the idea of the "everyday" from anthropology and apply it historically to understand how certain kinds of violence become more visible and memorable than others. Anthropologist Veena Das calls attention to the importance of the "everyday," which is often not spectacular or dramatic in the way "events" are. Das argues, however, that the everyday remains eventful in its own unique ways.[7] Following Das, this chapter explores how violence in coolie households was recorded in colonial archives and nationalist discourses alike as eventful (for the colonial and nationalist observers who witnessed it) and yet as an "everyday" and routine affair for the coolies.

The "everyday" here features as the platform upon which events in the lives of coolies was scrutinized, judged, and publicized as displays of gruesome and ruthless behavior involving sexual jealousy, violation of women, violence, and even murder. Colonial archives, in recording such violence as being an extraordinary but routine feature of coolie households, constructed an *extraordinarily violent and eventful* image of these households. In describing violence, the everyday, the event, the ordinary, and the extra-ordinary are not easily untangled. Therefore, I treat both "the everyday" and "violence" not as transparent and clearly defined concepts, but rather as categories with blurred definitional boundaries.

To elucidate, as readers of Ainsworth's memoir, we are informed about the ordinariness or routineness of intimate violence in coolie lines: violence, which nevertheless appears "spectacularly eventful" for Ainsworth and his intended audience. While we as an audience are guided to focus upon the visible violence between the coolie man and his wife, we fail to recognize other simultaneous kinds of violence that remain a constant within the same scene—that of the Empire and the colonial economy. The planters or managers of such plantations—far more privileged, socioeconomically, than their coolies—could have instituted strict patrolling of lines and ensured punishments for such acts. However, planters did not bother to do so. Furthermore, as some of the later cases will reveal, there were even incidents wherein women who felt threatened by their husbands approached local police officers to seek security and yet the officers carelessly sent them back to the same "abusive" spaces with the advice to either come back with more proof or to settle their affairs on their own.[8] Since less visible forms of violence, such as this failure of the colonial authorities to offer protection, remain hidden in the folds of the everyday, they tend to be occluded by the focus on spectacularly eventful displays of violence. The case studies in this chapter force us to focus on the intersections of protean varieties of violence in the everyday, and push us to explore what kind of alternative history can be evoked from them. It also forces us to think how particular ways of representing and *revealing* certain violent events can simultaneously become a way of *concealing* other kinds of violence.

THE COOLIE HOUSEHOLD: SPATIALITIES OF VIOLENCE

To better understand the realities of coolie domestic violence, it is necessary to explore the socioeconomic geographies of coolie lines, the ways these were experienced by coolies and represented by administrators and local newspapers as well as Indian nationalists. This will help in understanding the myriad characters that coolie "domestic" spaces assumed.

COLONIAL DESIGNS FOR COOLIE HOUSEHOLDS

The coolie households and lines functioned as a space of living, intimacy, shared accommodation, messing, and entrepreneurship. Coolie lines (Figure 3.1),

Figure 3.1 Coolie lines and workers on a rubber estate in Malaya, 1920

Source: Lim Kheng Chye Collection, courtesy of National Archives of Singapore.

therefore, were multipurpose spaces which did not provide coolie couples with an environment that could be categorized as "purely" private or domestic in the conventional sense of the terms. During the initial years (the late 1890s to the early 1930s), coolies, irrespective of their marital status, were crammed indiscriminately into matchbox-like rooms, with communal kitchens and lavatories.[9] These barracks were of different types: some were temporary structures with *attap* (palm leaf) roofs, some were semi-permanent, and others permanent dwellings resembling shop-house buildings. In line with the SS Labor Commission Report of 1890, the rooms in coolie lines were divided into cubicles and approximately eighteen coolies were accommodated into an area of 10 square feet each.[10] These lines were overcrowded, unhygienic, and allowed no privacy to coolies. The same commission also reported that planters housed coolie men and women indiscriminately: "... few estates housed up to eighteen men and women indiscriminately and at times three married couples were housed together in a single room and sometimes one or two couples along with single men."[11] Based on its survey, the commission insisted that separate rooms should be made available to every married coolie couple.[12]

While colonial administrators insisted on the provision of privacy to coolie couples, planters remained hesitant. A planter's comments published in the 1894 *Selangor Journal of Planters* reveals the adamant indifference of the planters toward the suggestions of commissions:

> Not more than six coolies should be put into each room, but the planter need have no apprehensions on the subject of mixing the sexes, as the Tamil cooly is most philosophical in this respect, a young unmarried woman not objecting in the least to reside with a family or even to sharing her quarters, if necessary with quite a number of the opposite sex.[13]

By such statements, the planters tried to persuade both fellow planters and local colonial administrators that coolies themselves found it acceptable to be housed together, irrespective of their gender: they had no need of privacy, nor did they desire "domesticity" in the conventional sense of the term. Despite such comments, the colonial government of British India remained concerned about the welfare of its subjects laboring in overseas colonies, particularly because the rising Indian nationalist movement in India was capitalizing on issues of morality and violence amongst migrant Indian coolies in plantation colonies of the British Empire.[14]

On yet another occasion, in 1910, the FMS Labor Commission asserted similar views to the 1890 commission and insisted that accommodation conditions of coolies in FMS estates were highly unsatisfactory particularly in regard to lack of privacy.[15] Subsequent commissions appointed by the Government of India to review labor conditions in Malaya such as the Marjoribanks Commission (1916) and Sastri Commission (1937) again reported a disturbing lack of privacy in coolie housing and asserted that this had a negative effect on the general quality of social and moral life amongst coolies on plantations.[16] Additionally, the Agent of the Government of India appointed to Malaya kept a close eye on coolie housing policies and regularly reported increasing concerns regarding privacy in coolie lines. For instance, Agent Rao Sahib R. S. Naidu noted regarding the conditions of Indian coolies:

> The Labor Law of this country imposed obligation on employers to provide their laborers with sufficient housing … not more than three single men nor more than a single family may, under the rules, be housed in a standard

room of ten feet by ten feet. Laborers living with their wives and children are to be housed separately from single men and bachelors as far as possible. These rules are observed generally; but married men are housed in the same lines as bachelors and as far as I could see there is not much privacy for married couples in the blocks of laborer's lines erected on plantations. The provision of separate housing or detached huts or dwellings will go a great way to encourage the labourers to bring their womenfolk and to save them from immoral habits.[17]

Further, in his 1927 annual report of the Agent of the Government of India in Malaya, Naidu criticized the Government of Malaya for its inefficiency in improving the housing of the estate laborers and for being responsible in pushing them toward immoral habits.

As time went on and these issues remained largely unaddressed, the annual reports of the Agent of the Government of India in Malaya, Crime Department reports, and local newspapers in Malaya claimed that coolie lines had become hotbeds of sexual jealousy and crime, and this became a bargaining tool for the growing anti-colonialist movement in India, which used it to challenge the legitimacy of the colonial government in India for failing to ensure the morality and well-being of Indian overseas laborers: an issue that is further discussed in the following chapter. Consequently, the Government of India pressurized the Government of Malaya to ensure privacy for coolie couples at least in domestic spaces and to check immorality on estates. Following a series of intra-colonial governmental negotiations and debates, the colonial administrators in Malaya, particularly the Labor Department, forced planters to make certain superficial arrangements during the 1920s to provide privacy for coolies. But privacy for coolie couples in housing was not addressed until much later. It was only in 1935 that the barrack-type housing for coolies was changed to detached and semi-detached single and double room cottages measuring 16 x 10 feet for married laborers living with their families.[18]

COMPLICATED REALITIES OF COOLIE HOUSEHOLDS

While superficial privacy was provided to coolie couples in terms of their domestic living spaces, the socioeconomic conditions of the estates—low wages and disproportionate sex ratios complicated the characteristics of such couples' domestic spaces. Coolie-couple households often took on a temporal character, shifting from being "private" at night to being "public" spaces of enterprise and social engagements during the day. As the cases discussed later show, coolie "husbands" and "wives" often collaborated as entrepreneurial partners in their efforts to ensure better living standards for the "family" by offering "messing," or dining, services in their houses to single male coolies. On some occasions, coolie couples even offered single male coolies cheaper lodgings than those provided by managers. Such efforts were based on entrepreneurial but technically fraudulent intentions of shrewd coolie couples, and on occasions, when such arrangements did not materialize as expected, violence broke out between the parties involved. Given the transient nature of domestic spaces and the complex relations between coolies, it becomes impossible to identify the nature of the space and relation at the given time of the violence. In other words, when an incident of violence occurred within a "domestic" space of coolie lines, or between coolie partners, it is often impossible to ascertain whether such incidents were purely domestic violence or violence arising from issues between entrepreneurial partners or even clients and patrons. In fact, given the transactional nature of coolie households, coolie domestic spaces were never entirely "domestic" to begin with. Rather, they were complex spaces in which domestic activity was enmeshed in other processes of entrepreneurship and the provision of services for reward, which made colonial ideas of domesticity irrelevant. In most cases, coolie household or domestic spaces provided a private space for physical intimacies for coolie couples, but simultaneously it was a shared public space that the couples shared with fellow coolies—for offering various kinds of accommodations and services. It was a household space not for a couple but for a larger community. As Sara Mills has convincingly argued, the nature of an individual's participation in societal spaces can hardly be understood by allocating their roles or the spaces to confinement zones of a particular character.[19]

VARIOUS DEPICTIONS OF COOLIE HOUSEHOLDS

While colonial administrative reports and planters' accounts created a stereotype of coolie households as being actually or potentially violent, other actors—like local newspapers, local residents, and Indian nationalists—contributed to the dissemination of such stereotypes.

Local newspapers in Malaya delighted in reporting gruesome domestic violence and immoral relations amongst coolies. Such initiatives by the print media undoubtedly helped boost newspaper sales, but also aided colonial administrators in promoting stereotypes about coolies. Even a cursory glance at local newspapers, particularly those in the English language such as the *Times of Malaya, Perak Pioneer, Malay Mail, The Straits Times, The Malay Mail,* and *The Singapore Free Press and Mercantile Advertiser,* from 1900 to the 1940s, reveals the regular, sensationalized reporting of cases of crimes of passion or domestic violence occurring within coolie households. Such cases, reported in these major dailies, were then picked up and discussed in dailies of various other states within Malaya, ensuring that the occurrence of such incidents was kept alive in the public mind all over the country. The most arresting aspect of the newspaper reporting was the dramatized headlines and catchwords used to underline the Indian identity of the individuals involved in such cases before sensational descriptions of the violence involved (see Table 3.1). Some headlines highlighted the crime itself, some highlighted the relation of the criminals to their victims; either way, the headlines vividly described the race and gender of the perpetrators of violence. The use of racially charged language to generate stereotypes about violence can be argued to be a form of violence in itself—a violence of stigmatization.

While incidences of ill-health resulting from malaria, epidemics, common diseases, toddy poisoning, or suicides from depression due to poor working and living conditions were equally frequent, they received much less media attention than incidents of violence.[20] Although ill-health was a statistically more significant cause of death amongst coolies than murder and suicide, it was the crimes and not the health issues that were reported. There were reasons beyond newspaper sales for such a focus. If issues of Indian coolies' health, wages, and living conditions were too frequently discussed, colonial authorities of Malaya would risk being criticized by Indian anti-colonialists and eventually also by the Government of India, as the Government of Malaya could hardly blame Indian coolies for their health and wage issues. Negative reactions from India would further endanger the labor inflow, which

Table 3.1 Headlines used while reporting Indian crimes in Malaya
(1905–1939)

Date	Title/Catchwords used for Crimes Committed by Indians	Newspaper
May 31, 1905	Murder and Suicide of a Kling*	*Perak Pioneer*
October 17, 1908	Murder by Klings	*The Straits Times*
June 12, 1909	Young Kling Girl Murdered—Husband Admits Crime	*The Times of Malaya*
August 10, 1910	Kling Kills Wife	*Perak Pioneer*
January 20, 1912	Tamil Nearly Hacked His Wife	*Perak Pioneer*
August 12, 1913	Drunkenness and Crime: Tamil Sentenced for Stabbing His Wife to Death	*The Times of Malaya*
July 31, 1914	Tamil Sentenced Five Years for Killing a Wife	*The Singapore Free Press and Mercantile Advertiser*
August 29, 1918	Tamil Sentenced—Husband Murders Wife	*The Singapore Free Press and Mercantile Advertiser*
June 9, 1926	Murder Charge Against Tamil Coolie	*The Straits Times*
July 28, 1927	Tamil Coolie Charged with Assault on Wife	*The Malay Mail*
December 10, 1929	A Coolie Stabbing—Tamil Admits Killing his Mistress	*The Straits Times*
October 23, 1930	Wife Murder on Estate: Tamil Tapper Sentenced to Death	*The Straits Times*
January 17, 1934	Killed His Mistress—Death Sentence to Tamil	*The Singapore Free Press and Mercantile Advertiser*
May 2, 1935	Young Tamil Faces Murder Inquiry	*The Times of Malaya*
March 24, 1939	Wife Alleges Husband Wanted to Sell Her: Indian Convicted for Attempted Murder	*The Singapore Free Press and Mercantile Advertiser*

Source: Collated from various newspapers as stated in the newspaper column with respective dates.

Note: * "Kling" is a derogatory word used to refer to Tamil coolies. There are various believed origins of this term for Tamil coolies in Malaya. Some claim that it is derived from the name "Kalinga" as many traders from the Kalinga Empire in south India (pre-colonial India) used to travel to Malaya to trade. Hence, one group of people claim that the word "Kling" has been in the Malayan vocabulary since then to identify the south Indians with. Another claim suggests that it is a more recent addition to the Malayan vocabulary and that it originates from the "kling kling" noise the anklets Indian women wore (some also say it is from the kling-kling noise of the bangles they wore). Such a suggestion hints at the colonial origin of the term and also the "gendered" nature of the term. Whichever may be the origin of the term, the reality remains that eventually it became a derogatory word to refer to Indians in Malaya.

was an increasingly significant issue by the early 1900s and especially during the rubber slump years from the late 1920s. By condemning coolies for their deaths—through acts of violence and homicides—the colonial administrators seemed to have nothing to lose, or so they thought.

Newspapers were not alone in popularizing such negative images about coolie households. Stereotypical images of coolies and coolie households as violent were widely accepted. Even lower ranks of the colonial bureaucracy and Indian middle and elite classes gave uncritical credence to stories of coolie men abusing their wives, whilst ignoring both the extensive cordial, cooperative relations amongst coolies and even stories of how colonial officials abused coolie women. Alexander Cuthbert, a former police constable in Selangor, FMS, recollects:

> Most Indian coolie men treated their wives like animals. We would intervene and protect them from their ruthless husbands. We became friends with these women coolies on the plantations as we would be on patrol and often spoke to them. Whenever we saw Indian men abusing their wives, we would intervene and protect them from their ruthless husbands. I clearly remember an occasion when I stopped a coolie man from killing his wife and the woman quite instantly fell in love with me and would leave no chance to express her love to me.[21]

The immediate urge of Cuthbert to rescue the coolie woman echoes the same reactions Ainsworth records in his narrative while witnessing marital violence at the coolie lines. Similarly, Dato Rasammah Bhupalan, an ex-Rani of Jhansi Regiment (RJR) recruit, in her interview with me recollected, "[T] hese women [referring to coolie women], you see, were treated so badly by their men. The men behaved as 'cruel animals' with their wives."[22] In fact, she assured me that this was one of the reasons why the coolie women joined the RJR during the Japanese occupation to escape the stranglehold of their men on their lives. Bhupalan argues, "It is in the RJR for the first time these women felt respect and were treated as equals to men and treated as human beings."[23] Indeed, this glorifies the RJR's contribution to these women's lives, but it also hints at the representation of the colonial image of the coolie community by the elite colonized community. Bhupalan seems to recall only the abuses on the plantations without any stories of cooperation, love, and cordial relations. As later discussed in Chapter 5, her account seems to echo the colonial construction of coolie women as victims and proposed that the coolie women were emancipated only after they joined the RJR.

Bhupalan's perceptions of coolie men and women reflected the opinion of the elite Indian community, including nationalists, in Malaya. In 1937, during a campaign to ensure the welfare of Indian coolies on estates in Malaya, the Central Indian Association of Malaya used the image of an Indian coolie man hitting his wife and children to show how certain "bad habits" of coolies encouraged by colonial masters had ruined the Indian coolie family.[24] While the aim of the association was to question the legitimacy of colonial rule, it also perpetuated the idea of the coolie household as a troubled and violent space and simultaneously used domestic violence as an othering feature to distinguish the various kinds of Indians present in Malaya.

Both Indian elites and colonial administrators or planters tried to dehumanize coolies and used the image of the coolie household as cruel and dysfunctional in their efforts to other and discipline them. Therefore, while analyzing representations of coolie household relations in colonial records, we need to question to what extent colonial constructions were true and to what extent they served to reflect elite superiority and to legitimize interventions into the private affairs and space of subalterns. Indeed, there were cases of coolie women being abused, tortured, harassed, and used by coolie men, yet at the same time the reality was not simple, but rather chequered. The pitting of coolie women against their men overlooks the instances where they helped each other against the common violence of the plantation system, including inadequate wages, inappropriate housing conditions, sex ratio imbalance on estates, inadequate logistical support for daily life, and judicial and administrative failure to protect the well-being of coolies.

The portrayal of coolie men as violent abusers and coolie women as passive victims concealed relations of cooperation between coolie men and women in standing against the oppression of colonial administrators and planters. Cooperation between coolie couples was never reported or highlighted in archives. Yet certain glimpses of collaborative relations amongst coolie couples remain as "silenced"[25] mentions in the archives which at times bubble to the surface, giving us enough scope to intersect the colonial and nationalist depictions of coolie households and focus on the complex and myriad intimate relations in which coolies engaged. As historian Anjali Arondekar has reminded us, the absence tells us more about the concerns and tensions within the empire.[26]

CONCEIVING THE POSITION OF COOLIE WOMEN IN COOLIE HOUSEHOLDS

Whilst housing for coolie couples was superficially private, married coolies were often encouraged to utilize their private spaces for activities which were rather public in nature, such as cooking and feeding single coolies.[27] In 1916, the Labor Commission in Malaya commented, "It is in the cooking of his food that the single Tamil laborer most feels the want of his womenfolk."[28] Based on such arguments, planters from the late 1800s and particularly from 1900 onward encouraged coolie women to not only cook for their households, but also to engage in communal cooking in return for extra earnings. In 1862, G. W. Earl, a member of the Malayan planting community, argued, "It is the custom of these people [referring to the coolies] to form themselves into messes ... the wives cooking and receiving a small fee for the service."[29] Thus evolved the *communal messing* infrastructure in coolie lines. While there was no written law to force coolie couples to engage in such entrepreneurial activities, the meager pay coolie couples earned and the constant encouragement of such arrangements by plantation authorities often influenced coolie couples to capitalize on the demand for such enterprises.

Using Victorian or Edwardian ideals of the dichotomous construction of private and public, domestic and work spaces to understand coolie relationships is, therefore, quite inappropriate. While planters and administrators seemed to design privacy for coolie couples in the new housing plans, the constant encouragement of communal messing made boundaries between "private" and "public" transient and complicated. In fact, planters on the majority of estates in FMS, by way of encouraging such arrangements, asserted, "what a bachelor pays to a married couple would amount to a small profit for the latter."[30] Furthermore, given the sex ratio imbalance on the estates, which meant that single coolie men vastly outnumbered both couples and single coolie women, communal messing infrastructure, whilst it cannot be said to have caused promiscuity or violence, facilitated the growth of jealousies, rivalries, and tensions, which were ultimately the product of the artificially produced sex imbalance. Such rivalries could be fed by frequent uncertainty regarding the status of coolie marriages—as to what extent they were genuinely committed relationships as opposed to temporary contractual settlements such as port or depot marriages (see Chapters 1 and 4).[31] If planters and colonial administrators had been genuinely concerned about violence in the coolie lines, they would have addressed such infrastructural problems and not promoted messing and lodging practices that were likely to lead to the escalation of already existing social problems. As Das has shown, the state and the intimate are tied together not physically or visibly as Siamese twins, but rather conceptually.[32] Thus, even though the administrators and planters remained un-confronted by the judges trying cases of coolie domestic violence, the structural design of coolie households and exploitation by the colonial plantation economy hint at the Empire's involvement in such incidents of violence. While the incidents of intimate violence amongst coolies were episodic and temporal, they were more visible than the routine and distilled forms of violence from the Empire and the colonial economy, which remained occluded.

At Gapis estate, a coolie couple, Narayan and Narayanee, regularly offered mess services to single male coolies. On September 2, 1931, one of their regular mess customers, Raman, allegedly killed Narayanee. Upon examination at the local magistrate's court, it was found that while messing at Narayan and Narayanee's coolie quarters, Raman and Narayanee developed intimate relations without the knowledge of Narayan. On the day of the murder, Raman went to visit Narayanee, knowing that Narayan would not be there at the given hour. On reaching the place, Raman claimed to have found Narayanee with another man in a compromising position. Seeing Raman, the other man fled the scene. Raman confessed that he was provoked by the situation and being overpowered by rage at Narayanee's disloyalty toward him, he killed her. The court found Raman guilty of murder and sentenced him to death.[33] Silent in her death, Narayanee's voice was not heard. Was it true that she was having an affair with another man and even with Raman? Was it a premeditated act by Raman resulting from frustration at his inability to have Narayanee as a partner? Or did Raman make up the whole adulterous story in the hope of receiving consideration from the court on the grounds of "grave and sudden provocation"—something that had become a common defense for men who murdered their partners?[34] As natural any of these questions seem, why did the magistrate not investigate such parameters?

While there can be no denying that Raman had killed Narayanee, the case evokes questions about several aspects of the everyday life of coolies in colonial estates, which implicitly contributed toward the escalation of such eventful and visible violence on estates: the disproportionate sex ratio causing jealousy amongst coolie men against those who had a partner; the intimate connections between coolie couples and single coolie men, especially when the latter depended on the former for something as basic as food. There were varied issues involved in this case: communal messing, adultery, and a situation that could be understood as "double-adultery" and jealousy. Finally, the fact that the court did not bother to explore the full story behind the violent episode shows yet another aspect of violence of the colonial legal order toward the coolies, wherein in their attempts to explain violence courts and journalists alike easily resorted to racist stereotypes of immorality or the "inherently violent nature" of coolie men.

On many occasions, communal messing provided opportunities for some coolie couples to make extra money by fraudulently alluring some of their dining patrons to become lodgers in their "married coolie" rooms. In 1935, Meenachi and her husband, Moorthy, offered messing services at their home in Menglembu, Perak. They lured their neighbour, Daniel (a Christian Tamil man), who lived in the same coolie lines in a single men's dormitory, to board at their house. Meenachi and Moorthy offered Daniel lodging and dining provisions at their "married coolie house" for ten dollars a month. To make the offer even more attractive, they had proposed—after one and a half years when the charges would have accumulated to 200 dollars—that they would offer their daughter Padoo in marriage to Daniel. Daniel willingly accepted. This was an attractive offer for any single Indian coolie on an estate in Malaya, as the sex ratio difference created challenges for any male coolie who aspired for a spouse. However, after one and a half years, the couple, Meenachi and Moorthy refused to marry their daughter to Daniel on the ground of religious difference. The couple threw him out of their quarters and Daniel went back to living in a single male coolie's accommodation right next to the couple's house.

After being continuously harassed and antagonized by Meenachi, her sister, and her younger daughter, Angoo, Daniel insisted that Meenachi return his money. Enraged by this, Meenachi, Moorthy, and their other local 'relatives' entered Daniel's quarters to assault him. In due course, Daniel, claiming self-defence, responded violently, killing Meenachi and Angoo. After hearing the case, the court convicted him of murder and sentenced him to death.[35] Evidently, it was a case of an aggrieved victim of a fraudulent transaction, who most likely felt trapped and frustrated with no available recourse to law (in the absence of any written contracts) and resorted to violence as a last means to avenge the injustice done toward him. Again, while the violence cannot be justified, the case foregrounds the complexities and problems inherent in the colonial plantations and judicial procedures, which made it extremely difficult for coolies to seek legal help to address their grievances.

Although the case exhibits fraudulent practices and the desperation of single coolie men to acquire wives, it also reveals that such acts of fraud and conditions of desperation were possible because of the nature of the plantation societies, which were characterized by low wages and sex ratio imbalance. Simultaneously, the case illustrates an example of coolie couples cooperating for their mutual benefit, something that remains silenced in the archival records, colonial and nationalist discourses alike.

In another murder case, in 1932, Kamachee and her husband, both employed as coolies on an estate in Sungei Siput, promised their daughter, Vellachee, in marriage to Karoopusamy, who had recently arrived as a coolie in the same estate. In exchange, Karoopusamy was asked to make some advance payments to the couple which they promised to use to set off the marriage expenses. As in the previous case, Kamachee and her husband offered Karoopasamy meals at their place. After a few months, Karoopusamy became restless and enquired when he could marry Vellachee. However, Kamachee kept putting off his questions. When Karoopasamy became a nagging "nuisance," Kamachee plotted with Vellachee (or so Karoopasamy claimed when accused) and invited Karoopusamy to their quarters late at night with the intention of teaching him a lesson. When he arrived at their house, Kamachee seized him and ordered Vellachee to cry for help from neighbors on the estate. When many people arrived, Karoopusamy supposedly felt threatened, took out a tappers' knife from his pocket, and in a fit slashed Kamachee, resulting in her death. Upon trial, the magistrate found the accused guilty and sentenced him to death.[36] As in the previous case, this case too reveals the everyday violence of the colonial plantation system toward the coolies. Further, it offers yet another example of collaborative, entrepreneurial relations between coolie couples, something that remains airbrushed from the social memory about coolies on colonial estates.

In 1933, Appache, a Tamil coolie, killed Thavani, a married coolie woman who, together with her husband, offered messing services at their room to single coolie men on Bukit Jelutong estate, Seremban. During his trial, Appache claimed that on the day of the murder, he had an argument with Thavani over the quality and quantity of the food she provided and demanded his money back. Thavani refused and he left. But, as he left, Appache claimed that he saw Thavani's husband killing her. In his witness, Thavani's husband and a few others argued that Appache's statement was a complete lie and that they believed Appache was enraged by Thavani's refusal and acting upon his rage, Appache killed her. The witnesses further opined that after the episode, Appache immediately went to the police station and reported that Thavani had been killed by her husband. Putting the statements from the witness in context with the evidence gathered from the police, the court arrived at the conclusion that it was most likely that in order to ensure that the police believed his deposition, Appache claimed that other coolies on the estate had often seen the couple fighting on earlier occasions. In the absence of any concrete proof, the case was dismissed.[37] This case offers an interesting example of colonial stereotypes regarding coolie couples and domestic violence being used by an alleged culprit to claim innocence and escape punishment.

The gendered presumptions that accompanied the colonial stereotypes about violence in coolie households also need to be questioned. The case of *Arumugam vs. Public Prosecutor* (1935) offers an example of over-simplistic gendered perceptions regarding domestic violence.[38] Arumugam, a Tamil coolie man, was convicted of murdering his coolie wife, Sinammah. While the case sounds like one where an enraged husband kills the wife, it is far more complicated.

During the trial, Arumugam had argued that his wife, Sinnamah, regularly neglected her "wifely duties," constantly hit him with "broomsticks," and forced him to live in a cattle shed for a month. To examine if this was true, the court called the couples' children who lived with them and their neighbours as witnesses. All witnesses confirmed the facts of "domestic violence" of the wife against the husband, and Arumugam was given immediate consideration for the murder on the grounds of severe provocation. While this shows how easy it was for a coolie man to get away with wife murder by making a case that he was severely provoked by an act of the victim, it also reveals that coolie men were not the only ones who could be or were abusive toward their partners in "domestic spaces." In fact, if anything, the case highlights how abused husbands could not take advantage of any channels of redress due to gendered notions of respectability and masculinity—an issue with which current societies continue to struggle.

The aforesaid cases complicate our understanding of the "natural" connection colonial administrators and planters created between coolie households and domestic violence and the presentation of coolie women as perennial victims. However, there were some cases of domestic violence wherein coolie women undoubtedly were victims. The reasons coolie men resorted to physical violence against their wives ranged from skewed patriarchal expectations to jealousy. In August 1924, Ananthan, a coolie at Merbau estate, Kuala Langat, murdered his wife, Kamachi. Kamachi had refused to cook him rice even after he had asked for it.[39] In another case in January 1935, Veersamy, a coolie at Stratharlie estate, Selangor, was convicted of stabbing his wife, Dhanapakiam, and her father, Murugam. Veerasamy reported that as Dhanapakiam was always negligent in performing her wifely duties, he had to finally resort to violence as no one would listen to him. Veerasamy complained to the magistrate that Dhanapakiam was seen with other men and was always unpunctual in giving him food, claiming that while his "fellow coolies got their food at 12 o' clock, he had to wait till two and even then often got no food." Veerasamy also mentioned during the trial that his wife even received encouragement for her "unwifely" behavior from her father, Murugan. At the end of the trial, Veerasamy was sentenced to twelve months' rigorous incarceration for his crime.[40] In 1940, another similar case occurred at Majidi estate. Periabuchi's husband resorted to violence for reasons similar to those claimed by Veerasamy in the previous case. Periabuchi, a coolie woman, while being accompanied by an eyewitness, sought police help upon being severely beaten by her husband for not serving him properly cooked food. The husband was then sentenced to rigorous imprisonment.[41]

There were also cases in which the colonial administrative infrastructure did not act as expected. On some occasions, the attitudes of the colonial administrators contributed to the occurrence of domestic violence and at times resulted in the death of the victims. In June 1937, Ponnusamy, a coolie at an estate in Selangor, was sentenced to rigorous imprisonment for killing his wife, Poorni. While newspaper reports captured the violent killing of a coolie wife by her ruthless husband, it did not do justice to all the other circumstances and subjects involved indirectly in this horrific incident. Poorni reported to the Controller of Labor office at Klang that she was regularly beaten and abused by Ponnusamy and wanted the officer to intervene. However, the officer advised her to give Ponnusamy another chance, promising that if the abuse continued thereafter, he would intervene. Ponnusamy, enraged at this act of Poorni, stabbed her forty-eight times, which resulted in her death.[42] Such cases show that coolie women, using available colonial infrastructural help like police, watchmen, and magistrates, took initiatives to report such abuses when they felt the need. However, as the case of Poorni hints, colonial authorities were only keen on registering such complaints and waiting for crimes to be committed and then using such examples to exhibit the problematic relations between coolie couples. By sending the victims back to face abuses instead of doing something substantial to ensure protection to the concerned coolie women, the colonial administrators at times knowingly or unknowingly promoted incidents of domestic violence within coolie households. But what was highlighted when such cases got reported in the newspapers was that a coolie man had brutally killed his wife.

The aforesaid case studies reveal the failure or inefficiency of colonial administrators to engage with the underlying problems which caused violent crimes within "domestic spaces." In most of these cases, the intervention of the Empire stopped at the doorstep of the coolie house but their prejudicial judgments did not. For instance, in the case discussed in the vignette, the planter refrains from intervening just as in the case described earlier, a coolie woman initiated a complaint to the police, but the police refrained from acting on it. The Empire, by normalizing violence within the domestic space rather than addressing it, performed its own kind of violence toward the victims of domestic violence. Such structural violence remains veiled, however, folded within the everyday due to its lack of physicality or visibility.

The mutilated, violated, or harmed bodies of the women were used to exhibit the demonic characters of certain colonized men and humiliate them (as has already been argued in other contexts in gender history). The cases show how, while the event of the violence, wherein the coolie man kills his wife, is highlighted, what remains concealed is that the root of this event lay in the everyday. The Empire's everyday engagement with coolies often caused such events, in that the Empire witnessed but chose not to address the signs of everyday violence. It almost appears as if the Empire waited so that the everyday signs of violence culminated into an act of violence—an event which could then be used by the colonial state to make legible only a particular kind of violence, that is, the violence of coolie men perpetrated toward their coolie wives or partners. Thus, the question that such cases invite us to ask is: why did the Empire fail to address such acts of violence—was it a reluctance to perform its expected role or was it more of an administrative failure? Perhaps there can be no single answer to this. Nonetheless, such cases lay bare how colonial everyday violence, although less visible, remained a constant factor in the "eventful" violence perpetrated by coolies.

Furthermore, the everyday lives of coolies were checkered with a plethora of experiences, and colonial maneuverings or distortions of facts led to sensationalizing a few particular traits of coolie households, which barely do justice to the complex nature of intimate relations within such households. A closer look at the households reveals the collective efforts of coolie women and men to counter the violence of the colonial administration and plantation system against them by becoming entrepreneurial partners to earn more profits in approved or deviant ways. This revelation contrasts with the pictures of coolies and coolie households recorded in the archives. What these cases force us to consider is, while many of the cases exhibited violence in domestic spaces, involving marital or intimate relations, they were not necessarily incidents of domestic (in terms of space and relation) or marital violence, largely because "domestic space" is an inadequate description of households that included complex and transient relations and activities.

These cases reveal how limiting and problematic our stereotypical categorization of domestic violence and victim identities can be. First of all, not all acts of violence occurring within domestic spaces can be classified as domestic violence. Second, gender-based perceptions of victims and perpetrators may not only be simplistic, but also erroneous. In fact, what most of the cases exhibit is that coolies who were involved in these violent incidents harboured transient identities of victim and perpetrator—at times alternating between them, at times harbouring both identities simultaneously. The cases of collaboration between coolie men and women and women perpetrators of violence thus prompt a reconsideration of gendered ideas of crime, agency, and cooperation within coolie households, which are so often described as one-way violent and oppressive relations in the ideological discourses of both colonialism and nationalism.

While the case of the coolie household is a story of unrelenting oppression, this examination reveals examples of how both coolie men and women negotiated the colonial state's control over the intimate lives of coolies. Certainly, racist and sexist social and legal structures of colonial society circumscribed the options for coolie men and women, but they did not eradicate their agency altogether. These cases also reveal women as active agents in shaping family dynamics, which they used for personal as well as household gain.

One characteristic feature that recurs in most of the aforesaid case studies is that while many of the acts of violence occurred within domestic spaces or involved relations within a given household, the violence resulted from a breach of contract or fraudulent transactions amongst coolies. As mentioned earlier, women were not always the victims, but sometimes the perpetrators of violence and at times they engaged in fraudulent transactions at the expense of other coolies. Resort to violence by aggrieved coolies can also be read as an act of frustration and resistance toward colonial administrators' intervention into their social, transactional, and domestic affairs. Without romanticizing this idea of resistance, it may be suggested that coolies who resorted to violence showed their lack of faith in, or rejection of, the way colonial law and administration functioned for them. In their effort to address their grievances of broken contracts, the aggrieved coolies found themselves caught between a hopeless colonial judicial system and the absence of proof for most of the contracts signed between them and their "partners." While women may have been the victims of the violent acts of coolie men, the aforementioned cases also reveal that coolie women acted as agents in their own right by initiating many of the transactional contracts or by denying "patriarchal privileges" to their partners.

The question then arises: why did colonial administrators and planters invest efforts in constructing such stereotypical representations of coolie households?

The answer perhaps lies hidden in the way society functioned in the metropole of the British Empire. Victorian society was particularly keen on categorizing people according to gender, status, and class. Such categorization involved stereotyping as a cognitive shortcut allowing individuals of a certain group to be mentally "filed" as a homogenous group which could be expected to behave in predictable ways. Categorization of "everyday violence" as a cognitive characteristic of a particular class and race was used as a differentiating point between the "respectable," urban, elite classes on the one hand and the working classes on the other. While male versus male dueling was seen as a logical outfall of conflict (although legally unacceptable), men using violence against women was perceived as "wrong," "immoral," and as a sign of an unbalanced social order.[43] Anna Clark has shown how the skewed gendered division of labor in working-class families was taken as a "given" contributor to domestic violence, as men alone could not run the house and had to depend on women and children, which caused an imbalance in domestic roles and behavioral expectations.[44] When colonial administrators and planters went to the colonies, they carried such Victorian categorizations with them and added to these the ranked elements of race and ethnicity. Although the housing conditions and wages given to the coolies were not conducive to family life and did not allow women to adhere to Victorian ideals of womanhood, in judging cases involving coolie households, colonial administrators remained heavily influenced by Victorian ideals of family life and femininity.

The entire colonial process of gendered recruitment of coolies, the physical arrangement of the coolie lines, the promotion of communal messing, the inefficient registration of marriages, and an inadequate justice system easily swayed by racist and classist stereotypical perceptions created a complex context in which tensions between coolies were highly likely to arise and, when they did arise, to lack any legal remedy.

COOLIE WOMEN AND THE POLITICS OF VIOLENCE

As historians, we may find ourselves perpetuating labels used by colonial administrators to describe coolie women, or using contemporary terms to identify the individuals we find in archives, who cannot speak for themselves.

This history of everyday violence in the lives of coolie women serve as a reminder that when we uncritically use such labels, we evoke a different kind of violence, a violence of language and knowledge production of the past. Violence was perpetrated in different guises and it is a mistake to give greater salience to the most visible forms of physical violence whilst ignoring the underlying structural violence that creates the conditions which produce physical violence. Therefore, the image of coolie women as victims of domestic violence at the hands of coolie men cannot be taken as a given. The various personal and entrepreneurial engagements into which coolie women entered reveal the impact of the socioeconomic conditions of colonial plantation societies on their everyday lives, on their sensibilities, intimacies, expectations, and decisions concerning how to engage with fellow coolies as spouses, partners, acquaintances, clients, patrons, or co-workers. It has shown how colonial politics and capitalist economics, as well as nationalist agendas, influenced the contours of the identities of coolie women on estates and how others perceived them.

Thus, the history of everyday violence which is explored in this chapter invites us to rethink given ideas about violence and spaces: to read and engage with acts of violence and judgments of culpability in more complex ways. The cause of violence by coolies was not necessarily gender, race, or flawed patriarchy, as colonial records suggest, but a variety of complex interrelated factors which make it difficult to categorize all incidents as purely domestic violence. The cases in this chapter illuminate the difficulties both men and women of immigrant working classes faced in reporting their concerns to colonial establishments or finding redress for grievances. It also reveals the biases of the colonial legal system based on patriarchal notions of what was "acceptable" violence. While certain categories of male violence could evoke sympathy for the perpetrator, it is hard to imagine similar considerations being given to women offenders, even though records remain silent about such cases, thus contributing to other forms of structural violence. As Johan Galtung has established, violence does not always have to be visible or enacted by a specific individual; it can be enacted indirectly by structures of power.[45] Therefore, the history of coolie women's experiences in coolie households invite us to think about the complexities of life on estates in general, the lives of those coolies who were affected by violence, to think about the colonial administrators, legal institutions, and planters who intervened in such circumstances and to think more critically about colonial and nationalist records which popularized and capitalized, in different ways and for different reasons, on insidious stereotypes of coolie households as violent and chaotic spaces. In so doing, it reveals that underlying the episodic, visible, and eventful incidents of coolie domestic violence persisted the everyday violence of colonial administration and plantation economy, which were at least as damaging, but much less visible.

4

NEGOTIATING INTIMACIES AND MORALITIES

ENTICEMENTS, DESERTIONS, VIOLENCE, AND GENDERED TRIALS

A sensational trial captivated readers of a British Malayan newspaper in January 1910. Letchmee, a coolie woman, had left her "husband," Deyal Singh, after a quarrel. She then went to live with Lal Singh, a police constable at Papan, Perak. Deyal Singh accused Letchmee of husband desertion, but Letchmee asserted that she had never been married to him. "I came with Deyal Singh from India as his mistress," she claimed, and their relationship had been a non-binding union of convenience.[1] Deyal Singh nevertheless considered Letchmee to be "his" woman and kidnapped her from Lal Singh's house with the help of friends. Lal Singh, with other police constables, managed to rescue Letchmee and filed a police complaint against Deyal Singh for trespassing on his domestic property with the intent of assaulting and kidnapping Letchmee. The case became a drawn-out affair in which witnesses changed their statements frequently. Marriage being unproven, Deyal Singh was fined fifty dollars for trespassing, and his friends who assisted him in his crime were fined five dollars each.[2]

Letchmee's act of "husband" desertion was not uncommon amongst the coolie communities in Malaya or in any estate colony across the British Empire, which depended on overseas coolie labor.[3] Continuing the discussion of domestic and familial relations begun in Chapter 3, this chapter ventures into various intimate relations in which coolie women were involved and explores the "moralities" colonial administrators used when describing or legally adjudicating cases concerning coolie intimacies. In so doing, it investigates how coolie women engaged with racialized and gendered understandings of morality and immorality in estate societies.

Colonial administrators and planters in various plantation colonies across the British Empire frequently voiced their outrage at coolie infidelities and "immoral" intimacies on estates, particularly with the act or threat of "wife-enticement," which according to the administrators and planters caused nuisance, social violence, and deaths in estate societies. In 1914, James McNeill and Chimman Lal in their report on the conditions of Indian immigrants asserted that "there is no doubt that the morality of an estate population compares very unfavorably with that of an Indian village."[4] Similarly, in 1916, a committee assigned to report specifically on the condition of indentured labor in Fiji, whilst explaining that the majority of Indian coolies in Fiji were docile and law-abiding subjects who exhibited no "murderous instinct," observed that they could become murderous as a result of sexual jealousy.[5] European overseers and planters shared such perceptions. An overseer in Fiji in his memoir expressed a low opinion of Indian coolie men and asserted that the coolie woman was nothing more than a "Hindu with the morals of an alleycat."[6] Plantations within other colonial empires which imported Indian coolie laborers, such as the French Reunion, recorded similar tropes.[7]

Administrators and overseers were not the only ones to voice such opinions about Indian coolies' intimacies. Reverend H. V. P. Bronkhurst, a missionary in Suriname, recorded in great detail the frequent cases of "immorality" amongst Indian coolies in Suriname.[8] In discussing the "cruel habits" of the coolies in Suriname, he cited a letter from a coolie man, published in the *Demerara Daily Chronicle*, which argued: "the coolie woman is always prone to be enticed away from her husband when superior intelligence and vain promises are brought to bear."[9] Based on the suffering of "coolie husbands," Bronkhurst argued that the government of Suriname should severely punish, preferably by hanging, "the rascals who try to lead astray or draw the wives away from their husbands." He argued this was the only way to set an example for the rest of the population and deter them from giving in to such immorality.[10] Similarly, C. F. Andrews, a Christian missionary and social reformer who had been vocally opposed to the use of indentured labor, argued that "Hindu" coolie women in Fiji were like "a rudderless vessel with its masts broken being whirled down the rapids of a great river without any controlling hand. She passes from one man to another and has lost even the sense of shame in doing so."[11] However, there is one subtle difference in the way Andrews and Bronkhurst depicted the coolie women. While both presented derogatory portraits of the character of coolie women, while casting them as mute bearers of Hindu culture, Andrews, perhaps unintentionally, by his claim that coolie women were unashamed of their behavior, offers a glimpse of the coolie women's fleeting agency in their ability to negotiate and choose partners depending on what those partners had to offer.

Even Indian nationalists used the perception of coolie intimacies as problematic as an argument to mobilize people to support the abolition of indentured migration and colonial rule. Indian nationalists sometimes differed little from Andrews in their depiction of the "immoralities" that plagued coolie communities in plantation colonies. In 1912, Gopal Krishna Gokhale, in his Legislative Council motion to abolish the indentured labor system, stated in front of the Governor-General of India that the indentured labor system, which was primarily male, had promoted the "prostitution of Indian women in colonies," which was "degrading to the people of India from a national point of view."[12] Gokhale's speech, evoking the image of coolie women as both helpless victims and as immoral women, was typical of nationalist discourses that placed the burden of embodying Indian national identity, culture, and labor migration on coolie women. The view of coolie women articulated by these middle-class nationalists was not far removed from that evident in the colonial discourses of British planters and administrators, seeing coolie women as victims of enticements and the immoral practices of coolie men, although it shifted the blame for this condition from coolie men to the colonial context.

When the intimate relations of coolies commanded the attention of colonial administrators in Malaya, they were dealt with in terms of gendered stereotypes of enticing male agents and enticed female subjects. The frequent recurrence of incidents involving acts of wife-enticement, sexual jealousy leading to homicides, adultery, or partner desertion amongst immigrant Indian coolies in Malaya sparked intense debate amongst colonial administrators in India and Malaya from 1900 to 1940. Such debates ignited tensions within the Empire. For instance, the annual reports of the Agent of the Government of India in Malaya during the 1920s–1930s documented the high frequency of domestic troubles arising from sexual jealousy, which were being brought to court by coolies in Malaya. The agents and the Government of India candidly blamed the administration in Malaya for such moral and social offences. In 1929, Agent

S. R. Naidu documented 272 cases of marital enticement and sexual-jealousy-based offences amongst Indian coolies. Similarly, Agent Rao S. M. K. Nair recorded 380 such cases between November 1930 and December 1933, and in 1934, Agent K. A. Mukundan reported 735 cases, the majority of which involved wife-enticement.[13] In their reports, these agents, as representatives of the Indian government in Malaya, regularly accused colonial administrators in Malaya of inefficiency and a slack attitude regarding the social and moral welfare of Indian coolies in the country. Agent Mukundan, discussing the hopelessness of solving coolie marital crimes in Malaya, went so far as to write in 1936, "It is doubtful if anything can be done in this country [Malaya] to remedy this."[14] Defending themselves, the Government of Malaya administrators responded with bold statements in their annual reports on crime in the FMS, which were often publicized and supported by local newspapers from 1934 to 1938, claiming that more than half of the murders in the FMS were caused by Tamil coolie men. These reports even asserted that, as most of these murders were unpremeditated and committed in fits of fury or passion, they were not preventable by police actions.[15] Consequently, as in other colonies, Indian nationalists seized upon the issue in Malaya, using the perception of colonial irresponsibility in ensuring the moral and social well-being of its subjects to question the legitimacy of colonial rule in India and beyond.

Administrators in India and Malaya, missionaries, and Indian nationalists alike downplayed the active engagement of coolie women in incidents of wife-enticement, adultery, and partner desertion as they pursued their political, administrative, and "welfare" concerns. Archival documents, including newspapers, planters' narratives, court records, and government departmental records, report these cases in a stereotypical manner wherein coolie men are always portrayed as the initiators of immoral acts, while coolie women are assumed to be easy prey and passive victims to "immorality," especially to acts of enticement. The question at stake remains: how were ideals of morality constructed in the given contexts? Were the alleged immoralities manifested in disputes over women an inherent and ineradicable trait of the colonized, as colonial discourses suggested, or did it result from the failure of the colonial government to fulfill its duty of care for its subjects, as nationalists claimed? Was it the loss of a romantic partner or the actual or potential loss of a woman as a "commodity" that motivated coolie men to behave violently in alleged cases of immorality? This chapter investigates the ways these claims were made by the protagonists, but goes on to ask the deeper question which is often avoided: to what extent were women really passive subjects of male manipulation, and to what extent were they active agents who sought to take control of their own destiny?

Most scholarly works on coolie lives in colonial contexts tend to promulgate colonial stereotypes of coolie intimacies and moralities, presenting coolie women as victims of coolie men's immoral acts.[16] I suggest that a deeper understanding requires, first, unpacking the construction of the morality–immorality discourse in these contexts to ask how applicable Victorian ideals of morality really were to the cases of coolie families. Second, if we reject the patriarchal portrayals of coolie women by colonial administrators and Indian nationalists as passive subjects, we need to question how much agency coolie women had in their intimate relationships and how they chose to exercise that agency. Using a tapestry of cases concerning intimate or conjugal problems between coolie men and women in Malaya, this chapter analyzes the variety of agencies coolie women exhibited in their intimate relations. It shows that while coolie women were sometimes subject to enticements, they were often far from passive in being "enticed." It argues that Indian coolie women often consciously acted upon fleeting opportunities to forward their own interests, but not necessarily to challenge or change the societal order. These cases reveal that despite the dreary image of coolie women's lives, which involved incidents of sexual jealousy, wife-enticement, adultery, and even wife-murder, coolie women were often able to take control of their interests in their intimate or conjugal lives, even if for a fleeting period.

In the afore-mentioned case, Letchmee claimed to have actively participated in a depot marriage of the type discussed in Chapter 1: a marriage of convenience undertaken as a survival strategy in difficult circumstances. Such a marriage, to Letchmee at least, did not entail the emotional, legal, or cultural bonds of a conventional marriage. In such cases, the standards of morality of the Victorian, or indeed Hindu, "conventional and traditional marriage" scarcely seem applicable. Scholars like Ann Laura Stoler and Jeffrey Weeks have shown that often such moral judgments were a by-product of morality training and baggage that administrators carried from their place of social and racial standing.[17] Similarly, historians such as Indrani Sen and Indrani

Chatterjee have shown how ideals regarding families, intimacies, moralities, and gender have been constructed in relation to both colonized women and colonial "white" women to produce overdetermined images that support particular colonial agendas.[18] Sen and Chatterjee note that such constructions consistently highlight disorderliness in the intimacies of colonized families, while celebrating the orderliness and morality of "white" families.[19] Neither nationalists at the time nor early academic studies concerning coolie intimacies questioned the basis of such stereotypical images and biased judgments.

Letchmee clearly chose to desert her partner to live with another man. Letchmee's agency was enacted not in directly challenging the patriarchal system of marriage or social order but rather in her situational choice: contesting her "husband's" control over her. As many more cases discussed later suggest, coolie women often managed to escape victimhood in one instance only to find themselves subsequently victimized again. Acknowledging the agency of such disenfranchised subjects encourages acknowledgment of other similar subjects in colonial history who exhibited situational agency through brief acts of self-determination and decision-making, attaining episodic breaks in long periods of oppression and suffering. Such brief moments of agency, without transformative goals, can be best described as a fleeting and situational agency, wherein persons used their agency to escape victimhood, even if only temporarily, with varying degrees of success. Whilst these coolie women did not seek to transform the structures that constrained them, tracing coolie women's situational agency in their intimate relations does shed light on these structures. It becomes apparent that judges in colonies were often caught in an administrative double-bind, between the Indian and local (in this case Malayan) governments, concerning which policies should be enacted to contain immorality and crimes of passion in coolie societies, and who should be responsible for implementing those policies.

COOLIE WOMEN'S INTIMATE RELATIONS AND COLONIAL JUDGMENTALISM

In stereotyping coolie intimacies as relations plagued with "immoralities" such as sexual jealousy, wife-enticement, adultery, and desertion,[20] most colonial discourses used Victorian ideals of "morality" and marriage to assess coolie relationships. In the process, they failed to acknowledge that many coolie marriages were non-binding or contractual marriages to begin with, to which morals of conventional "domestic" and "married" life could hardly be applied.[21] Moreover, Malayan dailies, official correspondence between the governments of India and Malaya, annual reports of the Labor Department and the Police Department (FMS), Legislative Council debates in Malaya, and Legislative Assembly debates in India, in their construction of coolie women as passive victims of immoral acts by coolie men, failed to acknowledge or chose to ignore that wife-enticements, adultery, and desertions always involved coolie women who *chose* to leave their partners to live with others, whether their own relatives or other men.

On many occasions, coolie women acted as victims of seduction, enticement, or other "immoral" acts by coolie men, to ensure their survival in an abusive and patriarchal society. It is crucial to note, however, that while many accepted the identity of victimhood during court proceedings, this did not necessarily reflect their understanding of themselves. The images of coolie women as repressed individuals or naïve victims that emerge in such cases can be misleading. Silence or submission to victimhood by coolie women could arguably be a reflection of their conscious strategies of self-representation in front of a particular audience, within a particular context, in order to achieve particular survival goals, that is, surviving not only the moment of the trial but potential chastisement by community or family afterward. The performance of victimhood, then, may reflect coolie women's awareness of their social position, gendered expectations, and perceptions of morality, responsibility, and criminality. Such implicit and strategic acts, which fused elements of survival strategies with implicit forms of resistance, can be best understood as acts of "survivance"[22] in which coolie women might choose to strategically camouflage their agency depending upon the situations in which they found themselves. In acts of survivance, coolie women neither completely accepted victim identity (although it might appear so in legal contexts) nor did they make visible their active resistance to patriarchal norms and colonial understandings of morality. Instead, through fleeting moments of consciously *acting* as victims, coolie women often managed to guarantee their immediate interest in escape, resistance, or survival.

Acts or threats of desertion occurred on various grounds and were not limited to "married" coolie couples. In August 1932, a Hindu coolie man, Periasamy, was convicted for murdering a Christian coolie woman, Therasama, at Kamunting, Perak. During the trial, it was established that Therasama had been Periasamy's mistress for some time and that recently she had given him an ultimatum that if he wanted to continue his relationship with her, he had to convert to Christianity. Periasamy had refused to convert and reportedly Therasama instantaneously deserted him. Enraged by this, Periasamy schemed with the head coolie of the estate to have Therasama fired. Thereafter, Periasamy followed Therasama and finding an opportune place and time, stabbed her to death. The Ipoh Supreme Court found Periasamy guilty and sentenced him to execution.[23] Thus, whether a mistress or wife, in a customary or a contractual marriage, coolie women exhibited fleeting and situational agency by deciding to desert relationships they no longer found suitable. Whilst courts and newspapers recognized such crimes of passion, the colonial judiciary did not explore the broader socioeconomic and political power dynamics that underlay such incidents in the intimate relations of coolies.[24] The fact that coolie women were more likely to move from one man to another than simply to separate, temporarily or permanently, from a partner, was a consequence of the fact that the colonial plantation system made it socially and economically impossible for coolie women to live alone whilst supporting themselves and their children, or to be "moral," especially under gendered wage and ration systems.[25]

While the previous case of partner desertion did not suggest that women engaged in adultery or that there was any form of "wife-enticement," there were other incidents in which such factors were present. On September 18, 1933, the Klang magistrate found Karuppen guilty of enticing away Annamalay's wife, Nagamah, and sentenced him to a fine of fifty dollars or three months of rigorous imprisonment. Annamalay reported to the police that while he had been hospitalized, his fellow coolie, Karuppen, enticed away Nagamah. Subsequently, Nagamah, in her witness statement, argued that she was ill-treated by Annamalay and, thus, in his absence, she asked Karuppen to take her away with him, without informing Karuppen that she was married. Thereafter, they both left the estate and lived in Segamat as husband and wife for three years. Interestingly, the Klang magistrate did not order the marriage between Nagamah and Annamalay to be proven, nor did the magistrate give any consideration to the fact that Nagamah consciously chose to leave her "husband."[26] Regardless of such evidence, the Klang magistrate found Karuppen guilty of wife-enticement even when the concerned woman declared she had willingly left her husband. The failure of colonial judges in such cases to take account of female agency, and their gendered reading of the evidence, may be a product of both their stereotypes of coolie households and their own patriarchal values and assumptions. As Weeks convincingly argues, a community's idea about what is moral is subjective and based on what they consider or are taught to consider as moral, irrespective of the views and lived realities of those being judged.[27]

Not all coolie women admitted their active engagement in adultery or enticement. There were many cases wherein coolie women consciously played the victim and exploited colonial preconceptions of coolie women as passive subjects. In a case presented before the Klang magistrate in February 1935, Periasamy, an estate coolie from Batu Tiga, charged a fellow coolie, Muthusamy, with enticing away his wife, Muthamma, during October 1932. During the trial, Muthamma in her witness statement claimed that after consuming some *curry* offered by the accused she did not know what happened and instantly became obsessed with Muthusamy and followed him to Teluk Anson, where they lived as a married couple. Muthusamy, denying such allegations, stated, "it was Muthamma who enticed him" and that he was unaware that Muthamma was ever married as she had begged him to be her husband and not being able to withstand her entreaties he took her away. When the magistrate demanded proof of marriage, Muthamma's father claimed that she was married to Periasamy. Once again, word of mouth, uncorroborated by any documentary evidence, was proof enough for the magistrate to find Muthusamy guilty of wife-enticement and sentence him to two years of rigorous imprisonment.[28] The evidence given by witnesses in this case appears contradictory and implausible. While Muthusamy feared imprisonment and fines, Muthamma arguably feared violence from her husband and chastisement from her family, who lived in Malaya. Evidently, it was a case of two consenting individuals in a *victimless act* of "immorality." Upon being dragged to court, both played victim as an act of survivance, but as a result of colonial perceptions of coolie women as victims of enticement rather than as enticers themselves, it was Muthamma's story that was believed.

A similar case, *Gopal vs. Thangavello*, was reported in 1933, wherein rather than curry, Veliamal, the wife of Thangavello, claimed to have been enticed upon eating a mango offered to her by Gopal, the alleged "enticer." In her witness, she skillfully narrated how her "feelings changed immediately after eating the mango" and she quite instantaneously fell in love with Gopal while being aware that she was married to Thangavello. After a series of witnesses being produced at the trial, the case finally concluded with the "enticer" being sentenced to three months of rigorous imprisonment.[29] The grounds upon which coolie marriages and wife-enticements were judged and proven were clearly problematic, in that they were based more on stereotypical gendered views of coolies than on the credibility of the evidence presented. Such cases provide evidence of how coolie women displayed fleeting signs of agency when they capitalized on gendered preconceptions, particularly of who was responsible for initiating the "enticement." In the course of trials, coolie women projected themselves as innocent victims of sinister manipulations of coolie men and portrayed their paramours, with whom they had collaborated, as villains, to save themselves from social, legal, and even familial chastisement. Such stories show the situational character of liaisons between coolie women and their partners.

Coolie women were not the only ones taking advantage of loopholes in colonial law. Coolie men escaped being convicted as "enticers" by capitalizing on the lack of documentary or oral evidence of marriage. As seen in several cases, the most significant challenge for judges was the validation of coolie marriages due to the absence of legal documents or reliable witnesses to prove the marriage. Forced to depend upon the oral accounts of witnesses, the judiciary struggled to establish the truth in many cases. As Agent Sahib reported in 1930, prosecution in the majority of the cases of marital crimes (such as "enticement") amongst coolies failed and "criminals" got away easily as marriages could not be validated.[30] Similarly, Agent Mukundan, in his 1934 annual report, asserted:

The common plea of the accused person when a husband alleges that his wife has been taken away by another man is that there was no regular marriage between the two, and on this plea the culprit very often not only escapes punishment but is also able to retain the woman.[31]

Mukandan was clearly unconcerned with the wishes of "the woman" herself, who is spoken of as if she were a piece of property, rather than an agent in her own right. In the attitudes of this Indian servant of the British Empire, the patriarchal assumptions of Indian and British imperial societies seem mutually reinforcing.

In 1930, Supramaniam, a coolie man at Bidor estate, Perak, accused Gandiah, another coolie, of stabbing Sanassiamah, a coolie woman, to death. It was reported that Sanassiamah was Gandiah's wife and, simultaneously, Supramaniam's mistress. While Gandiah reported that Sanassiamah was enticed away by Supramaniam, the latter claimed that he was enticed by Sanassiamah. According to Supramaniam, he did not know Sanassiamah before leaving employment on the said estate and meeting her at a station en route to his new place of employment, where Sanassiamah introduced herself as Parvathy, a single woman, and was eager to accompany him and live with him as "husband and wife" without going through a customary or legal marriage.[32] As the trial progressed, Gandiah claimed that on the day of the stabbing, he found Sanassiamah and had convinced her to return to him. Therefore, he claimed to have no reason to stab her. Gandiah further insisted that as Supramaniam lost his control over Sanassiamah, he became enraged with fury, stabbed her, and, to escape the charge of murder, blamed Gandiah. As there was no reliable evidence produced at the court to prove the marriage, the Counsel found neither man guilty and dropped the case.[33] It is evident that Sanassiamah capitalized on her marriage with Gandiah not being legally registered and eloped with Supramaniam. Simultaneously, Supramaniam capitalized on the same lack of documentation to claim that he was not responsible for enticing Sanassiamah as she did not claim to be married, nor was there any proof of her being married to Gandiah. Interestingly, the court seemed to have no concern with the need to punish the murderer, irrespective of the "enticement." Its focus was entirely upon the issue of wife-enticement and not the crime of murder.

Some cases tried at the magistrate's courts did not even involve any substantial acts of enticement or immorality, but merely the threat of it;

nonetheless, issues of morality and immorality were excavated from the cases and publicized by both administrators and local newspapers. On October 22, 1908, the *Perak Pioneer*, a popular daily in Malaya (FMS), reported a murder case:

> Of all the races living under the sun, the low Tamil is perhaps, *the most immoral* [author's emphasis] ... for jealousy, fury and ungovernable jealousy he beats all others. The latest in the case ... comes from Ipoh, where a Tamil ... hacked his wife to death. The deceased who was but eighteen, told her husband that she was tired of him and would seek another protector. It may have been an idle threat, made perhaps to secure a new *raokai* [partner], but it set the fire ablaze in the heart of her jealous husband, and losing all control over himself, he drew her on to his knee and with a grass cutter's knife, he almost decapitated her.... The unfortunate woman screamed for help but ere her father could arrive and disarm the murderer, her head had nearly been hacked from the trunk.[34]

The dramatic description and the sensationalized language of the newspaper account of this horrific event followed the stereotypical pattern of portraying coolie men as brutal and animalistic and coolie women as passive victims of such brutality. But it also offered a glimpse of the agency of the wife. She had consciously expressed her intention to seek another protector as she was tired of her husband: in so doing, she sought to negate the agency of her husband over her. Furthermore, as the woman's father lived nearby, she may have presumed his support and protection when she expressed her intention of deserting her husband. She had consciously stated her plan of action, proving that she was far from being a passive subject in the household. Cases like this suggest that coolie women with local relatives had a situational advantage in dealing with unsatisfactory husbands or partners since the women had the option of moving in with their family. In 1930, Ganapakium left her husband, Rangasamy (both coolies at Sungei Gapis estate, Selangor), to stay in the same estate with her mother because she was ill and refused to return to him thereafter. Enraged by what Rangasamy presumed to be immorality and desertion, he stabbed Ganapakium, killing her. The court sentenced Rangasamy to death on July 20, 1930.[35] While one cannot discount the fact that both Ganapakium and the eighteen-year-old victim in Ipoh were brutally murdered, it is also true that prior to being murdered, both women exhibited signs of situational agency by prioritizing their own interests in defiance of their husbands. It is likely that many similar cases that did not result in violence or murder were simply never reported.

There were also cases wherein coolie men murdered or attempted violence against fellow coolie men and when put on trial, claimed that they committed the crime as the other men had acted as "enticers" toward their wives and hence had become threats to their marriage. In June 1937, Devasagayam, a coolie at Sepang estate, was tried for the murder of Rengasamy. Devasagayam claimed that he committed the crime in self-defense as Rengasamy, Perumal, and their friends tried to murder him. However, when Perumal and his friends were brought to the stand, they alleged that while they repented the death of their friend Rengasamy, they were only trying to protect Perumal's wife, Meenachie. According to them, Devasagayam was an immoral man who had always had an eye on Meenachie and had tried to entice her away from Perumal multiple times. However, when Meenachie was brought to the stand, she denied ever being approached by Devasagayam.[36] The court found Devasagayam guilty of culpable homicide and he was sentenced to rigorous imprisonment. What is interesting to note here is that enticement, or the threat of it, was used by Perumal and his friends as a justification to engage in violence against a fellow coolie. We will never know if there was a real threat of enticement or whether Perumal and his friends attempted to cause harm to Devasagayam for other reasons, but this case suggests that coolie men understood that they were more likely to receive sympathetic treatment from colonial administrators if they cited the cause of enticement.

Such cases even raise the question as to whether the colonial judiciary and bureaucrats were implicitly sanctioning or even promoting crimes of passion amongst coolies through the randomness of their judgments or failure to act at all in regard to certain crimes. For instance, colonial judges often gave consideration to the "provocation" experienced by aggrieved husbands. On February 16, 1935, Ramasamy, a coolie at Chemor, Ipoh, was charged with killing his wife, Marie, with a *parang*. During the trial, based on oral evidence, Ramasamy and Marie's marriage was proven and the issue of Marie's intimacy with another man was raised but not proven. Charged with murder, a death sentence would have been customary, but the judge showed mercy and sentenced Ramasamy to ten years of imprisonment. Explaining his leniency, the judge commented that as Ramasamy was aggrieved and provoked by the extreme situation, he was eligible for judicial mercy.[37] In another instance, earlier in 1934, Manickam, a coolie at Fermanangah estate, Sepang, murdered his wife for misbehaving with other men. The marriage was proved and during the trial, Sepang asserted: "Yes, I committed the crime and I think six years' imprisonment will be sufficient."[38] While the jury convicted him for his crime, they also recommended him for the judge's mercy.[39] In another case, on March 22, 1907, Govendan, a coolie on the Matang Batu estate, was sentenced to death for murdering his mistress, Talimah. During the trial it was established that Govendan was provoked by an extreme situation wherein he walked in to witness Talimah having sexual intercourse with another coolie, whereupon he murdered Talimah. As the marriage was not proven, Govendan, unlike Ramasamy or Manickam, received no consideration for being provoked.[40]

The refusal of the colonial judiciary to engage with underlying social dynamics led to the apparent arbitrariness of their judgments in cases concerning intimate relationships amongst coolies. Some were judged as criminal cases of wife-enticement despite no convincing evidence of enticement being presented and even when there was no proof of marriage. Violence, even murder, by aggrieved husbands was more likely to receive leniency than acts of "enticement" by men, which also involved women's agency, but for which it was men who were held responsible. The cases reveal the inadequacies of colonial law in addressing the variety of incidences brought to the courts by colonized subjects. While in some cases, women were truly victims, in other cases, they chose to play the victim in order to escape legal and social punishments. Similarly, while some women chose to desert abusive relationships, others chose to act to secure a more desirable male partner, and whilst some women could be judged to be adulterous, for many, the informal nature of their partnerships and the impossibility of surviving alone meant that adulterous relationships were the only option open to them. If there is one common factor amongst these varied cases, it is that all coolie women were active and consensual participants in the relationships in which they chose to engage, but the failure or refusal of the colonial judiciary to see this led to many questionable judgments.

One characteristic feature that appears in all these cases is coolie men becoming anxious and violent upon losing "their" women. A woman had become not just a companion but also a status marker for a man due to the sex ratio imbalance in estate society. In fact, in such a socioeconomic formation, "having" a woman became a form of social capital for men, irrespective of their race, as women in general were scarce in immigrant communities in Malaya. Having a woman is likely to have privileged coolie men, providing them with some level of respectability in horizontal networks within estate society and at times even in vertical networks, such as cross-racial and cross-class hierarchies. This privilege, however, produced a simultaneous anxiety and a constant fear of loss. Having a woman, especially a "wife," elevated a coolie from the status of "boy" to "man" among his compatriots. Upon taking a wife, a coolie man who was the servant of the planters could claim to have his woman as his own servant, boosting his prestige amongst his peers. Securing a woman offered a man some ideological mobility in acquiring the status of master and protector. Ironically, such men continued to remain "boys" to the colonizers. Nevertheless, coolie men could feel some kind of pride in "owning" a woman—perhaps the only "thing" they could own on the estates. Having a woman of their own can be seen as especially prestigious for coolie men because even most of the colonial officers and planters in Malaya were not allowed to have wives, as their meager pay was insufficient to maintain a wife at a standard of living acceptable by "white" colonial standards.[41] For a coolie, however, losing one's woman to another meant a fall in one's social status, a demotion to a disgraced "boy" once again. This may be why coolie men, after avenging themselves upon enticers or wayward wives, sometimes killed themselves, rather than bear the disgrace.[42]

The frequent resort to crimes of passion by aggrieved coolie men could also be read as an act of resistance to colonial intervention in their domestic affairs. Without romanticizing this idea of resistance, it may be suggested that coolie men were showing their lack of trust in or their rejection of the manner in which colonial law functioned for them. In their effort to make sense of the social context of colonial estate lives, coolie men found themselves caught between the threat of losing their women and the hopelessness of the colonial judicial system, which could do little to address their grievances if marriage could not be proven. Frustrated, but simultaneously aware of how to use claims of provocation to appeal for leniency from the patriarchal judicial system, coolie men capitalized on loopholes in colonial law to punish perceived offenders, whether wife or "enticer," themselves. Whilst women may have been the victims of the violent agency of structurally subjugated coolie men, such cases also hint that for coolie men, coolie women were agents in their own right.

Coolie men who featured in courts as perpetrators of violence addressed coolie women as actors, rather than as abject victims. The violent actions these men engaged in were responses to the actions of the women involved. Why, then, when coolie men claimed that their women had been immoral or un-wifely, did the colonial administrators not address these women as immoral actors in their own right? Cases such as the one where murder was ignored in favor of the question of enticement suggest that the courts were not primarily concerned with saving women from ill-treatment, violence, or immorality; so what caused this reluctance? To answer this, it is useful to unpack the colonial attitude toward these issues by analyzing how women's agency was mapped against perceived men's agency, actions, and patriarchal forms of authority.

To begin with, enticement and adultery are participated in by the individuals involved, *not* undergone. But this was never recognized in colonial discourses. Evidently, while the colonial administrators were preoccupied with gendered ideas of morality and agency, coolie women adapted their survivance tactics according to the contexts in which they found themselves. In so doing, coolie women created flexible and situationally based variants of agency, which were apparently too deceptive for colonial and nationalist discourses to decipher. Whether in enticement or adultery, coolie women were always conscious agents of choice and action. The intention of survival and deliberate actions to seek more advantageous relations remained constant features of their behavior, whether it was desertion, adultery, or even in playing the victim.

IN THE NAME OF SOCIAL ORDER AND NATIONAL HONOR

While increases in the number of wife-enticement cases and related homicides became a concern for the colonial governments of both India and Malaya, each had different ideas regarding solutions to the problem. The

Government of India, through its Labor Enquiry Commissions to Malaya and later through the Agent of the Government of India in Malaya, suggested that Malayan administrators should implement a rigorous and systematic process of registering Indian marriages, enabling the courts to conclusively decide marital cases in estate societies, which in turn would deter coolies from engaging in immoral and violent acts.[43] In response, elite Indians in Malaya (some of whom worked for the colonial administration), while exhibiting their loyalty to the government of Malaya, hinted that better policing and selection of "eligible" immigrants from the ports of India would help control the occurrence of such issues. To them, the root cause of the problem was the careless nature of coolie selection and enlistment by coolie recruiters and port emigration officers.[44] The lack of a central or coordinated initiative from the governments of India and Malaya resulted from the reluctance of either to assume responsibility, and as the two governments' efforts to pass the buck degenerated into a blame game, the issues remained unresolved.

In 1924, pressure from the Indian government led Malayan colonial administrators to respond to the perceived rise in immorality and related homicides in Malaya by enacting the Marriage Registration Act for Hindus, which made it mandatory for all Indians in Malaya to register their marriage. It is important to note here that no such formal marriage registration was required in India itself. From 1925 onward, however, the Agent of the Government of India in Malaya annually reported that the complexity and expense of marriage registration made the Act unpopular amongst coolies.[45] Compiling data from the years 1930–1934, these reports also show that out of 676 reported cases of wife-enticement, 436 prosecutions (65.5 percent) failed due to lack of proof of marriage.[46] The Act failed, therefore, to bring any improvement. Faced with this failure, colonial administrators in India and Malaya chose not to explore the complexities of a problem which had social, cultural, and economic dimensions, nor to expose the avoidance of responsibility which had led to the blame game between them. Rather, they continued to avoid accepting responsibility by stereotyping violent and immoral behavior as an inherent trait of Indian coolies.

The cases examined here and other similar cases show that a protean range of factors led to incidents "immorality" and violence amongst coolies. First, as mentioned earlier, there is the question as to how many coolie marriages were genuine, in that they followed the customary or legal requirements of a marriage to begin with. Second, coolie women were not always or only victims, but also agents. Third, having a wife or a mistress offered certain coolie men a sense of pride and raised their status above that of their womanless peers. Hence, acts of violence amongst coolie men often involved gender and power politics, suggesting that neither attachment nor morality was the sole cause. Finally, living conditions for coolies in Malaya were unsuited to the Victorian ideals of "private" family life and morality, by which colonial administrators constantly judged them. For instance, single coolies of both sexes shared a common room with married couples in coolie houses, as such arrangements saved planters the costs of building separate housing for women and families.[47] Furthermore, as noted in Chapter 3, planters frequently encouraged single coolie men to eat at the houses of married coolies; coolie wives would cook and receive fees for their service.[48] Often, cases of adultery developed from such living arrangements, which allowed little privacy to couples and thereby laid the grounds for illicit relationships. It may be noted that similar issues applied to the working classes in industrial Britain, whose morality was also a perennial source of concern to the imperial ruling class.[49]

Judges rarely understood the lived realities of social and family arrangements in immigrant coolie communities. Outsiders to such communities, colonial judges saw such "immorality" and violence as an incurable disease which could at best be controlled. In their judgments of such cases, colonial bureaucrats, especially judges, tried to impose British moral standards, family ideals, and marital laws without considering the unique social dynamics in immigrant coolie communities. As a result, the legal treatment of such cases remained superficial, ad hoc, and sometimes absurd, uninformed by any systematic understanding of the underlying social causes. It was not that the colonial administration always neglected proper adjudication of law in such cases, nor was it simply that they were bereft of appropriate training, knowledge, experience, and resources to deal with the unique situations arising within immigrant communities in the colonies. Rather, the colonial judiciary was structurally unable to address the deeper causes of sexual competition and the resulting violence within coolie communities without acknowledging the Empire's role in creating those conditions. It was not just, therefore, that judges did not understand coolie life; rather, the structural position of judges in the imperial system meant that they *could* not understand the reality of coolie life and continued to regard themselves as impartial dispensers of justice.

The colonial strategy of demonizing Indian coolie households as inherently immoral and violent spaces backfired by opening the way for a nationalist critique of the colonial order that created such spaces. Rather than challenging the prevalence of violence and immorality amongst coolies, nationalists (both in India and in Malaya) criticized colonial governments for defaming their traditions and causing their fellow Indians of the coolie class to live in immoral conditions. An article in the pro-Indian nationalist newspaper in Malaya, *The Indian*, stated in 1936,

> [I]t is easy to blame him [the coolie] ... but those wiseacres [*sic*] who find fault in him are themselves responsible for his situation ... for past many years one could observe a steady increase in sex crimes among the laboring Indian in Malaya ... and the seeds have been sown by the policy of ... sex-ratio.[50]

A later report in the same newspaper highlighting the problem of sex ratio stated, "[T]he only women available for the immigrant bachelors to marry are the [already] 'married women.'"[51] The sexual morality of coolie women, therefore, became a battleground for colonial and anti-colonialist discourses. Anti-colonialists found unlikely allies in the imperial Government of India, which, in line with its policy of blame shifting, also accused the Malayan government of being responsible for immorality amongst coolies, as evidenced in the annual reports of the Agent of the Government of India in Malaya. It is possible that the Indian bureaucrats who produced such reports themselves had nationalist sympathies.

Moral issues surrounding coolie women became an early mobilizing cause for Indian nationalists to collectively challenge the legitimacy of colonial rule in India. According to Ashwini Tambe, it was precisely such issues in overseas colonies of the British Empire that were the "initial motivation" for M. K. Gandhi to assemble Indian nationalists and protest against the colonial government.[52] Gandhi blamed British policies and provisions on estates for encouraging immorality amongst overseas Indian women and invited Indians to save their culture and women through anti-colonial movements. Tambe argues that the politicization of women's issues and struggles for women's welfare were strategies enabling Gandhi to score significant victories for his nationalist campaign.[53] Nationalist concerns did not remain limited to protest movements. The representative members of the Indian National Congress, who were also members of the various local legislative assemblies in various presidencies in colonial India, engaged in intense and contentious debates in parliament with regard to these issues. In 1928, there was a heated question and answer session in the Madras legislative council between Gopala Menon and S. Satyamurti—local government representatives who were also members of the Indian National Congress—and the Panel Chairman, Khan Bahadur Sir Mohammad Usman Sahib Bahadur, regarding the problems of Indian emigrants in Malaya and Ceylon. Issues concerning sex ratios of migrant laborers and increases in mortality due to suicides in the FMS were amongst the most frequently debated. Menon and Satyamurti repeatedly demanded information concerning factors responsible for increased incidences of death on Malayan plantations during 1926–1927. They enquired if flawed colonial recruitment policies of the Government of Malaya and emigration policies of the Government of India, which led to imbalanced sex ratios on Malayan estates, were responsible for the incidents of immorality causing murders and suicides. The Khan Bahadur evaded all questions and stated, "[T]hose were confidential issues attained by government of India from its agent in Malaya, and that he was not authorized to give information out."[54]

The use of coolie women's issues as an entry channel into politics was not limited to male Indian nationalists. Shobna Nijhawan reveals through her readings of vernacular texts of the anti-colonial movement that Indian elite women made their way into national politics by asserting that the honor of migrant Indian women of the laboring class was being compromised by the colonial power. It was a well-strategized move by Indian elite women to facilitate their entry into colonial-nationalist politics as well-informed subjects and hint toward their eligibility as citizens.[55] Studies by Antoinette Burton, Mrinalini Sinha, and Barbara Ramusack convincingly argue, however, that Indian nationalists who gained political recognition by exhibiting concern for the moral degradation of Indian women ultimately acquiesced to the prevalent colonial discourses and did nothing for the colonized women.[56]

Following the trend established by Indian nationalists within India, elite-class Indians in Malaya also used concerns regarding immorality on estates to rise to political prominence. S. N. Veerasamy, for instance, the first Indian lawyer to sit at the Bar and become a member of the Federal Council in colonial Malaya, stated during a speech at the magistrates' meeting at the Federal Council, Kuala Lumpur, in 1929 that due to sex ratio discrepancies amongst Tamils in Malaya, enticing away married women had become too common, and as most marriages could not be proven as required by the court, most culprits went unpunished. Veerasamy even insisted that the Government of Malaya should become proficient in dealing with grievances of Indian laborers.[57]

Like colonial administrators, Indian nationalists and elites used gender politics to other the "socially backward" classes in order to achieve their respective goals. Indian nationalists accepted the stereotypes purveyed by the colonial administration and turned them against the colonialists. Nationalists never questioned to what extent the racialized and gendered stereotypes of lower-class Indians as immoral and violent were a realistic portrayal of migrant life. It may be that for every act of violence that came to the attention of the colonial authorities, there were scores of domestic disputes that were quietly settled without recourse to the courts by the agency of coolies themselves. No records of such cases are likely to be found, however, since by definition such incidents are not "news," and these were not stories either elite nationalists or British imperialists had any interest in telling.

(RE)VISIONING COOLIE WOMEN'S INTIMACIES

Re-visioning coolie women and their intimate relations in Malaya and beyond lays bare not only the ways in which historians of Empire have excluded coolie women from the center of their studies of colonial labor and migration, but also how much of the literature is imbued with a *victimology* approach that stresses images of coolie women as victims,[58] rather than paying attention to actions taken by such women in their own interests. The close examination of cases such as those mentioned earlier makes it evident that coolie women were constantly enacting their own survival strategies and negotiating claims to autonomy and agency. Such efforts, however, are fleeting and temporal, making their collaborations, agency, and identities situational.

Focusing on depictions of coolie women's roles in various intimate relations as described within court cases reveals evidence that the concerns of both colonial administrators and Indian nationalists regarding Indian coolie women were never really about women's morality or victimhood. Rather, such concerns were gendered political strategies used in a game of power politics in which the winners were those who could establish themselves as the protectors of women. Such gendered political strategies were not unique to Malaya or India. On the contrary, the colonial history of Malaya is closely related to the wider history of racial and sexual politics in plantation colonies and also in the class and sexual politics of the colonial metropole—England. As Lata Mani, Mytheli Sreenivas, and Ann Laura Stoler assert, intimate relations were effectively politicized to serve the interest of the state, or those who held power in the state.[59]

Operating within multiple hegemonies that often made "immorality" inescapable, coolie women strategically manipulated the colonial infrastructure and their position within it to survive or escape unfavorable situations, even if only for brief periods. As the cases here have shown, even in being "enticed," coolie women exhibited choice, determination, calculated survival strategies, and, at times, brief moments of resistance. However, as academics and social beings who generally prefer our stories to have clear-cut conclusions, we are often obsessed with ideas of longevity and permanence and most of these temporal acts of agency, which were momentary and fleeting, remain ignored. In addition, as patriarchal notions of agency and victimhood heavily influenced most newspapers reporters, administrators, and nationalist activists, all refused to acknowledge coolie women's kaleidoscopic roles and participation in such "enticements." Furthermore, in almost all the cases discussed here, there emerge images of coolie women aligning, at least partially, with dominant power structures so that their autonomy and resistance are never absolute but rather remain implicit and ambiguous. Nonetheless, through a complex web of collaboration, silence, conscious strategizing, and decisive acts, coolie women displayed signs of fleeting and situational agency. More importantly, these cases help us understand how individuals can change their strategies without losing their autonomy. They show that coolie women were often *not* passive and voiceless; they were simply not registered, seen, or heard.

5

BECOMING "RANIS"

COOLIE WOMEN AS RANI OF JHANSI REGIMENT
RECRUITS IN WORLD WAR II

We were real soldiers! I and many girls and women from the plantations joined the Rani Jhansi Regiment. I joined the *Jan Baz* Unit, the suicide unit. We trained well, I could shoot rifles, Bren guns, pistols, bigger guns, everything. I was not weak like you see me today. I was fit, strong and trained well for the fight. We were happy, fearless and full of energy.

—MeenachiPerumal,
former soldier in the Rani of Jhansi Regiment[1]

This is how Meenachi Perumal began her account of an exciting chapter in the lives of many coolie women—their service in the Rani of Jhansi Regiment (RJR), a regiment formed by Indian nationalist leader Subash Chandra Bose in 1943 across Japanese-occupied Southeast Asia, to fight for India's independence. Born in Bukit Keming estate, a rubber plantation in Malaya, Meenachi Perumal, like many other Indian women from the estates, joined the RJR in Japanese-occupied Malaya, between 1942 and 1945. Meenachi was sixteen years of age when she joined the regiment's suicide unit and was already a married woman.

Before carrying the story of Meenachi and the RJR forward, it is necessary to explain the context of this chapter and its place in this book. Between the 1920s and late 1930s, Indian coolie women in British Malaya found themselves central to power struggles between the British imperial governments and the Indian nationalists, as described in Chapter 4. These struggles were transformed by the entry of Japan into World War II in December 1941 and its rapid conquest of Singapore, British Malaya, and Burma in order to gain control of the region's rich resources of rubber and tin and deny their use to the Allies.[2]

The loss of Singapore, renamed Syonan by the Japanese conquerors, was a humiliation for the British Empire and was later described by Winston Churchill, the British Prime Minister at the time, as "the worst disaster and largest capitulation in British military history,"[3] thus revealing the psychological impact of the world's most powerful empire being easily defeated by a much smaller Asian army. Eighty-five thousand British, Australian, and British Indian soldiers surrendered to a Japanese army of only 30,000 men. Whilst Churchill was "stupefied" and "stunned" by the scale and rapidity of the defeat,[4] Indian nationalists were encouraged and the Indian Independence League (IIL) perceived an alliance with the Japanese to defeat the British as the surest route to Indian independence.[5] Bose's plan was for the Indian National Army (INA), including the RJR, to assault the British army in India at the northeast frontier, where the British army least expected any attack. Bose began recruiting soldiers and logistical support for the INA and RJR in Malaya in 1943, and historian Tim Harper asserts that Malaya under Japanese occupation became a "recruiting ground" for India's independence movement.[6]

Accounts given by RJR leaders, such as Dato' Rasammah Bhupalan, who joined the RJR with her sister at sixteen (the same age as the coolie Meenachi) but rose up the ranks quickly because of her skills and leadership qualities, and Lakshmi Sahgal (Swaminathan), a doctor by profession and one of the "older" women recruits, who was personally recruited by Bose, along with the few other studies of the RJR, have all accepted that the majority of women who joined the RJR from Malaya were either Indian coolie women or their children who lived in the estates. There has been little exploration, however, of what drove such women to join the RJR and how the RJR experience affected their lives.[7]

Until recently the RJR did not even feature as a subject of historical study in South Asian, Indian, or Southeast Asian history. Of the scholars who have studied RJR, some have depicted it as a feminist movement while others interpret it as a reflection of the extraordinary leadership of Bose in the Indian nationalist movement.[8] Most studies concerning the RJR focus on Bose, whom they present as the dedicated founder and leader of the regiment.

Two studies that mention estate women in the RJR do so in a rather fleeting manner. Joyce Lebra and Nilanjana Sengupta say little about life within the RJR or the lasting effects of the experience on RJR veterans. Lebra and Sengupta briefly discuss four women from the estates who joined the RJR, but the information—largely drawn from Lebra's interviews with these women—seems tailored to fit the mainstream celebratory narrative focused on Bose and the image of the RJR as a revolutionary and egalitarian organization.[9] Lebra's interviews captured vivid recollections of the training for battle, the RJR's retreat from Burma, and the qualities of Bose as a leader, but none of these studies reveals much about the women from the estates in RJR. Consequently, these studies shy away from the opportunity to evaluate and engage with the experiences of estate women who participated in the RJR. The full breadth of women's experience in the overseas Indian nationalist movement and particularly in military service remains to be examined.

Even popular histories of the RJR barely do justice to the complex history of the regiment and of its coolie women recruits. *The Rani of Jhansi Regiment: Fighting for India*, for example—a television documentary which aired on the History Channel, Asia, on February 16, 2012—was widely discussed by my friends and acquaintances in India, Malaysia, and Singapore. They marveled at the courage displayed by the recruits joining this extraordinary women's army, but none seemed to notice the troubling silence about the women who joined the RJR. The thirty-minute-long episode included reenactments of major incidents in RJR history, views from scholars, interviews with RJR officers such as Dato' Rasammah Bhupalan (henceforth Bhupalan), Dr Lakshmi Sahgal (henceforth Sahgal), and Maryawati Arya, along with observations by two lower-ranking veterans who had joined the RJR from the estates, Meenachi Perumal and Anjalai Ponnusamy.[10] The manner in which the show presented the views of the estate women and the relatively brief time allotted to them (approximately four minutes, compared with seventeen minutes for RJR veterans from privileged backgrounds) raises questions about the untold history of the estate women and their engagement in the RJR. The show did offer Anjalai and Meenachi a fleeting opportunity to identify themselves with a transient revolutionary moment in history. But by following mainstream narratives and highlighting the actions and opinions of elite participants, the show created notable silences.[11] Silences are significant and, as Michel-Rolph

Trouillot convincingly suggests, are manufactured by historical accounts as they are produced and consumed.[12]

When I discovered the presence of Meenachi and other estate women in RJR, I wondered how these women, most of whom were born in Malaya as children of estate coolies and had never set foot on Indian soil, related to Bose's patriotic calls. Why did they join the RJR and risk their lives? Was Bose's charisma as hypnotic as nationalist discourses claim? Investigating the context in which coolie women joined the RJR and how they and others remember the regiment, this chapter goes on to ask the deeper questions which nationalist discourses and some recent studies have all avoided: what really motivated coolie women in Malaya to join the RJR? What did everyday life in plantations under Japanese occupation look like vis-à-vis everyday life in the RJR camps? Finding answers to these questions also threw light on Bose's own complex and textured motivations and ambitions regarding the RJR and the estate women upon whom he relied. Having addressed the roles and experiences of coolie women in spaces of labor, domesticity, and intimacy in previous chapters, in this chapter I unpack coolie women's fleeting and situational agency within the space of nationalist politics and armed military service.

Addressing the aforementioned questions, the chapter provides us ground to explore and understand ways in which *situational agents*—in this case, the estate women who joined the RJR—acted and how their engagements with the regiment were constituted, socially and politically, through power-laden discourses, practices, and memories. Furthermore, without dismissing the important role Bose played in the nationalist movement of India, the chapter provides deeper insights into Bose's use of gender politics in warfare, and simultaneously highlights the class-based biases in social memory of the RJR, particularly by discussing how RJR recruits from other social classes perceived the coolie women from the estates. Two hitherto unexplored themes emerge from this exploration. First, while the RJR was overtly created as a revolutionary army, the apparent motive behind it was to draw women into the nationalist movement—a politicization of gender also seen in many other nationalist movements. Second, the RJR offered a situational opportunity to RJR recruits to access survivance within the context of uncertainty, suffering, impoverishment, and danger resulting from the Japanese occupation. As the following discussion reveals, in many cases, the initial motivation of coolie women to engage with the RJR was not political in nature; rather, it was in pursuit of survival. Nonetheless, it can be argued that during their time with the regiment, women developed patriotic sentiments and nationalist identities as a product of the social process of participation in the regiment and the broader nationalist movement.

While the previous chapters have dealt with coolie women within the context of British colonialism, here we engage with a period in Malaya when the coolie women were facing an entirely new context—Japanese occupation. Thus, before progressing any further, it is crucial to answer two central questions: First, why was the RJR founded and what strategies and ideologies underlay its formation? Second, what did everyday estate life look like in Malaya under the Japanese occupation?

FORMATION OF THE RANI OF JHANSI REGIMENT (RJR)

The RJR was a female infantry unit formed in Malaya which later served in Singapore and Burma. The RJR was named after Rani Laxmibai of Jhansi (Figure 5.1), whose death fighting the British army in 1857 in an effort to defend her kingdom made her a celebrated symbol of heroism and patriotism. The RJR enlisted more than a thousand recruits in Malaya, the majority of them young coolie women from the estates.[13] Some scholars have indicated that 80 percent of RJR recruits were from the rubber estates of Malaya.[14] The ex-RJR members I interviewed could not provide exact figures, but they confirmed that the majority of the members of the RJR were illiterate women from the estates and largely second-generation residents of Malaya.[15]

On July 12, 1943, while encouraging Indians in Malaya to join his nationalist efforts, Bose made the first public call to Indian women in Malaya to join the RJR:

It is not important how many rifles you carry on your shoulder or how many cartridges you fire. It is the spiritual force, which will be generated by your heroic example that is important. Indians—both common people and members of the British Indian Army—who are on the border areas of India, will on seeing you march with guns on your shoulders, voluntarily

Figure 5.1 Members of the Rani of Jhansi Regiment with a portrait of Rani Laxmibai of Jhansi at the center

Source: Puan Sri Datin J. Athi Nahappan Collection, courtesy of National Archives of Singapore.

come forward to receive the guns from you and carry on the struggle started by you.... I therefore request all those who want to join the Rani of Jhansi Regiment to come forward and give your names.[16]

Bose explained that women in India were already participating in the national freedom movement in various capacities, and that it was time for Indian women living outside India to participate on equal terms with men as soldiers.[17] While Bose may have personally believed in gender equality, his efforts to engage women in the war for Indian independence were also politically motivated.[18] Bose was neither the first nor the only leader in the Indian nationalist movement to make the mobilization of women a part of the nationalist agenda. In 1913, M. K. Gandhi had already used women to mobilize support for his Satyagraha movement, although he limited women's activities within the freedom struggle to "feminine roles" and constantly glorified Sita[19] as an ideal for Indian women.[20] In forming the RJR, Bose (Figure 5.2) showed that both men and women could respond to nationalist appeals to engage in armed struggle, but the discourses surrounding the RJR also show how notions

Figure 5.2 Subash Chandra Bose reviews "Rani of Jhansi" Regiment and other Indian National Army officers, 1943

Source: Puan Sri Datin J. Athi Nahappan Collection, courtesy of National Archives of Singapore.

of gender were used for propaganda purposes. I will present hereafter a more detailed analysis of how Bose used gender politics involving women from the estates. First, however, it is crucial to understand the context within which Bose sounded his clarion call to Indian women in Malaya, for the trajectories of estate women joining the RJR cannot be understood without referring to the everyday life of Indian coolies on estates under Japanese occupation.

EVERYDAY LIFE FOR INDIANS IN MALAYA UNDER JAPANESE OCCUPATION

British intelligence records are among the few written sources regarding the Japanese occupation that are available to historians. Undoubtedly, these reports reflect particular perspectives, but when set alongside the oral history accounts from survivors in Japanese-occupied Malaya and Singapore, they provide a reasonably reliable glimpse of the everyday life experiences of people during the Japanese occupation.

Initially, most Indians in Malaya and Singapore, including those from the working class, welcomed the coming of the Japanese military, with the hope that their lives would improve.[21] However, they were soon disenchanted and developed a degree of hostility toward the Japanese due to the latter's violent treatment of the people in Malaya and Singapore. Even though the Japanese were less hostile toward Indians than Chinese, simply being racially Indian did not protect them from abuse.[22] The Japanese threw their support behind the IIL, and Indians in Malaya soon understood that IIL membership could provide a measure of security from the Japanese soldiers. Consequently, IIL donation and recruitment drives attracted considerable support from Indians of all socioeconomic backgrounds.

All Indians, irrespective of class, faced hardship during the Japanese occupation, but the experiences of Indians living on estates were unquestionably the worst.[23] By the end of 1942, eighteen Japanese rubber companies had joined together to form the Syonan Rubber Syndicate, which took control of the rubber industry in Singapore and Malaya.[24] The syndicate allowed laborers to work only for ten to fifteen days a month and paid them wages at a per-day rate that was 30 to 40 percent less than pre-war wages in British Malaya.

The estates in Malaya also underwent a fundamental change in administration under the Japanese occupation. Most Europeans, including estate planters, fled or became civilian internees or prisoners of war. To counter the loss of managerial staff for the estates, the Japanese appointed Indian *kirani* as managers and *kangany* as estate clerks and overseers.[25] In many cases, the newly promoted staff, particularly the *kirani*, took advantage of their newly acquired positions to exploit the workforce under them. Ravindra Jain suggests that the *kirani* presumed that by being harsher with their laborers, they could attract more appreciation from the Japanese and obtain rewards. Jain reports instances where, due to the meager wages and lack of regular food, many laborers absented themselves and the *kirani* would raid coolie lines to locate defiant coolies and force them to work. Jain cites instances when the *kirani* entered coolie houses without notice, mentioning that in some instances "coolie women had to run out covering themselves only with gunny bags."[26] Even with pay cuts and coercive labor practices, the rubber syndicate failed to make profits as the Japanese were unable to access world markets to sell manufactured rubber. In April 1943, the Japanese government made massive cuts in the estate workforce, leaving large numbers of coolies unemployed.[27] Alongside rising unemployment, the cost of living reached unprecedented heights during the war. When rice became scarce in 1943, the controlled price for one bag rose to 50 dollars, but inadequate supplies forced people to purchase rice on the black market, where prices ranged between 100 and 150 dollars per bag. The price of other commodities also rose precipitously.[28] Unemployed Indian laborers on the estates could not pay such high prices and the result was impoverishment, hunger, and diseases associated with malnutrition. In 1943, a British Intelligence report stated that from late 1942 to early 1943, "tens of thousands of Indian rubber estate coolies were thrown out of work and many starved to death."[29] The Japanese also rolled back medical care on estates. A post-war report by the Medical Department of Selangor indicates that malaria killed many estate workers between 1941 and 1946 because the Japanese were unable to maintain existing anti-malarial measures.[30] Without work, food, and medical care, sheer survival was a constant challenge for people living on the estates. Michael Stenson notes that the Indian population of Malayan estates fell by 7 percent during the Japanese occupation.[31]

By 1943, the Japanese had launched large-scale construction projects to improve communications and strengthen defenses in the region. Faced with labor shortages on these projects, the Japanese recruited Indian men from the estates to work on construction projects, including the infamous Thailand–Burma "death railway." Some women were taken to work sites but most remained on the estates and had to support themselves by growing vegetables. In the absence of men on the estates, incidents of Japanese soldiers harassing and raping Indian estate women increased. While the number of such episodes was small compared to the number of cases reported for the Chinese community, the constant threat haunted Indian women living on the estates.[32] A British Intelligence report from 1943 captured the fears of Indian estate women in suggesting that many of them were afraid to leave their houses, but also feared staying at home without their husbands or male relatives.[33]

Survivors with first-hand experience of estate life during the war recall the atmosphere of fear. Pachaimmal, an ex-estate laborer, remained on the estate while her husband, Marimuthu Sabapathy, was taken by Japanese soldiers and forced to work on the death railway. Describing her wartime experiences to me, she said:

> We had a good life when the British were here; they treated us fine. They used to come regularly to the estates and send police to inspect the law and order in the estates—we were safe.... During the Japanese, there was no plantation, no food, and it was dangerous. Men were taken to the railway and we were taken to work on dockyards to bind fences.... It was only after the British came back, life went back to being normal again.[34]

A "normal" life for Pachaimmal meant that work, food, and safety were assured. When I asked her to describe her situation before the war, Pachaimmal did not give the impression that her life was entirely happy, but when I asked her to compare her experiences under British rule and during the Japanese occupation, she insisted that life under British rule was undoubtedly better.

Jain's study of the Pal Melayu estate under the Japanese occupation offers yet another revealing glimpse of terrifying episodes experienced by coolie women. There were reports of *kirani* and Japanese soldiers separating newly married coolie couples by sending the men to work on the railway and forcing the wives to become their mistresses. In one instance, a *kirani* named Sivan ordered all women on the Pal Melayu estate to consider him as their husband since their real husbands had been taken to the death railway.[35] Jain also gives examples of Japanese soldiers torturing women by forcing them into a room, stripping them naked, tying them to chairs, and beating them.[36]

Paul Kratoska cites similar reports but also mentions instances when Japanese officers intervened to protect workers, mentioning for example an incident when a *kirani* made inappropriate advances to an Indian estate laborer who had approached him about work on his estate. She complained to the foreman, who ignored the complaint, and then she walked 19 miles to the town of Muar and reported the incident to the Japanese officers. They brought her back, gave her food, and then beat up the *kirani* and ordered him off the estate.[37] Events of this sort notwithstanding, the women on estates could not depend on either the *kirani* or Japanese soldiers for protection, and constantly faced the threat of harm with little prospect of redress.

The situation in urban areas was no better. Even socially and economically privileged Indians living in cities had uncomfortable encounters with the Japanese. In an oral history interview with the National Archives of Singapore, A. K. Motiwalla, an Indian businessman who sold stationery and eventually became a stationery supplier to the INA, stated that the Japanese constantly interfered with the way businessmen ran their businesses. He said that the primary reason he associated himself with the IIL was to ensure his safety and allow him to carry on his business with less interference from the Japanese. He explained that once people were known to be collaborators or members of the IIL, the Japanese usually left them alone.[38]

How, then, were nationalist sentiments and bonds constructed in such a diverse and challenging context? Malayan lawyer S. Chelvasingam MacIntyre reflected on the *artificiality* of such bonding in his memoir, suggested that many Indians joined the IIL under compulsion in the hope that participation would help them survive, a circumstance that the IIL disguised as an indication of enthusiasm for Indian independence.[39] The advantages of collaborating with the IIL were clear and persuasive. But there were fundamental differences in the ways that privileged and less-privileged Indians associated themselves with the IIL and its army. For members of the elite, donations to the IIL, friendship with IIL officials, and business alliances with the IIL served as evidence of strong links to the organization, but such channels were not available to Indians on estates. Estate Indians could barely feed themselves and hence were in no position to make substantial donations to the IIL. In this context, many estate men and women became emboldened to become involved in the INA and the RJR.

NEGOTIATING (IN)SECURITY: ESTATE WOMEN, AGENCY, AND ACTS OF SURVIVANCE

Often in history, when women partake in wars, violence, or riots, various mainstream discourses have made efforts to rationalize such participation as resulting from dedication to protection of their nation or community.[40] Such discourses tend to situate women as following masculine leadership for the "greater good," implying a difficulty in perceiving women as having chosen violent roles of their own volition. In the case of RJR women, the pattern seems no different. In narrating the attraction of the RJR for estate women who had never set foot in India and had not necessarily been aware of the nationalist movement in the country, the memoirs of elite members of the RJR often represent estate women as naïve, being swayed, manipulated, or hypnotized by Bose's nationalist discourse to join the RJR. The frequent emphasis upon Bose's oratory skills appears to resist assigning agency to estate women who joined the RJR on their own volition after weighing the threats and insecurities of their position on the plantations against the potential opportunities that they could access once enlisted in the RJR.

Historian Temma Kaplan has established, in the history of collective action, that women participants in RJR, while contributing towards a larger revolutionary goal, were simultaneously driven by their own sociopolitical consciousness and radical needs.[41] Identification with a long-distance Indian national movement arguably did not come naturally for many Indian women in Malaya, and their motives for joining the RJR varied according to their personal situations. Socioeconomic circumstances predating the influx of Indian nationalists into Malaya and Singapore influenced the choices of Indian women in the estates, and many of these women joined the RJR in pursuit of personal safety rather than for patriotic motives. Other women, faced with similar concerns, had also attempted to capitalize on the opportunities offered by RJR. Sahgal, a medical doctor practicing in Singapore and Malaya when the war broke out, became an RJR commander entrusted by Bose with the task of recruiting. Sahgal recalled that many Malay and Chinese women pleaded to be allowed to join, but she refused them as they were not Indians.[42]

When I asked Dato' Bhupalan why Indian women living on estates joined the RJR, she suggested various socioeconomic realities that underlay the supposed commitment of the participants to Indian nationalism. First, she explained her own motives:

If you ask me what inspired me to join Netaji [referring to Bose], let me tell you first, my parents—both were teachers—were great supporters of Gandhiji's non-violence movement. But I had the good fortune of reading books on the Jallianwalah Bagh massacre in India—my father being a lover of English literature and history used to bring books. The Jallianwalah Bagh book was inspirational to me and we were already learning about political developments around the world in our schools. In a school tutorial of about six students, I remember learning of the 1857 revolt in India. We were being taught that it was a mutiny, but I argued and insisted that it was not a mutiny but was the first war of independence. And even the Satyagraha movement inspired me.... So, when Bose came in and delivered his spectacular speech, we were absolutely motivated to join the RJR. But my family thought me and my sister were stupid to join and it was only after the impressive convincing from the commander of RJR, Laxmi Sahgal, that my mother allowed us to join.[43]

Only after detailing her own motives for joining the RJR did Bhupalan move on to explaining why Indian women from the estates joined. Could this have been a conscious structuring of her narrative to emphasize that at least some women joined the RJR because of their attachment and dedication to the Indian nationalist movement? Perhaps. Eventually, when Bhupalan began to describe why estate women joined the RJR, she said:

Many of them hadn't even heard of India's national independence movement. They were uneducated, they were totally exploited. They were in misery. They were not aware of certain things that were taking place, but they were somewhat aware of Gandhi.... Because of the extreme deprivation they had, it was easy for them to understand that they were in a slave situation and enslaved from dawn to dusk. Even in their families, the women in the estates were treated like slaves. When Netaji spoke of being "free" they were moved. Because of the extreme exploitation and deprivation they faced, they were able to understand what freedom from such an enslaved situation would be. Even in their families their husbands tended to be the "lord" of their lives ... but here came a movement that proved that they were humans and had rights. Netaji gave them the status for which they could give their lives.... *For estate women it was a bonanza*, it was a new world, a rainbow.... The men had a superior, inflexible hold over their wives but I think—when you see in an estate about *forty women or even ten women* wanting to join, then you realize as a man that you cannot control them. But there were times when estate women were faced with stone-wall–like husbands; in such circumstances, the wives would come to the IIL or the Regiment camps and somebody from the army would accompany those women to their estate house and persuade the men.

Once in the RJR, estate women were given arms training and made to feel like real heroes in control of their lives. *For women like us who had education it was easy to associate with the RJR but even the women from the estates, there was inspiration to join.* (Emphasis added)[44]

While Bhupalan seemed attached and empathetic toward the women from the estates, her narrative, like other nationalist discourses, represented the estate women as *objects* of estate economy, patriarchy, and finally nationalism. While we get faint glimpses of their agency, these appear constrained and overpowered by stereotypes created about estate women and their lives. Moreover, in creating generalized ideas why the estate women joined the RJR, elite members of the RJR like Bhupalan, perhaps unconsciously, have devalued the agency of the estate women in conflict and chaos and have thus contributed toward their disempowerment.

Sahgal states in her memoir and in her oral history interview that invoking patriotic sentiments to recruit women from the estates was particularly challenging because they were indifferent to India's freedom struggle. The fact that the majority of the younger women living on estates had been born in Malaya or Singapore and had no first-hand experience of India was one of the major obstacles she faced in recruiting.[45] Like Bhupalan, Sahgal too claimed:

Coolie women were literally treated *as animals*, they were abused and used by the men on the plantations for satisfying various needs. The Regiment for the first time made them feel as "humans" who had more value than being objects of desire for sexual or labor purposes. (Emphasis added)[46]

However, she differs with Bhupalan on one crucial point. According to Bhupalan, estate women spontaneously joined the RJR to escape domestic troubles, but Sahgal found that it required a lot of effort and persistence to persuade them to join the RJR as soldiers. In one of her recruitment drives, Sahgal encouraged the women on estates to join the RJR by arguing:

You know women have a bigger role to play, not just being wives and mothers
... it is not just your kitchen pots and looking after children, cooking food for
your husbands. If you go to the army and your husband does not join, then
he too can see what it is like to cook and look after children.[47]

While both seem sympathetic and supportive of the estate women, their
stereotyping of them as particularly abused and exploited by their men
illustrates how class identity remained woven into the narratives of the
nationalist movement. In contrast to Pachaimmal, neither Bhupalan nor Sahgal
paid much attention to how food scarcity and personal safety influenced estate
laborers.

As evident from these remarks, educated recruits showed a hint of
"othering" in their views of estate women. Their stereotypical view of marital
relations within estate families and the suggestion that estate women were
burdened with work as wives or mothers evoke memories of the way the
British observers stereotyped Indian male laborers as violent and oppressive
toward their docile wives and female relatives.[48]

Accounts by various survivors of the period, both men and women, provide
further evidence concerning the reasons women joined the RJR. For instance,
Seva Singh, who refused to join the INA on the grounds that he had a young
wife and small children at home, recalled:

There were many who joined with their families.... Wives joined the Rani
Jhansi Regiment.... [T]he military recruits were treated better [as compared
to civilians]. But the ones that didn't join they were not treated better. They
were given very poor rations.[49]

In his explanation of why women joined the RJR, Tan Ban Cheng, who
attended a boarding school adjacent to the training ground of the RJR,
claimed:

I think most of them did it because that's the way they could get a good
meal each day, provided with uniforms and so on and given certain privileges
which the local population did not have.... The women soldiers seemed to be
very proud of themselves. And they used to walk with a sort of swagger

because we were all living under very sort of poor conditions. And they were well provided away with nice uniforms and they were well-fed. So they seemed to be enjoying their privilege as soldiers in those days.[50]

As noted in Sahgal's recollections discussed earlier, not all estate women joined the RJR, nor did all those who were recruited join as soldiers. Both Bhupalan and Sahgal mentioned that many women from the estates were asked to join the RJR as cooks or nurses, knowing well that they could not be soldiers.[51] Sahgal recalled that many women she rejected on the grounds of their age were insistent on joining the RJR and proposed joining as cooks.[52] Similarly, Bhupalan told me that many women from the estates became involved in the RJR by collecting food packets, making bandages, and collecting funds. Bhupalan added that all RJR members were treated alike, whether or not they were soldiers: "[O]nce a woman became a recruit (of whatever rank or role) she was considered to be a Rani and was assured the same supply of provisions and protection that the soldiers were given."[53] Focusing on the assurance of protection in the RJR, K. R. Menon, an ex-officer of the IIL who claimed in his oral history interview that he presented an insider's view of the RJR, asserted that women joined the RJR because they wanted to "keep themselves safe from the hands of the Japanese. As they knew the Japanese were not going to leave them as they were...."[54]

The aforesaid observations reveal that the women from the estates were drawn to the RJR in part to secure benefits that were beyond the reach of other women and in part to escape the dangers of the Japanese occupation. This indicates that the estate women used the nationalist ideology, which became dominant amongst Indians in Malaya under Japanese occupation, to improve their own lives and guarantee their survival.

Pachaimmal recalled that her family, not being particularly keen for her to enlist in the INA, donated money and jewelry to the RJR and INA recruitment officers to show support for Bose and also to ensure that they were seen by the Japanese as collaborators with the INA and the RJR.[55] My conversations with Pushpa, another former estate woman and friend of Pachaimmal, supported Pachaimmal's recollection. Pushpa was young at the time of the RJR/INA activities in Malaya, but she could recall vividly that her mother and other acquaintances donated their savings and rations to the IIL. When I enquired why they did so, especially when life on the estates was difficult during the war, Pushpa explained that they wanted the British to be defeated. She further suggested that her family also wanted to have some association with the INA or the RJR.[56]

Pushpa was very young and could only remember the family jewelry going into the donation tins, but her friend David (Dave) Anthony (a Christian Tamil Malaysian), who was present at the same interview, provided some useful insights in this regard. The son of the owner of the estate where Pushpa's parents worked as laborers, Dave grew up with Pushpa and they remain friends. Dave explained to me:

You see everyone used them [referring to the Indian plantation workers)— the British, the Japanese, the rich Indians, and even the Indian nationalists, like Subhash Bose. Bose was a very manipulative man—he used the plantation workers to fulfil his dream to free India.... You see, people say he was liberating women by taking them to the regiment but emancipating these people was not in his mind, he only wanted India's freedom.[57]

Expressing his disapproval, Dave also suggested that Bose and his men lured coolies into donating all their savings in the hope that they would be saved from the Japanese. Although Dave came from a privileged background, he witnessed life on the estates and his views resonate with those of MacIntyre and Stenson, who suggest that support for Bose and the IIL was often coerced, and that Bose "demanded" and ensured that he received donations from the Indian population in Malaya.[58]

The aforementioned recollections and conversations show the myriad capacities and roles in which estate women joined and supported the RJR. But more importantly, it also suggests that estate women weighed likely benefits and costs, potential opportunities, constraints and dangers before choosing whether to participate in the RJR and thereafter deciding on how to participate. The RJR leaders' narratives took away from the estate women their situational agency in negotiating and capitalizing on the context of the war and insecurity to bravely negotiate channels of autonomy and self-determination. Instead, such biased narratives transformed them into puppet-like figures who were spellbound by Bose to contribute to the war. Such depictions represent estate women as instruments in the hands of masculine figures—first, their own husbands and, then, Bose and other nationalist leaders—thus reducing the estate women to subjects without agency and choice of their own.

Interestingly, when I asked Meenachi what drew so many young women to support the RJR, her views seemed to fall somewhere in between the views of elite RJR leaders and the views of men and women from the estates who supported Bose's war efforts but did not physically participate in it. Meenachi described the RJR as a happy, thrilling, and a whole *new* experience for her and many others from the estates. She explained:

> It was the excitement, the adventure! It gave us prestige to join an army of women only. We were not scared, never worried, always happy and excited. Each day was a new and exciting day. We would travel by night and hide during the day. Why wouldn't any young woman want such kind of adventure and excitement? But do remember, not everyone became soldiers, some joined in with heart, they donated all their savings, they cooked, they stitched, they cared for the sick. They too were a part of us even though they didn't take up the arms.[59]

While Meenachi spoke warmly of Bose and the RJR, the spotlight in her narrative was the adventure and excitement that the RJR life offered the women from the estates. She neither referred to patriotic sentiments as a driving force nor brought up any of the stereotypical reasons that Dato' Bhupalan and Sahgal cited. Nor did Meenachi share the views of Menon, Singh, and Dave. Could Meenachi's silence, regarding whether estate women saw association with the RJR as a strategy to guarantee their survival and safety, be read as a strategic avoidance to resist engaging in sensitive topics? We will never know. Eventually, I rephrased and asked her the same question, "What opportunity you think the RJR promised the estate women during the occupation?" After a pause, she briefly exclaimed, "Excitement, my child! It was an exciting and new opportunity." One could read such a response as a reflection of how dominant discourses and memories circulating in a society influence individuals' responses and at times perhaps implicitly oblige them to be silent or continue the same discourse. Nonetheless, arguably many women like Meenachi made sense of the events happening around them in

Japanese-occupied Malaya, and upon weighing the options of staying in the estates or joining the RJR, found the regiment more promising, if only for the lure of excitement and adventure. Such decisions remain telling examples of situational agency. Women were not passively lured into the nationalist movement; they did not simply submit to persuasions. Instead, they exercised their power of decision-making and capitalized on the opportunities presented to them by the chaotic situation.

The themes, the highlighted memories, and the reasons offered in all the aforesaid narratives were diverse. But, by creating a dialogue between the views of Bhupalan, Sahgal, Meenachi, MacIntyre, Menon, Motiwalla, Singh, Pachaimmal, Pushpa, and Dave, it seems reasonable to suggest that women were not joining the RJR only to escape troubled marriages or the "lordship of their husbands" as claimed by Bhupalan, but also and perhaps primarily to escape the hardships and dangers of estate life. The RJR offered regular meals and substantial quantities of food along with some income and provided a safe haven from the *kirani*, *kangany*, and Japanese soldiers. Men in the INA and women in the RJR were paid equally, something that women coolies had never experienced on the estates,[60] and the opportunity to be trained in warfare, a typically "masculine" field, added to the appeal (Figure 5.3). Clearly, RJR women had a protean range of reasons to join the RJR, and each member articulated a different claim and choice while exercising their situational agency in joining the RJR. The same is undoubtedly true of those who considered their options and chose not to join.

THE REWARDS OF PARTICIPATION

Situational forms of agency do not necessarily work in a unilinear, straightforward, or universal way. With the end of the war and the death (or as many claim, disappearance) of Bose, the RJR ceased to exist and former coolie women were forced back to the estates: their hopes of a new life of freedom dashed, at least temporarily.

By May 1945, the RJR's fate was sealed. While they made it to the war zone and took part in Japan's attempted invasion of India, the decisive defeat of the Japanese forces, including the INA, by the British Indian Army (BIA) at

Figure 5.3 Rani of Jhansi Regiment soldier in training
Source: Puan Sri Datin J. Athi Nahappan Collection, courtesy of National Archives of Singapore.

Imphal forced a retreat from India and Burma. The memoirs of RJR veterans emphasize that the Ranis were shattered when they were not allowed to fight in the conflict for which they had trained, but women recruits from the estates had to face another shock when they returned to Malaya. While the experience of war came as a shock for all Ranis and provided a reality check regarding their real role in the conflict, for recruits from the estates, disbandment brought a sense of a directionless future. At the end of the war, different arrangements made for RJR recruits on the basis of their social class became the most telling example of the class and caste differences camouflaged within the RJR. Bose diverted funds belonging to the IIL to benefit members of the RJR, but the money went to elite women. He made arrangements for Ranis to be admitted to boarding schools where they were allowed to pursue whatever subjects they wanted to study,[61] but this plan only benefitted recruits who were educated and came from privileged backgrounds. There were no provisions to improve the lives of Ranis who came from the plantations and had no plans for their future.

Bhupalan described the aftermath of the war in this way:

Even though we returned to Malaya demoralized and devastated having lost the chance to fight the enemy, we were seen to be "real warriors" by the masses. The Ranis had a lifetime opportunity to rediscover themselves and understand their value in society. I believe every woman who was in the Rani of Jhansi Regiment came back changed. Changed for the better, empowered to be a part of the world, to be respected and be understood, and to be given the freedom which for centuries had been denied to women. We came back enthused with these convictions and it became a part of us, our persona.[62]

While Bhupalan universalizes the empowering effect of the RJR, there is no denying that the less-privileged Ranis returned to the estate life they had perhaps hoped to escape. They did not receive scholarships, and they are scarcely mentioned in the autobiographies and memoirs of elite RJR veterans such as Bhupalan, Sahgal, and others who have featured in magazine or newspaper articles or appeared in public forums. Both Bhupalan and Sahgal became important players in politics and social service in Malaya and India respectively, using their experience and association with Bose and the RJR to craft vibrant political lives for themselves. They maintained contact with other members of the RJR's officer corps, but they can barely recall the names of any non-elite recruits from the estates. This is another telling example of the limitations of situational and fleeting agencies. Many coolie women seized the moment brought about by the confluence of the Indian nationalist movement with the chaos of war and Japanese occupation, but their capacity to reap benefits from participation in nationalist activity was massively constrained by their class position.

THE RANIS AS A DISCURSIVE RESOURCE FOR INDIAN NATIONALISTS

Bose used the recruitment of women into the RJR to stress the urgency of war against British rule in India. Involving women had other advantages as well. Bose believed that the RJR could be a powerful psychological weapon for the

INA when it encountered the numerically larger BIA. The RJR symbolized the strength and courage of colonized women in challenging the "masculine"[63] nature of colonial rule. Bhupalan asserted in one of her interviews with me that "Bose intended to attack the masculinity of BIA."[64] According to Bhupalan, Bose intended to use gendered notions of power and courage upheld by Indians at large to shock the BIA. She insisted that Bose was confident that upon seeing Indian women bearing arms and prepared to fight Indian men, the BIA would experience shame and ridicule, which would influence them to join the nationalist cause.[65] In the event, British Indian troops at Imphal were not demoralized by their encounter with the INA/RJR at Imphal and their defeat of the Japanese and INA forces was a turning point in the Burma campaign, putting an end to Japanese dreams of conquering India.[66]

Could it then be argued that the RJR was simply intended to provide a shield for the INA, especially as it was numerically small and could not rationally hope to defeat the BIA in battle? Could it also be a calculated risk, taken at the possible cost of the lives of Ranis, if the male soldiers of the BIA were not demoralized by the sight of Indian women bearing arms? Perhaps a definitive answer can never be found, but if the purpose of the RJR was to serve as a moral boundary or security shield, Bose was not the only nationalist to use women for such purposes. Scholars have extensively discussed how women's bodies have been used as battlegrounds in the politics of nationalism.[67] For instance, Anne McClintock has shown how colonial administrators, Boers, and African nationalists throughout South African history used women's bodies and identities as symbols of moral and racial boundaries against their respective "outsiders."[68] Similarly, Nira Yuval-Davis and Floya Anthias, in their edited volume, *Woman–Nation–State*, captured the three main ways in which nationalist leaders implicated women: as symbolic signifiers of biological–ethnic boundaries for national groups (established by restricting sexual or marital relations to "their" community), as active transmitters and producers of national culture, and as active participants in national struggles.[69] It is possible that Bose did not design the regiment to ensure political agency for the women he recruited, but rather to exhibit them as symbolic bearers of the nation and to serve as an auxiliary unit within the INA.

According to Menon, women joined the RJR to offer services to the INA, the "real army," and not to fight as soldiers. He said:

It [the RJR] was a mere puppet show. And not a single woman knew how to wield a knife properly. They knew how to wield the kitchen knife, but not the knife for the battle. And they had no other source because every day this propaganda going on and asking Indian women to come and join. They are not going to fight, you know, but they are going to do other service for the army—the regular army....[70]

Motiwalla likewise denied that the RJR was truly a fighting force. He said:

It [the RJR] was just propaganda. What Bose actually told us was, these were a handful of Indians [referring to RJR], which I have selected ... [they] are not going to conquer India. And not only that, I don't trust each and everybody. Because once they cross the border, they might go home. Only some of them will stay. My purpose out of these recruits ... is to transfer armour [sic] this British Indian Army in India to rebellion.[71]

Offering a slightly different account, Mamoru Shinozaki, a Japanese diplomat stationed in Singapore during the Japanese occupation, stated in his memoir that the women recruits who were young mothers participated in the daily drills in the RJR camp at Bras Basah Road with their children in their arms, and that when the trainers called for breaks during the daily training, the young mothers attended to their children and breastfed infants.[72] This could be read in various ways, as a reflection of the strong determination of these women to participate in the RJR as soldiers, or that the drills were not serious, given that women with children in their arms could not perform them effectively.

Surprisingly, Sahgal herself said in a speech in 1943:

Indian women here have a supremely responsible part to play, in the furtherance of the Indian Independence Movement and in affording relief to their brethren in need.... It was primarily the task of Indian women to attend to the needs and comforts of the Indian troops in Syonan [Singapore], and this, could be efficiently done only through the creation of a well-organized women's section within the Indian Independence League, and subsequently a country-wide women's movement.[73]

5

Again in early 1945, while recording the experience of the RJR at the war front, Sahgal said:

> The INA soldiers brought to the hospitals, where the Ranis offered them care and support, were touched to the core to find a woman offering him a cool drink of water or sponging his feverish limbs. The wounded bit their lips and stifled their screams and curses, when they found their most painful and foul smelling dressings being changed by gentle hands and not the tough hands of the male orderlies.[74]

That the commander of the RJR made these comments about the RJR's role is shocking, for it supports the view of the INA soldiers that the RJR existed to serve the needs of the real army—the INA—and was not a true fighting unit. Even though the Ranis had gone through military training, in the war zone they were assigned tasks such as nursing, cooking, and providing logistical support for the men of the INA. According to one ex-INA soldier, Damodaran s/o Kesavan, who was present in the Arakan camp, the RJR women acted as nurses and otherwise supported the "real army," which did the fighting.[75] In fact, RJR veterans themselves admit that they found themselves reduced to "corps of nurses" on the battlefield, and in interviews they vented their frustration at not being given a chance to fight in the war for freedom.[76]

Whether the RJR was a mere propaganda army or a genuine fighting unit, it offered overseas Indian women of all classes a way to participate in anti-colonial politics. The morality and security of overseas Indian women, and particularly of unskilled laborers, had been a subject of previous political negotiation between colonial administrators and Indian nationalist leaders,[77] but the women themselves had not directly participated in colonial politics and confrontation: the RJR gave them that opportunity.

(UN)COVERING THE HISTORY OF ORDINARY WOMEN IN EXTRAORDINARY TIMES

Silence and voice have recently been increasingly debated as sites of agency, particularly in gender and women's history research within the context of conflict and war. Methodologically, this chapter's attempts to "hear" voices of coolie women in national movements enforced the usage of different source materials, since the voices of these women in nationalist discourses, archival records, and even in memoirs have customarily been underrepresented. Drawing on a wide variety of voices, this chapter has examined the various ways that silence and voice can be brought into dialogue, to present a more holistic narrative of periods within which archival records are particularly scant and close to absent. The chapter has also shown that historians sometimes have the advantage of engaging with and recording *living archives*—the survivors who have witnessed and experienced the moments of history one studies. By collecting such oral history narratives and curating them, historians can contribute toward making them archival artifacts, expanding the limits of the archives and, in the process, saving histories before they are lost. In their own studies, using such sources, historians can also analyze how interviewees interpret history and their own lives within the given contexts of the past, and how they use them as a source of knowledge. Using such sources and placing them in conversation with recorded histories can, in many instances, even lead to a radical re-historicization and decolonization of colonial histories.

Conceptually, this chapter has shown how giving privilege to presence over absence and to voice over silence has impacted our understanding of the complex ways in which agency was performed, particularly in situations of conflict and insecurity. In the process, it has also shown how fleeting agencies can be identified in an individual's silence.

While the moments of transition, insecurity, and chaos created by war offered estate women opportunities to develop and exercise subtle forms of agency and survivance, their agency and voices were constrained by myriad hierarchical structures of power in the post-war period. Coolie women's choice to join the RJR or support its efforts was often, although not always, based on their socioeconomic background and the dangers the Japanese occupation posed to them. Their decision was as much an act of survivance as it was a demonstration of autonomy. RJR membership undeniably had an empowering dimension for coolie women, regardless of whether this was Bose's primary intention. For the first time, they were rubbing shoulders with privileged men and women and were experiencing life outside the estates. We can see the exercise of autonomy, choice, and situational agency fused together in coolie women's decision to join the nationalist movement.

This chapter has, thus, sought to challenge the dominant and linear narratives of agency, based on voice alone as a necessary precondition for understanding or negotiating fleeting moments of agency and temporal empowerment. It highlights how the estate women who joined the RJR were aware that they were making history and yet had limited means available to document and record those histories. This chapter deepens our understanding of situational agency by allowing us to see the implicit histories of strength, self-determination, and autonomy within an extreme context of war, chaos, insecurity, and instability. Above all, this chapter honors those Indian women soldiers who have yet to make it to the history books.

CONCLUSION

The critical task of this book has been to consider the importance of the everyday experiences of migrant women laborers in national histories, transnational histories, and colonial migration histories. The work has shown that much of the scholarship on coolie communities has uncritically accepted stereotypes of coolies and of coolie women which have their origins in colonialism but were also propagated by elite nationalist opponents of British imperialism. This study has shown that real identities are more complex, situational, and changeable than such stereotypical categories suggest. Importantly, this work has shown, through the everyday histories of coolie women, that identities ranging from "innocent victim" or "abused worker" to "entrepreneur," "moral Indian woman," or "anti-imperialist soldier" could be strategically adopted as and when they were useful to improve an individual's situation and, in some cases, to ensure their survival. I have shown that the enaction of such identities involved complex and fluid forms of "agency" and, in so doing, I have sought to democratize understandings of agency in extremely oppressive situations. Furthermore, I have shown how re-evaluation of coolie women's history can help the rewriting and re-visioning of migration histories along with the histories of South Asia and Malaysia.

(RE)THINKING AGENCY

In thinking about agency in oppressive situations, this book has broadened the definition and understanding of the architecture and mechanics of agential acts, in order to make the definition of agency more inclusive. It has achieved this by accepting situational and fleeting actions, maneuvers, or strategies implemented by vulnerable and oppressed subjects as acts of agency in their own right. By analyzing coolie women's everyday encounters with colonial infrastructures of power, patriarchy, and gendered forms of Indian nationalism, I have demonstrated that in extreme situations of constraint and oppression, agency cannot be expressed in conventional ways; rather, the subjugated individuals perform their agential acts through modified acts of choice, preference, and self-determination, which may or may not appear as a pronounced and visible form of "free action." Thus, in understanding the agency of subjugated individuals in such situations, we must modify conceptions of what count as agential acts to include the implicit, the covert, and the non-oppositional as well as open and defiant acts of resistance. I have achieved this by focusing on the temporality of agency as expressed in fleeting, momentary, and situational acts of agency by coolie women seeking short-term relief or advantage, rather than long-term societal transformation. In so doing, I have not attempted to exclude the importance of agential actions which are more visible and long-lasting, but rather have pointed out that such open, visible, and, therefore, potentially dangerous actions are likely to be a very small proportion of all the acts of agency undertaken within such oppressive contexts. In this context, even the decision by many coolie women to take up arms in the RJR, described in Chapter 5, has been shown to be motivated as much by the desire to escape immediate oppression by the Japanese in Malaya as by the longer-term aim of overthrowing British rule in India.

These fleeting yet strategic moments of agency suggest that coolie women in Malaya, despite their absence from conventional histories, had a sense of their position, the claims they could make, to whom they should direct such appeals, and the kind of appeals that were likely to be effective.

An important contribution of this book has, thus, been to follow the histories of coolie women in their fleeting acts of agency, in the ways they accorded meanings to their lives, made sense of the rights and privileges they believed they enjoyed, or should enjoy, within the dominant society, and struggled in a protean way to vindicate these rights while still remaining subject to oppressive conditions, socially, politically, and economically. This book has thus argued for the need to display intellectual awareness and sensitivity toward the agential acts of suppressed individuals in oppressive conditions, especially in the archives where these fleeting voices and acts are easy to miss.

Each chapter of this book has offered a different lens to reconceptualize perceptions of migrant coolie women and their everyday lives on estates. Challenging long-established stereotypes and biased presumptions, each chapter has dealt with variations in two central and ongoing questions. First, does agency always have to be associated with visibly rebellious activities, which have long-lasting impacts on participants involved? Second, were the migrant coolie women merely passive victims of, or dependents of, their male relatives? While answering these questions through a narration of the everyday lives of coolie women, each chapter has shown, in different ways, that coolie women's apparent conformity to colonial or patriarchal stereotypes was often a conscious strategy, constructed to secure their own interests or negate others' power over them whilst simultaneously protecting themselves from further exploitation.

The framework of conventional historical analysis has, so far, disallowed access to the lives, choices, and agencies of coolie women, deployed individually and collectively, explicitly and implicitly. Many previous accounts of coolie women have misrepresented them by ignoring traces that can only be found by an in-depth reading of archives. Such reading reveals that coolie women exhibited situational agency in multitudinous ways, including depot marriages, collaborative efforts with coolie men in both work and domestic spaces, engagement in illicit relations, desertion of partners or husbands, or choosing to take up arms for a nationalist movement. *Fleeting Agencies* identified and analyzed these displays of agency, often less theatrical and less explicit than open rebellion, but also potentially less risky and more effective in producing concrete, if limited, improvements in the lives of particular coolie women. The work has shown how coolie women actively engaged with a range of challenging situations and contexts—with labor recruitment and migration, work on estates, socialization, personal life, and long-distance Indian nationalism—always seeking to make the most of adverse situations in their everyday lives.

In each chapter, *Fleeting Agencies* acknowledged the laboring women's victimization as well as their situational agency, and thus recognized the nuances in the fluid nature of economic, political, social, and intimate relations between individuals within exploitative situations. It unveils multiple ways in which migrant laboring women and men interacted, cohabited, collaborated, and at times challenged each other. Each chapter has asserted that while coolie women's agency remained mostly implicit, such acts were often carefully calculated strategies, executed either through fleeting collaborations with other members of estate society or through individual efforts to capitalize upon favorable situations and extract the best possible opportunities from them.

PLACING COOLIE WOMEN IN COLONIAL AND NATIONAL HISTORY

This book has shown that a single dominant narrative cannot effectively represent the history of Indian labor migration in Southeast Asia. Instead, it has shown that under the most accessible, but often deceptive layers of history, which are easily available in the archives maintained by the dominant forces in a society, may be found far more complex and tangled stories. It is the responsibility of historians to engage with such diverse entanglements and seek to draw them into the light, rather than simply accepting the dominant narrative that emerges from a surface-reading of the archives. In re-historicizing coolie women and re-conceiving the images of coolie women that dominant narratives have presented, this book has revealed important implications for understanding gender, labor, migration, nation, and community, not only in colonial Malaya and India but across the British Empire. The case studies of coolie women in this book help us foreground the significance of gender in interlinking various regional and transnational histories during the colonial past. On another level, exploring colonial history through coolie women's lives, this book has illuminated how gender and migration, particularly in relation to the Indian women laborers in Malaya, became an important ground for debate in colonial and postcolonial imaginations. Whilst many descendants of coolies in contemporary Malaysia seek to downplay or occlude their coolie heritage, some surviving coolies continue to take pride in their roles in building the "Empire of Rubber" on which the modern postcolonial Malaysian state was built. Therefore, recognizing the broad range of coolie women's experiences in the past not only allows us to foreground the importance of coolie women to national and colonial histories, but also allows us to see connections between past and present trends in the gender politics of labor and social relations, which in turn offers to generate a rich site for proliferating discourses on the entanglements of the past and present dynamics of labor migration.

Paying attention to women labor migrants' everyday lives allows us to foreground the "messy" ways that gender dynamics were implicated in the production of transnational migration patterns and networks, which in turn offered grounds for endless political debates during colonial rule. This book has also shown that a focus on women laborers can make visible the interaction between colonial migration policies, the various modes of organizing and recording intimate relations amongst migrant communities, and the ways these relations became grounds for proliferating transnational and transregional nationalist discourses and movements. Thus, to some extent *Fleeting Agencies* not only re-historicizes coolie histories, but also the histories of South Asia, Southeast Asia, and migration therein.

(RE)IMAGINING SOUTH ASIAN HISTORY

By bringing South Asian and Southeast Asian history into a common analytical space alongside British history, this book unsettles imagined boundaries which treat these histories as separate. In particular, this book has illuminated how the experiences of South Asian labor migrants globally became an important ground for debate within Indian nationalism and colonial politics, showing that the history of South Asia itself cannot be completely understood if the histories of global South Asians are neglected. Furthermore, this book shows that writing a history of coolie women involves a rewriting of many other related histories. By foregrounding the roles of migrant women laborers in sociopolitical and economic structures, tissues of connection between the histories of "different" spaces, the borders of which have been enforced on our imagination by imperial actors, are brought into view. The lens of coolie women's histories can bring to light many lesser-known textures hidden in colonial history, migration history, and global

South Asian history. Examples brought to light in this work include changes in colonial labor migration policies from the recruitment of unaccompanied men to the recruitment of women and families to Malayan plantations; the deployment of stereotypes of coolie women and coolie gender relations to serve the political agendas of competing elites, colonial administrators on the one hand and Indian nationalists on the other; and Bose's use of the RJR as a form of gendered propaganda directed at the BIA. This history from below, then, can recognize ignored aspects of colonialism and anti-colonialism and address the long-overdue need for regionally specific histories to not only look inward, but to simultaneously look outward and include vital connections beyond perceived borders. In other words, it emphasizes that the histories of a space, a nation, a region are not only made within its "imagined" boundaries, but also beyond them.

The questions this study has posed, and the answers it has found, constitute an invitation to create a more nuanced analysis of subaltern agencies amongst migrant laborers but also within other marginalized or subordinated groups. Such analysis may move beyond essentialized representations of categories and identities to reveal the real ways in which individuals and groups seek to survive and even prosper in difficult or oppressive circumstances.

EPILOGUE

ACKNOWLEDGING "PAST CONTINUITIES"

Examining the past experiences of coolie women in colonial histories illuminates connections and entanglements between past and present histories. I close this volume with a brief excursion into the present-day experiences of coolie women on estates of Malaysia, suggesting how certain trends in gendered dynamics in migration and labor politics echo past colonial designs.

Today, many ex-coolies, who toiled through the colonial period on estates, have escaped estate life and are proud of the socioeconomic mobility they have achieved. Here, I once again return to Pachaimmal's story. Pachaimmal was first a child coolie, then graduated to becoming a coolie woman at Sungai Buaya estate, Selangor. At the age of eighty-four years, Pachaimmal narrated to me how she had migrated to Malaya with her parents as an infant in the 1930s. She insists, "Life was good but difficult on the estates. It will always have a place in me, which I cannot explain. I have spent most of my life on the estates." Gesturing around her large and well-decorated living room in a double-storied house in Kelana Jaya, she said:

All this is new. My sons and daughter insist. We are accustomed to simpler ways of life. But, I am happy. You know, when you see your children not having to labor through the day in the hot sun, in the rain, under the fear of being fined, it gives you happiness. It makes you feel you have done your best and I can now go in peace.[1]

Selvaraju Sandrakasi (Raju), who was born in Perak in 1985, hails from a family of ex-estate coolies. Today he is well-known for his role as a midfielder in the Malaysian Hockey League. While playing hockey, Raju also earned an engineering degree from Universiti Kuala Lumpur Malaysia France Institute. Many hockey clubs in India, Australia, and Europe have sought to recruit him. Currently, he lives in Malaysia, but travels to Italy every year to play for the Pistoia Hockey club, which he refers to as his "second home." Unlike many others who try to ignore their family histories of laboring on the estates of Malaysia, he takes pride in acknowledging the hard work and persistence through daily struggle that got him and his family where they are now. He explained:

It was not easy. But me and my parents made it. Even then, Indians here who are poor and have grown out of plantation background are still in a very bad condition. They still suffer. Today people know me because I play hockey and represent Malaysia: would they know me if I wasn't? No. I would be one of the many nameless people who do not get acknowledged and are treated with disrespect—sometimes just because of their race. You know, one time, I had a friend on the backseat of my motorbike, who happened to be a Malay woman. We were just returning from somewhere and a police on the street stopped to check if I had kidnapped her. It is crazy! Just because I Indian, she Malay, people just think. We are like dirt and criminals in their eyes. Yes, we are not on estates anymore, but race and class divisions are killing us [referring to Malaysian-Indians]. There are so many of us who are still on the estates struggling to even be alive.[2]

Explaining the difficult situation of Malaysian-Indians in Malaysia, Raju said:

It is really difficult, like we are floating in the middle. When we go to India we are treated like *kings from foreign* [author's emphasis] but here we are treated like rats. We are not totally Indians neither totally Malaysians and yet our parents worked so hard for this country and India too. We make Malaysia and still get treated like some black-skin demons.[3]

My discussions with Raju echoed narratives I had read in archives regarding the racial discrimination and prejudices Indians faced on estates; they also constantly reminded me of Willford's seminal work in which he reminds us that Tamils are living in a "cage" in postcolonial Malaysia.[4]

While Pachaimmal and Raju prefer to be humble in acknowledging their and their families' escape from the estates, some are more expressive. Pushpa and her family, aspects of whose stories appear in the Introduction and Chapter 5, had successfully escaped the clutches of an oppressive estate society. Today, with pride and gratitude toward her parents, Pushpa narrates how they struggled to ensure that she and her siblings got "good education." With joy and pride in her eyes, she showed me a picture of her daughter and said:

> She is more smart than me. She received higher education and recently got married to an American, an Indian American, a citizen of USA. I am very proud of her. Good she went out of here, what has this country to offer? She made it to the land of opportunities.[5]

My discussion with Pushpa made me curious about what her parents would have thought of Malaysia when they migrated there—perhaps a land of opportunity too? But today Pushpa's words suggest that Malaysia is rather a land from where some are eager to escape. This question and Raju's comment on the current situation of Malaysian-Indians on estates soon led me to the stories of many Malaysian-Indian families who still lived on the estates.[6]

On my numerous visits to estates (mostly palm oil plantations and some rubber plantations) in Selangor and Ipoh, I found overwhelming echoes of the past.[7] I came across many families who have lived on the estates for generations but who did not share the good fortune of Pachaimmal, Raju, or Pushpa. Saroja, a sixty-year-old female estate worker in Dunedin Rubber Plantation, lives in the estate accommodation lines with her mother Selamma (102 years in 2011), her sisters, and their families (Figure 6.1). Saroja was born on the same estate and recalls that her parents arrived on an estate during British rule and ever since they have lived and worked on estates. While narrating the situation in the plantation, she broke into tears and explained:

> This plantation, I worked all my life here but suddenly they have decided to close the plantation and make a housing project here. Where will we go?

Figure 6.1 Saroja, her sister, and their mother, Selamma, in their Dunedin estate, Putrajaya, 2011

Source: Author's personal photograph.

Saroja exposed me to yet another layer of reality: that Malaysian-Indian estate workers today are constantly dealing with closure of estates. She explained:

> I never studied, I don't know what else to do. The plantation closes and I have nowhere to live and no place to work.... Life on estates is anyway hard. But at least under the British they had work, now, in a few days we won't even have that. How will we survive?[8]

Along with the closure of estates, there were many other challenges for the estate workers in Malaysia, some being specific to the estate women, such as physical and sexual abuses by overseers and managers. Such incidents remind us that even present-day estate women continue to suffer, although their everyday experiences continue to be overlooked even in many contemporary studies. Nonetheless, while scholarship has seldom engaged with the present-day hardships of estate life for women in Malaysia, some alternative literature has been produced that make us aware of their situation. K. S. Jomo and Josie Zaini's fictionalized *Meena: A Plantation Child Worker* and K. S. Maniam's *Between Lives* have laid bare some of the real and everyday challenges that Malaysian-Indian estate women are forced to engage with in post-independence Malaysia.[9] In particular, Jomo and Zaini made painstaking efforts to turn true stories of women's lives on plantations into a fictionalized comic-book account as a part of a movement to raise consciousness on the issues that women and children estate workers in Asia still regularly face. Meena's story included the daily struggles of estate girls and women—including physically exhausting work, health hazards, and sexual abuse, which remain rampant in present-day Malaysia.[10] However, the Institute for Social Analysis (INSAN), which supported the production and publication of such literature, has since been abolished, leading to further silencing of such realities.[11]

During my visits to the estates, it appeared strikingly visible that the present-day "coolie" population primarily consists of women of Indian descent (now second-, third-, or fourth-generation) and their children. Most of their male relatives have now left the estates to live and work in factories in suburban or urban areas of Malaysia. The plantations are once again dependent upon coolie women to produce and reproduce labor. The estate authorities today, mostly Chinese-owned private corporations, compensate for the out-migration of estate men by employing temporary migrant male laborers from Bangladesh and sometimes from south India. The long absence of male partners and husbands from the estates and the presence of "other" men on the estates have led to social problems on estates reminiscent of those during the colonial era. It is reported that illegitimate intimacies have often developed between estate women and migrant men, and "when the husbands of the concerned women found out, violence, murder and chaos" broke loose on the estates.[12] Once again, one finds a reflection of the structural violence (as discussed in Chapter 3) that sometimes incited violence among coolie couples in the colonial period.

Furthermore, present-day gendered migration schemes, both internally and internationally, have affected the social relations and intimacies of estate women. The watchman of an estate in Semeyenih explained to me that whilst relations are a problem in themselves, they become impossible to handle if children are born out of "casual affairs" between estate women and Bangladeshi men. According to the watchman, these children often become a burden for the women; in most such cases the woman is left alone with the child once the Bangladeshi man returns to Bangladesh at the end of his contract.[13]

Economically too, the situation has changed little for present-day estate women. For instance, during my visits to Abaco Rubber Estate, Semenyih (Figure 6.2), many estate women, who engaged in work similar to that of migrant male workers, expressed their frustration at being paid much less than migrant men. According to the women with whom I spoke, despite the same workload, the Bangladeshi group of laborers, as per inter-governmental understandings and International Labour Organization standards, receive wages following certain strict guidelines; they are paid 1,000–1,200 ringgits per month whereas the women received approximately between 600–750 ringgits per month. Furthermore, with no schools in the vicinity, the children,

Figure 6.2 Women and child estate workers on Abaco rubber estate, Semeyenih, 2011

Source: Author's personal photo.

especially daughters, tend to follow in their mothers' footsteps, serving as helpers to their mothers and young tappers on the estates.[14] For many estate families, then, the cycle of child labor and limited educational opportunities results in a lack of any alternatives for young women to a life of hard labor on the estates.

The question that arises here, then, is: has Malaysia's independence from British rule changed anything for the Malaysian-Indian estate workers? The answer appears to be that little has changed, especially for the women estate workers who continue to work in similar conditions for different owners. The past and present thus remain inseparably entangled in one another. However, current studies of estates, which are mostly at the stage of data collection and analysis, have overlooked the continuities between the past and the present, and consider what they witnessed on present-day estates as "contemporary" features.[15] This failure to consider the historical roots of contemporary labor practices suggests that without knowing the past, we become prisoners of the present. In their efforts to voice the sufferings of the Indian estate community, these scholars shy away from historicizing the condition of women estate workers, constricting their ability to understand the causes of present circumstances and problems.

Focusing on the history of coolie women thus allows us to unravel the power relations within labor and migration policies that, throughout the colonial era and beyond, have depended upon coolie women and, more broadly, on gender politics. Such a historical focus illuminates the gendered implications of such policies that the estate women continue to endure and engage with. In the process, it disrupts more commonplace, generic, and homogenizing narratives of Malaysian-Indian estate workers. Placing together the past and the present-day lives of coolie women in Malaya/Malaysia, thus, forces us to contemplate what happens to a community ensnared in the debris of colonization and decolonization within a now independent nation that, however, remains deeply enmeshed in exploitative global capitalist networks whilst maintaining racial hierarchies rooted in the colonial past. While this book has focused on the past experiences of coolie women on rubber estates of Malaya, the analysis it presents and the questions it raises are pertinent not only to labor and migration histories, but to contemporary sociological and anthropological studies too.

Although more about the lives of Indian coolie women in Malaya has been covered and uncovered in this book than in previous works, there can be no denying that this is only a fragment of their many roles and shades of experiences in estate, local, national, regional, and global histories. Nonetheless, *Fleeting Agencies* has shown that without a more organic view of silences, voices, absences, and presences in archives, the history of subaltern global migrants cannot be effectively written. Moreover, the discussions in this book have made it evident that the history of coolie women can often become a key to unlocking multiple histories of gender, class, race, power, and migration in colonial and, indeed, postcolonial contexts. The work has reinterpreted the history of estate societies and redefined the position of coolie women in colonial history, seeking to penetrate the silencing of subaltern voices and reveal their agential engagements in pursuit of their own goals as well as their contributions to the broader networks of which they were part. Over all, *Fleeting Agencies* has sought to take a step toward recording *a* history of ordinary yet exceptional women, to whom both history and memory have yet to do justice.

GLOSSARY

ayah	A native maid or nursemaid or caregiver.
attap	Roof made with palm leaves.
certu-k-kolu-tali	A form of fake or illegal liaison/marriage which migrants entered into in order to migrate without attracting unwanted attention and investigations from immigration officers. It was a marriage of convenience wherein an actual traditional/customary marriage did not take place, but the parties claimed to be married on record.
Chetty/Chettiar	It is a "title"/surname used by various mercantile, agricultural, and land-owning castes in south India, particularly in Tamil Nadu. During the late nineteenth and twentieth centuries, many Chettiars migrated to colonial plantation colonies to venture into the moneylending business and even try to become planters themselves.
coolie lines	Housing arrangement for coolies on estates. Coolies on estates were housed in matchbox-like barracks, which were guarded and kept under strict surveillance by planters. As these houses were systematically constructed in the form of a line, the British military terminology of "lines" was adopted to describe them.
Dewali/Deepavali	One of the most popular Hindu festivals, which is also known as the festival of lights. It is celebrated in autumn and it symbolizes the victory of light over darkness, knowledge over ignorance, good over evil.

devadasi	Literally the term translates to "female servant of God" in Hindi; however, in reality it is a woman "dedicated" to worship and the service of a priest in a temple for the rest of her life. After the influx of colonialism, the term *devadasi* attained a new texture almost always being associated with prostitution.
indenture	A formal agreement/contract between an employer and employee for a fixed term, usually a minimum of three years.
kangany	A recruiter and overseer of plantation labor in India and Malaysia. A *kangany* was often a plantation laborer or foreman who returned home to recruit workers on commission.
kanji	Malay name for congee, which is a type of rice porridge or gruel popular in many Asian countries
kling	A derogatory word used in parts of Southeast Asia to refer to a person of South Asian origin, especially from south India. There are conflicting claims about the origin of the term. Some claim it was used to describe Indian immigrants from the Kalinga kingdom, while others claim it originates from the sound of the glass bangles south Indian women wore which then became stereotyped as a characteristic feature of the Indian community in Southeast Asia.
latex	The milky fluid found in some trees. The latex from rubber trees is the chief source of natural rubber.
mess	Military term adopted to describe an informal arrangement wherein an individual takes meals in a particular place for a small service fee.
parang	A kind of machete/knife used across the Malay archipelago.
planter	While the term "planter" was used to refer to European individuals in charge of the plantations in Malaya, not all

those referred to as planters were owners of plantations. The term was sometimes applied to overseers or managers who were recruited and sent from Britain by large private plantation companies based in Britain.

raokai — Intimate partner; lover.

rotan/rattan — A long cane.

Shudra — The fourth caste in the Hindu caste hierarchy, ranking below Brahmins, Kshatriyas, and Vaishyas. Shudras were entrusted with the work of serving the castes above them, had almost no rights in society, and lived at the mercy of the castes above them.

tapping — Method of drawing out latex from rubber trees.

thali/tali — A traditional necklace worn by south Indian married women as a sign of marriage.

toddy — An alcoholic drink made from fermenting palm, sugar, and water.

NOTES

INTRODUCTION

1 I use the word "subaltern" following Antonio Gramsci's definition to refer to individuals who are subordinated by those in power on the basis of caste, race, class, gender, language, or culture. Antonio Gramsci, *Selections from Prison Notebooks*, ed. and trans. Quinn Hoare and Geoffery Nowell Smith (London: Lawrence and Wishart, 1971).

2 Gerald Vizenor, *Manifest Manners: Narratives on Postindian Survivance* (Lincoln: Nebraska, 1999). Following Vizenor's definition, by "survivance" I refer to active and agential acts of survival by subaltern individuals, which suggest that individuals do not simply accept the situations they find themselves in but constantly and actively engage with the contexts to improve their situations.

3 I use the phrase "*a* history" because I focus on fragments of histories of coolie women's lives, which can only reflect "a" variant of their multiple histories. Hence, I consciously use "a" instead of "the". I thus resist the temptation to write a generalizing history that privileges only certain actors. Lynn McDonald has argued that androcentric scholars, swayed by an obsession to produce empirical knowledge, have often criticized feminist scholars and scholarship as subjective and value-based. As McDonald explains, knowledge in itself is a constructed reality; thus, value-free research is neither possible nor required. Scholars like MacDonald and others rather urge feminist scholars to be consciously partial and not necessarily aim for creating universal truths through their studies, as theoretically being "general" implies being partial to the privileged actors in the society.

See Lynn McDonald, *The Women Founders of the Social Sciences* (Ottawa: Carleton University Press, 1994); Maria Mies, "Towards a Methodology for Feminist Research," in *Theories of Women's Studies*, ed. Gloria Bowles and R.D. Klein (London: Routledge and Kegan Paul, 1983), 117–139, 118; Rita Mae Kelly, "Liberal Positivist Epistemology and Research on Women and Politics," *Women and Politics* 7 (Fall 1987): 12–27; Mary McCanney Gergen, "Toward a Feminist Metatheory and Methodology in the Social Sciences," in *Feminist Thought and the Structure of Knowledge*, ed. Mary McCanney Gregen (New York: New York University Press, 1988), 87–104, 88.

4   For further discussion on this, see Chapter 2.

5   Pushpa in discussion with the author, May 10, 2011 (Selangor), October 15, 2013 (Selangor): Pushpa's parents had migrated to Malaya as coolies and labored in rubber estates at Ipoh. She was born on the estate, but upon receiving education, she moved out of the estate and settled in Selangor. Although she was never a coolie, she vividly recalls her parents toiling as coolies and has vivid memory of the last years of the Japanese occupation of Malaya and the ensuing British recolonization. She recalled how her parents struggled to make sure she got a good education. Eventually, she moved out of the estate, married, and settled down in Selangor. Her parents and elderly relatives still live in Ipoh. She has a daughter, who has received higher education and recently married an Indian in the United States of America. Although Pushpa relates to her coolie origins, she takes much pride in "making" her daughter go "beyond" Malaysia to settle in the United States, which she calls "the land of opportunities."

Pachaimmal in discussion with the author, May 10, 2011, in Selangor: Pachaimmal (ex-coolie woman at Sungai Buaya estate, Selangor; she was 84 years old at the time of interview) had migrated to Malaya as an infant in the 1930s with her parents. She recalls serving the estate in different capacities at different stages in her life: as a line ayah on the Sungai Buaya estate when she was a child, then as a weeder, and finally worked as a tapping coolie until the 1960s.

6   In my personal interactions with second- and third-generation Indians in Malaysia (specifically in Kuala Lumpur, Selangor, Ipoh, Cameroon Highlands, and some in Singapore), I got a different impression. Most of

these individuals, which included members of the Parti Sosialis Malaysia, members of the Sisters in Islam, and journalist friends, when narrating their family history to me, referred to their parents as rubber-estate workers, and seemed to consciously avoid the term "coolie." Furthermore, while witnessing street quarrels or even while interacting with some Malaysian friends of non-Indian ethnicity, I often noticed that the term "coolie" was used in a derogatory way to refer to poor or lower-class backgrounds of individuals or groups of Indian origin. Some Malaysian-Indian acquaintances and friends from middle-class backgrounds, on learning that I was studying the social history of coolie women in Malaya, ensured that I did not mistake them for "coolie sons or daughters," by making brief references to their ancestors' occupation, such as—"my father came as a clerk in the post office," "my grandfather was a watchman on the estates," or "my family used to own a shop here."

7   Government of India, Legislative Department, "Mr. Gokhale's address to the Council, 'Indentured Labor,'" in *Proceedings of the Council of the Governor General of India*, Calcutta, March 4, 1912.

8   Gaiutra Bahadur, *Coolie Woman: The Odyssey of Indenture* (Gurgaon: Hachette Book Publishing, 2013), xxi.

9   Selvakumar Ramachandran, *Indian Plantation Labor in Malaysia* (Kuala Lumpur: S. Abdul Majeed & Co., 1994); K. S. Sandhu, *Indians in Malaya: Some Aspects of Their Immigration and Settlement* (Cambridge: Cambridge University Press, 1969); Arasaratnam Sinnappah, *Indians in Malaysia and Singapore* (Bombay: Oxford University Press, 1970); Ravindra K. Jain, *South Indians on the Plantation Frontier in Malaya* (New Haven: Yale University Press, 1970); R. N. Jackson, *Immigrant Labor and the Development of Malaya, 1786–1920* (Kuala Lumpur: Government Press, 1961); Usha Mahajani, *The Role of Indian Minorities in Burma and Malaya* (Bombay: Vora &Co. Publishers, 1960); Amarjit Kaur, "Indian Labor, Labor Standards, and Worker's Health in Burma and Malaya, 1900–1940," *Modern Asian Studies* 40, no. 2 (2006): 425–475.

10   Eric Hobsbawm, *The Age of Capital 1848–1875* (London: Weidenfeld & Nicolson, 1975). In discussing the high tide in the age of capital and migrants "moving" in the nineteenth century, Hobsbawm only discusses "men moving." While it is true that men "moved" more than women, there

were also substantial movements and migrations of women that are absent from his work.

11 The examples concerning South Asian migrant men's histories are enough to show the trend. Rana P. Behal and Marcel van der Linden, *India's Laboring Poor: Historical Studies c.1600–c.2000* (Delhi: Cambridge University Press, 2007); Brij V. Lal, *Chalo Jahaji: On a Journey through Indenture to Fiji* (Canberra: Australian National University Press, 2000); Frank Heidemann, *Kanganies in Sri Lanka and Malaysia* (Munchen: Anacon, 1992); Ramachandran, *Indian Plantation Labor in Malaysia*; Kenneth O. L. Gillion, *Fiji's Indian Migrants: A History to the End of Indenture in 1920* (Berkeley: University of California Press, 1962); Rajesh Rai, *Indians in Singapore, 1819–1945: Diaspora in the Colonial Port City* (Oxford University Press, 2014); Yasmin Khan, *India at War: The Subcontinent and the Second World War* (Oxford and New York: Oxford University Press, 2015); Nayan Shah, *Stranger Intimacy: Contesting Race, Sexuality and the Law in the North* (Berkley: University of California Press, 2011).

12 Rhoda Rheddock, "Indian Women and Indentureship in Trinidad and Tobago 1845–1917: Freedom Denied," *Caribbean Quarterly* 54, no. 4 (2008): 41–68; Verene Shepard, *Maharani's Misery: Narratives of a Passage from India to the Caribbean* (Kingston: University of West Indies Press, 2002); Samita Sen, *Women and Labor in Late Colonial India: The Bengal Jute Industry* (Cambridge: Cambridge University Press, 2004); Bahadur, *Coolie Woman*.

13 Ashuthosh Kumar, *Coolies of the Empire: Indentured Indians in the Sugar Colonies, 1830–1920* (Delhi: Cambridge University Press, 2017); Nitin Varma, *Coolies of Capitalism: Assam Tea and the Making of Coolie Labor* (Berlin and Boston: Walter de Gruyter GmBh, 2017).

14 Today, gendered migration patterns, particularly in domestic service, garment industries, and construction industries are overwhelmingly visible in Malaysia and Singapore. Malaysia and Singapore allow only women from Indonesia and the Philippines to immigrate to serve as domestic workers and keep an intrusive watch on their intimate relations. In fact, if a migrant domestic maid is found to be pregnant while in Singapore or Malaysia, they are by law immediately deported. On the other side

of the gendered migration policy line are the Bangladeshi and south Indian construction workers who migrate to Singapore and Malaysia. Interestingly, the recruiting agencies of domestic servants in the Philippines and Indonesia are even reported to attempt to brainwash women against any kind of possible attraction toward South Asian male migrants in Singapore and Malaysia. Bangladeshi women migrants in Malaysia, who work in the garment and textile industry, are said to be kept under a similar official "watch" as migrant maids. See Anja Rudnick, *Working Gendered Boundaries: Temporary Migration Experiences of Bangladeshi Women in the Malaysian Export Industry from a Multi-Sited Perspective* (Amsterdam: University of Amsterdam Press, 2009).

15 G. Roger Knight, *Commodities and Colonialism: The Story of Big Sugar in Indonesia, 1880–1942* (Leiden and Boston: Brill, 2013), 75–80; G. Roger Knight, "Gully Coolies, Weed-Women and Snijvolk: The Sugar Industry Workers of North Java in the Early Twentieth Century," *Modern Asian Studies* 28, no. 1 (1994): 51–76.

16 Elise van Nederveen Meerkerk, *Women, Work and Colonialism in The Netherlands and Java, 1830–1940: Comparisons, Contrasts, Connections* (New York: Palgrave Macmillan, 2019).

17 Shobita Jain and Rhoda Rheddock, eds., *Women Plantation Workers: International xperiences* (Oxford: Berg, 1998).

18 Amarjit Kaur, *Wage Labour in Southeast Asia since 1840: Globalization, the International Division of Labour and Labour Transformations* (New York: Palgrave Macmillan, 2004).

19 Ramachandran, *Indian Plantation Labor in Malaysia*; Sandhu, *Indians in Malaya*; Sinnappah, *Indians in Malaysia and Singapore*; Usha Mahajani, *The Role of Indian Minorities in Burma and Malaya*.

20 Brij V. Lal, "Kunti's Cry: Indentured Women on Fiji Plantations," *Indian Economic and Social History Review* 22, no. 1 (1985): 55–71; John D. Kelly, "Fear of Culture: British Regulation of Indian Marriage in Post-indenture Fiji," *Ethnohistory* 36, no. 4 (1989): 372–391; John D. Kelly and Uttra Kumari Singh, ed. and trans., *My Twenty-one Years in the Fiji Islands, and, The Story of the Haunted Line* (Suva: Fiji Museum, 2003); Sandhu, *Indians in Malaya*; R. K. Jain, *South Indians on the Plantation Frontier in Malaya*; Gail R. Pool and Hira Singh, "Indentured Indian Women of the Empire: Between

Colonial Oppression and the Brahmanical Tradition," *Journal of Plantation Society in the Americas* 6, no. 1 (1999): 1–46; Ashrufa Faruquee, "Conceiving the Coolie Woman: Indentured Labor, Indian Women and Colonial Discourses," *South Asia Research* 16, no. 1 (1996): 61–76.

21 Marina Carter, *Lakshmi's Legacy: Testimonies of Indian Women in 19th Century Mauritius* (Stanley, Rose Hill, Mauritius: Editions de l'Océan Indien, 1994); Marina Carter, *Women and Indenture: Experiences of Indian Labor Migrants* (London: Pink Pigeon Press, 2012).

22 Clare Anderson, *Subaltern Lives: Biographies of Colonialism in the Indian Ocean World, 1790–1920* (Cambridge: Cambridge University Press, 2012).

23 Piya Chatterjee, *Time for Tea: Women, Labor and Post-colonial Politics on an Indian Plantation* (Durham: Duke University Press, 2001); S. Sen, *Women and Labor in Late Colonial India*; Shobita Jain, "Gender Relations and the Plantation System in Assam, India," in *Women Plantation Workers: International Experiences*, ed. Shobita Jain and Rhoda Rheddock (Oxford: Berg, 1998), 107–128.

24 P. Chatterjee, *Time for Tea*.

25 S. Sen, *Women and Labor in Late Colonial India*.

26 S. Sen, *Women and Labor in Late Colonial India*; P. Chatterjee, *Time for Tea*.

27 Jo Beall, "Women under Indentured Labor in Colonial Natal, 1860–1911," in *Women and Gender in Southern Africa*, ed. C. Walker (Cape Town: David Philip, 1990), 146–167; Kalpana Hiralal, "Rebellious Sisters: Indentured Women and Resistance in Colonial Natal, 1860–1911," in *Resistance and Indian Indenture Experience: Comparative Perspectives*, ed. Mauritz Hassankhan et al. (New Delhi: Manohar Publications, 2014), 241–270.

28 Hiralal, "Rebellious Sisters"; Bahadur, *Coolie Woman*; Jain and Rheddock, *Women Plantation Workers*.

29 Lomarsh Roopnaraine, "Review of Coolie Woman: The Odyssey of Indenture," *Journal of Intercultural Studies* 35, no. 4 (2014): 464–466; Richard B. Allen, "Review of Women Plantation Workers: International Experiences," *The Historian* 62, no. 2 (2000): 432.

30 Ramachandran, *Indian Plantation Labor in Malaysia*; Sandhu, *Indians in Malaya*; Sinnappah, *Indians in Malaysia and Singapore*; R. K. Jain, *South Indians on the Plantation Frontier in Malaya*; Mahajani, *The Role of Indian Minorities in Burma and Malaya*; Kaur, "Indian Labor, Labor Standards."

31 James F. Warren, *Rickshaw Coolie: A People's History of Singapore* (Singapore: Singapore University Press, 2003); James F. Warren, *Ah Ku and Karayuki-San: Prostitution in Singapore 1870–1940* (Singapore: Singapore University Press, 2003).

32 Kelvin E. W. Low, *Remembering the Samsui Women: Migration and Social Memory in Singapore and China* (Vancouver: University of British Columbia Press, 2014).

33 Lai Ah Eng, *Peasants, Proletarians and Prostitutes: A Preliminary Investigation into the Work of Chinese Women in Colonial Malaya* (Singapore: Institute of Southeast Asian Studies, 1986); Kenneth Gaw, *Superior Servants: The Legendary Cantonese Amahs of the Far East* (Oxford: Oxford University Press, 1989).

34 Ramachandran, *Indian Plantation Labor in Malaysia*; Sandhu, *Indians in Malaya*; Sinnappah, *Indians in Malaysia and Singapore*; R. K. Jain, *South Indians on the Plantation Frontier in Malaya*; Mahajani, *The Role of Indian Minorities in Burma and Malaya*; Kaur, "Indian Labor, Labor Standards"; Sunil S. Amrith, "South Indian Migration, 1800–1950," in *Globalising Migration History: The Eurasian Experience*, ed. Leo Lucassen and Jan Lucassen (Leiden: Brill, 2013), 122–148; Sunil Amrith, "Indians Overseas? Governing Tamil Migration to Malaya, 1870–1941," *Past and Present* 208, no. 1 (2010): 231–261.

Note: Absence of more contemporary literature on "coolies," especially coolie women in colonial Malaya, is reflected in Kaur's study, "Indian Labor, Labor Standards" (2006), which is one of the few contemporary works on coolies, and even she does not refer to any recent literature.

35 Peter J. Rimmer and Lisa M Allen, eds., *The Underside of Malaysian History: Pullers, Prostitutes, Plantation Workers* (Singapore: Singapore University Press, 1990).

36 Aparajita De, Amrita Ghosh, and Ujjwal Jana, eds., *Subaltern Vision: A Study in Postcolonial Indian English Text*s (Cambridge: Cambridge Scholars Publishing, 2012); Stephanie Cronin, *Subalterns and Social Protest: History from Below in the Middle East and North Africa* (London and New York: Routledge, 2012); Ritu Birla, "Postcolonial Studies: Now That's History," in *Can the Subaltern Speak?: Reflections on the History of an Idea*, ed. Rosalind C. Morris (New York: Columbia University Press,

2010), 87–99; Abdul Janmohamed, "Between Speaking and Dying: Some Imperatives in the Emergence of the Subaltern in the Context of U.S. Slavery," in *Can the Subaltern Speak? Reflections on the History of an Idea,* ed. Rosalind C. Morris (New York: Columbia University Press, 2010), 139–155; James C. Scott, *Weapons of the Weak: Everyday Forms of Peasant Resistance* (New Haven: Yale University Press, 1985); Ranajit Guha, "The Prose of Counterinsurgency," in *Subaltern Studies: Writings on South Asian History and Society,* ed. Ranajit Guha, Vol. 2, 45–86 (Delhi: Oxford University Press, 1983).

37 Rosiland O Hanlon, "Recovering the Subject Subaltern Studies and Histories of Resistance in Colonial South Asia," *Modern Asian* Studies 22, no. 1 (1988): 189–224.

38 Gyan Prakash, "Postcolonial Criticisms and History: Subaltern Studies," in *The Oxford History of Historical Writing: Volume 5: Historical Writing since 1945 to the Present,* ed. Axel Schneider and Daniel Woolf (Oxford and New York: Oxford University Press, 2011), 74–92.

39 Sumi Madhok, *Rethinking Agency: Developmentalism, Gender and Rights* (New Delhi: Routledge, 2013); Durba Ghosh, *Sex and the Family in Colonial India: The Making of Empire* (Cambridge: Cambridge University Press, 2006); Lila Abu-Lughod, "Return to Half-Ruins: Memory, Postmemory and Living History in Palestine," in *Nakba: Palestine, 1948 and the Claims of Memory,* ed. Lila Abu-Lughod and Ahmad Sa'di (New York: Columbia University Press, 2009), 77–106; Sherry B. Ortner, *Anthropology and Social Theory: Culture, Power and the Acting Subject* (Durham, NC: Duke University Press, 2006); J. C. Scott, *Weapons of the Weak*; James C. Scott, *Domination and the Arts of Resistance: Hidden Transcripts* (New Haven: Yale University Press, 2008); Judith Butler, *The Psychic Life of Power* (Stanford: Stanford University Press, 1997).

40 Allen, "Review of *Women Plantation Workers: International Experiences.*"

41 Shobita Jain and Rhoda Rheddock, "Plantation Women: An Introduction," in *Women Plantation Workers: International Experiences,* ed. Shobita Jain and Rhoda Rheddock (Oxford: Berg, 1998),1–16; Rhoda Rheddock, "The Indentureship Experience: Indian Women in Trinidad and Tobago 1845–1917: Freedom Denied," in *Women Plantation Workers: International Experiences,* e, ed. Shobita Jain and Rhoda Rheddock (Oxford: Berg, 1998),

29–48; Rheddock, "Indian Women and Indentureship in Trinidad and Tobago, 1845–1917."

42   Shaista Shameen, "Migration, Labor and Plantation Women in Fiji: A Historical Perspective," in *Women Plantation Workers: International Experiences*, ed. Shobita Jain and Rhoda Rheddock (Oxford: Berg, 1998), 49–66; Verene A. Shepherd, "Indian Migrant Women and Plantation Labor in Nineteenth and Twentieth-century Jamaica: Gender Perspectives," in *Women Plantation Workers: International Experiences*, ed. Shobita Jain and Rhoda Rheddock (Oxford: Berg, 1998),89–106.

43   Rachel Kurian, "Tamil Women on Sri-Lankan Plantations: Labor Control and Patriarchy," in *Women Plantation Workers: International Experiences*, ed. Shobita Jain and Rhoda Rheddock (Oxford: Berg, 1998), 67–88.

44   For survivance related discussion, see Chapters 4 and 5.

45   Lila Abu-lughod, *Writing Women's Worlds: Bedouin Stories* (Berkley: University of California Press, 2008); Lila Abu-lughod, "Return to Half-Ruins: Memory, Postmemory and Living History in Palestine," in *Nakba: Palestine, 1948 and the Claims of Memory*, ed. Lila Abu-Lughod and Ahmad Sa'di (New York: Columbia University Press, 2009), 77–106; Madhok, *Rethinking Agency*; Butler, *The Psychic Life of Power*, 10; Indrani Chatterjee, ed., *Unfamiliar Relations: Family and History in South Asia* (New Brunswick: Rutgers University Press, 2004); Sherry B. Ortner, *Anthropology and Social Theory: Culture, Power and the Acting Subject* (Durham, N.C: Duke University Press, 2006); S. Sen, *Women and Labor in Late Colonial India*.

Lila Abu-Lughod convincingly argues that conventional understandings of the term "agency" suffer from the failure to recognize less "fancy" acts of autonomy as agency. Abu-Lughod further explains that as most scholars romanticize and privilege the act of "resistance" as agency, simpler, individualistic acts of autonomy, which do not necessarily aim to resist or transgress the order of society, fail to be recognized. Similarly, Sumi Madhok in her recent work, "Rethinking Agency," while studying an exploited group of Indian women in rural Rajasthan, advances a captivating idea that individuals take up a variety of "agential practices" in "manifestly oppressive contexts." Thus, both Madhok and Abu-Lughod resonate in more explicit terms the understanding of agency in oppressive conditions forwarded by Butler in a much earlier work, which argued that a subject's identity, in such oppressive contexts, is constructed by those in power but that does not take away the agency of the concerned subject.

46 Padma Anagol, "From the Symbolic to the Open: Women's Resistance in Colonial Maharashtra," in *Behind the Veil: Resistance, Women and the Everyday in Colonial South Asia*, ed. Anindita Ghosh (Hampshire and New York: Palgrave Macmillan, 2007), 21–57.

47 It, thus, relates closely to Spivak's much discussed work, "Can the Subaltern Speak?" wherein she insisted that often subaltern individuals, while engaging in an "act" to ensure their survival, did not necessarily consider themselves as actors "challenging" or negating the agency of others. Gayatri Chakravorty Spivak, "Can the Subaltern Speak?" in *Marxism and Interpretation of Culture*, ed. Carl Nelson and Lawrence Grossberg, 271–316 (London: Macmillan, 1988), 276.

48 Elizabeth Kolsky, *Colonial Justice in British India: White Violence and the Rule of Law* (Cambridge: Cambridge University Press, 2010), 13.

49 This study is, thus, based on an extensive multi-sited archival research at: the National Archives of India, Delhi; the West Bengal State Archives, Kolkata; the Netaji Research Bureau, Kolkata; the Tamil Nadu Archives, Chennai; the National Library, Kolkata; the Singapore National Archives, Singapore; the Arkib Negara, Kuala Lumpur; the British Library, London; the National Archives, Kew; the Women's Library in London Metropolitan University, London; the School of Oriental and African Studies Library, University of London, London; and the Carl A. Kroch Library, Rare and manuscript section, Cornell University, Ithaca.

50 Michel-Rolph Trouillot, *Silencing the Past: Power and the Production of History* (Boston: Beacon Press, 1995).

51 Ann Laura Stoler, *Along the Archival Grain: Epistemic Anxieties and Colonial Common Sense* (Princeton and Oxford: Princeton University Press, 2009); Ann Laura Stoler, "Archival Dis-Ease: Thinking through Colonial Ontologies," *Communication and Critical/Cultural Studies*, 7, no. 2 (2010): 215–219.

52 Anjali Arondekar, *For the Record: On Sexuality and the Colonial Archive in India* (Durham: Duke University Press, 2009).

53 Warren, *Ah Ku and Karayuki-san*, 389.

54 Antoinette Burton, *Dwelling in the Archive: Women Writing House, Home and History in Late Colonial India* (Oxford: Oxford University Press, 2003).

55 William Henry Scott, *Cracks in the Parchment Curtain and Other Essays in Philippine History* (Quezon City: New Day Publishers, 1982).

56 One common suggestion I kept hearing from archivists in all these archives was that records on colonial Malaya, especially those concerning Indian coolie women, are difficult if not impossible to find. I was often told by archivists about the story of the "bonfire of colonial official files on Malaya," instituted by colonial officials just before granting independence to the country. Although I did accept such a claim, I barely gave much heed to it until the recent publications of the story in *The Guardian* (See "Revealed: The Bonfire of Papers at the End of Empire," *The Guardian*, November 29, 2013; "Britain Destroyed Records of Colonial Crimes," *The Guardian*, April 18, 2012). This explains why some of the most controversial files regarding the morality and sexuality of colonial officers are missing from all archives although they may be mentioned in other official correspondences and postal records.

57 Spivak, *In Other Worlds*, 197, 198.

58 Spivak, "Can the Subaltern Speak?" 281.

59 Gayatri Chakravorty Spivak, "The Rani of Sirmur: An Essay in Reading the Archives," *History and Theory* 24, no. 3 (1985): 242–272, 270.

60 G. W. De Silva, ed., *Selected Speeches by S. N. Veerasamy* (Kula Lumpur: Kyle, Palmer and Company Ltd., 1938). S. N. Veerasamy was appointed at the Bar at Law, Kuala Lumpur, in 1928. He was the first Indian member of the Federal Council and was known for stepping forward to help fellow Indians from all classes.

61 Similar historical enquiries have been made by James Francis Warren and Lenore Manderson in their respective seminal works. Warren, *Ah ku and Karayuki-San*; Lenore Manderson, *Sickness and the State: Health and Illness in Colonial Malaya, 1870–1940* (Cambridge: Cambridge University Press, 1996).

CHAPTER 1

1 E. Hobswam, *Age of Capitalism, 1848–1875* (London: Abacus, 1975), 228–244.
2 National Library of Singapore (NLS): *The Straits Times*, October 22, 1935, 19.

3 NLS, NL3596: *The Singapore Free Press and Mercantile Advertiser*, September 26, 1938, 5.

4 Sunil S. Amrith, *Crossing the Bay of Bengal: The Furies of Nature and Fortunes of Migrants* (Cambridge: Harvard University Press, 2013).

5 Sandhu, *Indians in Malaya*, 21–30.

6 I call them neglected because, although the British Empire established its economic connections and trading base in 1771 at Pulau Penang and established Georgetown in 1786, it was not until 1824 (the Anglo-Dutch Treaty) that Malaya came under complete British control. The British interest in Malaya was primarily to develop it as a place for colonial investment, employment generation, and profit making.

7 From 1824 to 1858, British Malaya was directly governed through the East India Company (EIC) in colonial India. However, with the dissolution of the EIC in 1858, India was placed under the direct rule of the Crown. By this time, the colonial administrators of Malaya began lobbying to be placed directly under the Colonial Office of the Crown. Finally, in 1867, British Malaya was separated from the colonial Government of India and placed directly under the Crown. This ensured colonial administrators in Malaya greater autonomy in administering affairs of Malaya but it also strained the relations between the colonial Government of India and the colonial Government of Malaya.

8 Compiled from George Netto, *Indians in Malaya: Historical Facts and Figures* (Singapore: George Netto, 1961), 16.

9 Sandhu, *Indians in Malaya*; Netto, *Indians in Malaya*.

10 Arkib Negara, Kuala Lumpur (AN) 1957/0103354: "Correspondences Regarding Recruiting of Indian Labor from Northern India," 1902.

11 AN 1957/0429173: "Licensing the Recruiters of Indian Labor: Forwards Correspondence for Information and Guidance," 1902.

12 R. B. Krishnan, *Indians in Malaya: A Pageant of Greater India* (Singapore: The Malayan Publishers, 1936), 19–20.

13 Ibid., 19–20; Hugh Tinker, *A New System of Slavery* (London: Oxford University Press, 1974).

14 Heidemann, *Kanganies in Sri Lanka and Malaysia*.

15 Sinnappah, *Indians in Malaysia and Singapore*.

16 It was at times referred to the "second wave of slavery" or "the slavery system under a new name."

NOTES

17 The indenture system was abolished for Malaya in 1910, but for other colonies under the British Empire, abolition came much later.

18 Sinnappah, *Indians in Malaysia and Singapore*, 13–15, 19, 35. For every recruit, the *kangany* was paid a fixed amount. On some estates, if the workers under the *kangany* worked every day regularly, the planters paid the *kangany*s "head money" as bonuses. Thus, *kangany*s became oppressive at times not only to demonstrate their sociopolitical status over coolies but also to ensure receiving the daily bonus.

19 AN 2006/0019647, Book No. 6: Indian Immigration Committee Meetings Minutes, February 1932–February 1938, November 1934 Minutes; Sinnappah, *Indians in Malaysia and Singapore*, 18–19; J. N. Parmer, *Colonial Labor Policy and Administration A History of Labor in the Rubber Plantation Industry in Malaya 1910–1941* (New York: Association of Asian Studies, 1960), 50.

20 Jackson, *Immigrant Labor and the Development of Malaya, 1786–1920*, 238.

21 P. Chatterjee, *Time for Tea*, 80–82; Janaki Nair, *Women and Law in Colonial India* (New Delhi: Kali for Women, 1996), 99–104.

22 Most other plantation expeditions had been short-lived and less extensive than rubber. Rubber plantations being more long-lived and being established at a time when tensions between the governments of British India and British Malaya were high, labor procurement became a particularly alarming problem for the planters and administrators in Malaya.

23 This anticipation of the planters turned out to be true; during the slump years whenever the Indian laborers repatriated, it was seen that the majority of the repatriates were single male laborers, while coolie families stayed on, often with the encouragement of the planters. See Graham Saunders, *The Development of a Plural Society in Malaya* (Kuala Lumpur: Longman Malaysia, 1977), 17.

24 National Library of India, Kolkata (NLI), G.P. 325.254: Government of India, Department of Revenue and Agriculture, "Terms of Agriculture, Wages and Conditions of Service," Emigration and Immigration, India (Calcutta: Government of India, Central Printing Office, 1894); NLI, G.P. 325.254026 IN2: Government of India, The Emigration Act, 1922; NLI, G.P. 325. 254 In 2 Cem: Government of India, Ministry of External Affairs, "Indians Emigration Rules 1923 and Special Rules to Ceylon and Malaya."

180

Note: The Emigration Acts of 1864 and 1922 required that all recruiters of unskilled Indian labor for overseas colonies must ensure that unaccompanied men did not exceed one in every five emigrants. However, Malaya and Ceylon were constantly favored and exempted by the colonial Government of India. See Sandhu, *Indians in Malaya*, 116.

25 AN 1957/060448: *Supply of Indian Labor for Estates in the Malay Peninsula.* 1917, 5.

26 Ibid.

27 AN 1957/0516564: *Permanent Exemption of Malaya from the Operation of Rule 23 of the Indian Emigration Rules, 1923*, 1931.

28 AN 2006/0019648, Book No. 6: Indian Immigration Committee Meetings Minutes, February 1932–February 1938, May 16, 1934, minute book and November 14, 1934, minute book.

29 AN 2006/0019648, Book No. 6: Indian Immigration Committee Meetings Minutes, February 1932–February 1938.

30 The cause of Indian overseas laborers became one of the strategic and influential clarion calls made by Indian nationalists to mobilize support for the anti-colonial movement in colonial India.

31 Heidemann, *Kanganies in Sri Lanka and Malaysia*, 47.

32 NLS: *The Straits Times*, October 31, 1901.

33 NLS: *The Straits Times*, November 2, 1901.

34 LS: *The Straits Times*, November 22, 1901. See also AN: *Perak Pioneer*, November 28, 1901.

35 The Montague Chelmsford Reforms, 1918, proposed that self-government institutions would be eventually developed in colonial India. This reform made it clear to the nationalists that the colonial government had no intention of ensuring complete freedom to India and hence a full-on independence movement began.

36 The Indian Emigration Act of 1922 required countries importing Indian labor to improve the working and living conditions of the laborers and also improve the sex ratio amongst the emigrating labor population as it was believed that most of the problems of the laborers were caused due to the sex ratio imbalance.

37 NLS: *The Straits Times*, September 5, 1922.

38 Exact dates are not available for when the organized recruitment of coolie women began for colonial Malaya, but the recruitment schemes and

various incentives provided to the recruiters for recruiting coolie families and single women suggest that from the early 1900s the planters of Malaya were eager to recruit more women coolies. Census reports from 1901–1921 provide ample evidence for this. Intensive institutionalized incentives to recruit more women became more visible in the 1920s.

39 There was no census recorded for 1941 as World War II had begun by then.

40 National University of Singapore Library (NUSL): George Thompson Hare, *FMS Census of the Population, 1901* (Kuala Lumpur: Government Print Office, 1902), 34–35.

41 AN 1957/0286315: C. W. Parr, *Report of the Commission Appointed to Enquire into the Conditions of Indentured Labor in the Federated Malay States* (Kuala Lumpur: Government Print Office, July 13, 1910), 5–6.

42 Cornell University Kroch Library (CUKL), Film 9186: *Annual Report on Indian Immigration and Emigration, FMS, for the Year 1908* (Kuala Lumpur: Government Print Office, 1909), 9.

43 NUSL: A. M. Poutney, *FMS Review of the Census Operations and Results* (London: Darling and Son, 1911), 28.

44 AN: *The Census of British Malaya, 1921*, 139.

45 NUSL: C. A. Vlieland, *British Malaya: A Report on the 1931 Census and on Certain Problems of Vital Statistics* (London: Malayan Information Agency, 1932), 85–86.

46 Visible from all vagrancy reports on arrests, housing of Indian coolie vagrants from 1920 to 1930 in FMS. See Vagrancy Reports in Arkib Negara, Kuala Lumpur.

47 Brij V. Lal, "'Kunti's Cry: Indentured Women on Fiji Plantations," *Indian Economic and Social History Review* 22, no. 1 (1985): 57; Jan Breman, *Labor Migration and Rural Transformation in Colonial Asia* (Amsterdam: Free University Press, 1990), 35–47. See also John D. Kelly, *A Politics of Virtue: Hinduism, Sexuality, and Countercolonial Discourse in Fiji* (Chicago: University of Chicago Press, 1991), 27–29.

48 Temple servants who in British India were socially degraded, being seen as temple prostitutes.

49 Shobna Nijhawan, "Fallen through the Nationalist and Feminist Grids of Analysis: Political Campaigning of Indian Women against Indentured Labor Emigration," *Indian Journal of Gender Studies* 21, no. 1 (2014): 115–118.

50 Abbe Dubois, *Hindu Manners, Customs and Ceremonies* (New York: Cossimo Classics, 2007), 336.

51 P. Subramanian, *Social History of the Tamils* (Delhi: D.K. Printworld [P] Ltd., 2005), 74–75.

52 British Library (BL) W7870/20: Government of India, *Census of Madras Presidency 1891* (Madras: Government Press India, 1892), 129.

53 BL: Madras Devadasi Association, *Manifesto of Madras Devadasi Association* (Madras: Aurora Press, 1927), 8.

54 R. Azhagappan, *Periyar EVR* (New Delhi: Sahitya Academy, 2006), 101, 103, 105–107. Geraldine Forbes argues that the focus on women by the Self-Respect Movement and other similar social reform movements of the region emerged with their quest to ensure a broader public and political support for their respective parties. Forbes establishes that, by including women's issues, these parties claimed to be more "universal" in their nationalistic demands and thereby legitimized their uniqueness. See Geraldine Forbes, *Women in Modern India* (Cambridge: Cambridge University Press, 1996), 73–76.

55 S. Ramanathan, "Social Reform Movements in South India and Mahatma Gandhi: A Critical Study," PhD dissertation, Department of Political Science, Shivaji University, 2011, 143–150.

56 NUSL, BL: A. Mukkarains, Officer of the Honorary Commissioner for Depressed Classes for SS and FMS, *Report on the Traffic between South Indian Ports and Malaya 1925* (Kuala Lumpur: Government Print Office, 1926), 2–3.

57 Jackson, *Immigrant Labor and Development of Malaya, 1786–1920*, 123.

58 Heidemann, *Kanganies in Sri Lanka and Malaysia*, 65.

59 Ibid.

60 Sandhu, *Indians in Malaya*, 141–151.

61 NLS: *The Straits Times*, March 21, 1917.

62 NLS: *The Straits Times*, March 23, 1917.

63 BL: Government Order No. 568, July 16, 1907.

64 AN 272/1896: Government of British Malaya, *Report on Labor Commission 1890–1900: SS & FMS (1901)* (Kuala Lumpur: Government Print Office, 1901), paras 280–283. Note: *Kanganies* tried to make the women aware of the work they would have to do upon migration and accentuated their potential wages. This promised economic independence was alluring for

women. Furthermore, they were listed in migration records as "coolie women" or "coolie wives" and not as dependents.

CHAPTER 2

1   Personal interview with Pachaimmal, May 10, 2011, Selangor.
2   See British Library, India Office Records (BL, IOR): *The Agent of the Government of India in Malaya Reports (1926–1940)* and *Labor Department Reports of FMS (1920–1940)*.
3   Leopold Ainsworth, *The Confessions of a Planter in Malaya: A Chronicle of Life and Adventure in the Jungle* (London: H.F. & G. Witherby, 1933); Pierre Boulle, *Sacrilege in Malaya*, trans. Xan Fielding (Kuala Lumpur: Oxford University Press, 1958).
4   Boulle, *Sacrilege in Malaya*; Ainsworth, *The Confessions of a Planter in Malaya*; *Planters' Magazines* (1923–1940).
5   Boulle, *Sacrilege in Malaya*, 46. Pierre Boulle is best known as the author of books including *Planet of the Apes* and *Bridge on the River Kwai*. Boulle served as a technician on British rubber plantations in Malaya during 1936–1939. Boulle wrote the book *Le Sacrilege Malaise* (English translation: *Sacrilege in Malaya*) based on his experiences in Malaya, particularly on rubber plantations.
6   Ainsworth, *The Confessions of a Planter in Malaya*, 61, 63–64.
7   Ramachandran, *Indian Plantation Labor in Malaysia*; Sinnappah, *Indians in Malaysia and Singapore*; R. K. Jain, *South Indians on Plantation Frontier*; Amarjit Kaur, "Tappers and Weeders: South Indian Plantation Workers in Peninsular Malaysia, 1880–1970," *South Asia: Journal of South Asian Studies* 73, no. 1 (1998): 73–102; Kaur, "Indian Labor, Labor Standards."
8   Ashwini Tambe, "Gandhi's 'Fallen' Sisters: Difference and the National Body Politic," *Social Scientist* 37, no. 1 (2009): 21–38, 32; Madhavi Kale, *Fragments of Empire: Capital, Slavery, and Indian Indentured Labor Migration in the British Caribbean* (Philadelphia: University of Pennsylvania Press, 1998), 168–171; Nijhawan, "Fallen through the Nationalist and Feminist Grids of Analysis"; Lal, "Kunti's Cry"; John D. Kelly, "Gaze and Grasp: Plantations, Desires and Colonial Law in Fiji," in *Sites of Desire or*

Economies of Pleasure: Sexualities in Asia and Pacific ed. M. Jolly and Lenore Manderson (Chicago: Chicago University Press, 1997), 72–98; Kelly, "Fear of Culture"; Faruquee, "Conceiving the Coolie Woman,"; Pool and Singh, "Indentured Indian Women of the Empire." Also see M. K. Gandhi, *The Collected Works of Gandhi* (Delhi: Publications Division, Ministry of Information & Broadcasting, Govt. of India, 1958), 15, 75.

A telling case is that of "Kunti's Cry" (1913): Kunti, a coolie woman in an estate in Rewa, Fiji, was reportedly sent to weed in an isolated patch, and the white overseer took advantage of the situation to make inappropriate advances and also to discipline Kunti. Kunti managed to escape the clutches of the overseer and jumped into a river nearby, where a fellow Indian, Jagdev, who happened to be there, saved her from drowning. Kunti thereafter tried to register a complaint against the overseer but the manager rejected her report, insisting that Kunti's character was questionable and that she had a personal grudge against the overseer. Nonetheless, Kunti's case was picked up and heavily popularized by the press in colonial India. Kunti's case became a clarion call used by Indian nationalists to gain popular support for their challenge against the legitimacy of colonial rule in India. See Lal, "Kunti's Cry."

9   Tambe and Nijhawan have explained that sexual abuses and other morality issues regarding Indian coolie women in overseas colonies of the British Empire was Gandhi's "initial motivation" to assemble Indian nationalists and protest against the wrongs of the colonial government that they claimed resulted in the moral and sexual degradation of Indian coolie women. Colonial administrators responded by asserting that the abuse of coolie women was largely carried out by other Indians, that is, either by *kanganis* and head coolies or by their male relations.

See Tambe, "Gandhi's 'Fallen' Sisters"; Nijhawan, "Fallen through the Nationalist and Feminist Grids of Analysis."

10   Sandhu, *Indians in Malaya*; Kaur, "Tappers and Weeders"; Kaur, "Indian Labor, Labor Standards"; Ramachandran, *Indian Plantation Labor in Malaysia*; Sinnappah, *Indians in Malaysia and Singapore*; R. K. Jain, *South Indians on Plantation Frontier*; Ravindra K. Jain, "Migrants, Proletarians or Malayans?" PhD dissertation, Australian National University, 1966; Mahajani, *The Role of Indian Minorities in Burma and Malaya*. Most of

these earlier studies presume that coolie women were dependents on coolie men or were at best secondary laborers.

11 Many historians, such as Gauitra Bahadur and Rhoda Rheddock, have noted that in most colonial plantation societies, coolie women were assigned lower-ranked and physically less-demanding jobs. But this was not the case in Malaya. See Bahadur, *Coolie Woman*, 91; Rheddock, "Indian Women and Indentureship in Trinidad and Tobago 1845–1917."

12 Sandhu, *Indians in Malaya*; Kaur, "Tappers and Weeders."

13 BL: A. T. Edgar, *Manual of Rubber Planting* (London: Incorporated Society of Planters, 1947).

14 BL: J. B. Carruthers, "Report of the Director of Agriculture FMS for 1906," *Agricultural Bulletin of Straits and FMS* 6, no. 9 (1907): 287.

15 Colin Barlow, Sisira Jayasuriya, and C. Suan Tan, eds, *The World Rubber Industry* (Oxon: Routledge, 1994), 150, 330.

16 BL: Edgar, *Manual of Rubber Planting*.

17 The payment by result or piece-rate system paid tappers by the number of pounds of latex each tapper brought in at the end of the day.

18 AN, 1957/0187600: *Annual Labor Department Reports of FMS* (reports from years 1912–1921); BL, IOR L/E/7/1341, *Annual Report of the Labor Department, FMS* (all years from 1922 to 1927); BL, IOR L/E/7/1532: *Annual Report of the Labor Department, FMS* (all years from 1928 to 1929); BL, IOR L/PJ/8/258–259: *Annual Report of the Labor Department, FMS* (all years from 1930 to 1936); BL, IOR V/24/1184–85: *Annual Reports of the Agent of Government of India in Malaya, 1926–1940*; Eng, *Peasants, Proletarians and Prostitutes*, 69–71; Parmer, *Colonial Labor Policy and Administration*.

19 BL, IOR V/24/1184: *Annual Report of the Agent of the Government of India in Malaya 1928*, 12; Jackson, *Immigrant Labor and the Development of Malaya, 1786–1920*, 108. A tapper's job usually began before sunrise and ended by afternoon as the latex of the rubber trees dried up with the increase in temperature during the day, making the trees un-tappable.

20 BL, IOR L/E/7/1532: *Annual Report of the Labor Department, FMS for the Year 1929*, 10.

21 Ibid.

22 BL, IOR V/24/1184: *Annual Report of the Agent of the Government of India in Malaya 1928*, 12.

23   BL, IOR L/PJ/8/259: *Annual Report of the Labor Department, FMS for the Year 1935*, 41.

24   BL, IOR L/E/7/1341: *Annual Report of the Labor Department, FMS* (all years from 1922 to 1927); BL, IOR L/E/7/1532: *Annual Report of the Labor Department, FMS* (all years from 1928 to 1929); BL, IOR L/PJ/8/258–259: *Annual Report of the Labor Department, FMS* (all years from 1930 to 1936).

25   BL, IOR V/24/1184–85: *Annual Report of the Agent of the Government of India in Malaya 1929*, 9; *Annual Report of the Agent of the Government of India in Malaya 1931*, 8.

26   Whichever may be the reality, it is clear from the wages that tapping was an important task on the estates. This becomes more evident by the system of "fines" levied on tappers, that is, if they were found tapping trees inefficiently. Such fine systems were not in practice in the weeding tasks on the plantations or rubber creping tasks in the factories.

27   Shepherd, "Indian Migrant Women and Plantation Labour in Nineteenth and Twentieth Century Jamaica."

28   Shameen, "Migration, Labour and Plantation Women in Fiji."

29   Kurian, "Tamil Women on Sri Lankan Plantations."

30   Nair, *Women and Law in Colonial India*; P. Chatterjee, *Time for Tea*; Jennifer L. Morgan, *Laboring Women: Reproduction and Gender in New World Slavery* (Philadelphia: University of Pennsylvania Press, 2004).

31   Patricia E. Tsurumi, *Factory Girls: Women in the Thread Mills of Meiji Japan* (New Jersey: Princeton University Press, 1990); Louise Tilly and Joan Scott, eds, *Women, Work and Family* (New York: Methuen, 1987); Donald Mackenzie and Judy Wajcman, eds, *The Social Shaping of Technology: How the Refrigerator Got Its Way* (Milton Keynes: Open University Press, 1985); Susan Hanson and Geraldine Pratt, eds, *Gender, Work and Space* (New York and London: Routledge, 1995); Laura E. Ruberto, *Gramsci, Migration, and the Representation of Women's Work in Italy and the U.S.* (Lanham: Lexington, 2007); Morgan, *Laboring Women*.

32   AN, 1957/0402597: *Abstract for Labor Laws relating to Indian Laborers 1927–1928*, see Extracts from the Labor Code, section 49.

33   BL, IOR V/24/1185: *Annual Report of the Agent of Government of India in Malaya 1936*, 10.

34   NLS: *The Straits Times*, July 6, 1937.

35 AN, 1957/0610415: Letter from A. S. Jelf to High Commissioner for the FMS.

36 BL, IOR V/24/1184: *Annual Report of the Agent of Government of India in Malaya 1930*, 14; AN, 1957/0259526: Letter from Undersecretary to FMS to Secretary to Resident of Selangor, "Line Ayah's Creches Attendant Ayahs and Education of Children of South Indian Laborers"; Netto, *Indians in Malaya*, 28.

37 BL, IOR V/24/1185: *Annual Report of the Agent of the Government of India in Malaya 1936*, 11.

38 Personal interview with Pachaimmal, May 10, 2011, Selangor. Eventually, as she grew older and younger siblings came along, her mother allotted her the task of taking care of her siblings and other children on their line. Narrating the circle of life, Pachaimmal also mentioned that when she had her children, she often left them with an elderly lady on her estate while she tapped trees.

39 Ibid.

40 BL, IOR V/24/1185: *Annual Report of the Agent of Government of India in Malaya 1935*, 12.

41 BL, IOR V/24/1184: *Annual Report of the Agent of Government of India in Malaya 1930*, 14. The profits from toddy sales were also used to sponsor construction and maintenance of temples on estates and also to sponsor coolie religious festivities (mostly Hindu festivals).

42 As discussed in Chapter 1.

43 Carter, *Lakshmi's Legacy*, 115, 121.

44 AN, 2006/0019640: *Report of the Executive of the General Labor Committee, British Malaya on Indian Labor and Laborers 1920*, 6; BL, IOR L/E/7/1341: *Annual Report of the Labor Department, FMS* (all years from 1922 to 1927). Even the Planters' Association of Malaya in a report to the government of Malaya on the condition of Indian laborers on estates in Malaya, in 1928, recorded coolie women independently, like the administrative records. See AN: *Interim Report of the Special Labor Committee on Matters Relating to Wages for Indian Estate Labor* (Kuala Lumpur: Planters Association of Malaya, 1928).

45 This became a crucial point of contention in the event of rising wife-enticements, especially because of the absence of any records that proved coolie marriages. This topic is examined in Chapter 4.

46 See annual Labor Department records and Agent of the Government of India in Malaya reports.

47 Jackson, *Immigrant Labor and the Development of Malaya, 1786–1920*, 137–138.

48 Also, in all Labor Department records and Agent of Government of India in Malaya reports coolie women regularly featured as "independent" units of labor with independent wage structures.

49 Ibid.

50 BL, IOR V/24/1185: *Annual Reports of the Agent of Government of India in Malaya 1932*, 8; BL, IOR V/24/1185: *Annual Report of the Agent of Government of India in Malaya 1931*, 9.

51 BL, IOR L/PJ/ 16/2/39: Correspondence between G. S. Bajpai and the Secretary to the Government of India, *Indians in Malaya*; BL, IOR L/PJ/ 589/39: *Indians in Malaya: Negotiations between Government of India and a Delegation from Malaya on the Question of Rates of Wages* (1939).

52 Donald Reid, "Reflections on Labor History and Language," in *Rethinking Labor History*, ed. Lenard R. Berlanstein (Urbana and Chicago: University of Illinois Press, 1993), 39–54.

53 William H. Sewell, "Toward a Post Materialist Rhetoric for Labor History," in *Rethinking Labor History*, ed. Lenard R. Berlanstein (Urbana and Chicago: University of Illinois Press, 1993), 15–38.

54 Joan Scott, *Gender and the Politics of History* (New York: Columbia University Press, 1999), 71.

55 AN, 1957/0288045: *Report by Controller of Labor Malaya, K. L. November, 1937.*

56 Most estates had designated letter-writers employed by the Controller of Labor whose sole duty was to write letters for the laborers employed on the estates. See AN, 2006/0019640: *Report of the Executive of the General Labor Committee, British Malaya on Indian Labor and Laborers, 1920.*

57 National Archives of India (NAI): Department of Commerce and Industry Emigration Records June 1913, Part B, No. ¾, Treatment of Laborers in Federated Malay States, Letter from Murugan; NAI: Department of Commerce and Industry Emigration, March 1913, Part B, Nos 29–30.

58 Ibid.

59 Ibid.; NAI: *Bengalee*, July 26, 1913; NAI: "Letter of Murugan" in Official Correspondence between the Controller and the British Resident in Selangor.

60   Ibid.

61   NAI: Department of Commerce and Industry Emigration Records June
1913, Part B, no. ¾, Treatment of Laborers in Federated Malay States,
Letter from Murugan; NAI: Department of Commerce and Industry
Emigration, March 1913, Part B, Nos 29–30.

62   BL, IOR V/24/1184: *Annual Report of the Agent of Government of India in
Malaya 1929*, 21.

63   Michael R. Stenson, *Industrial Conflict in Malaya: Prelude to the Communist
Revolt of 1948* (London: Oxford University Press, 1970), 29.

64   Judith Butler, *Vulnerability in Resistance* (Durham and London: Duke
University Press, 2016), 6. For Butler, vulnerability is not powerlessness, but
rather the experience and space wherein acts and strategies of resistance
are imagined and made.

65   J. C. Scott, *Weapons of the Weak*, 29.

66   See *Annual Labor Department Reports* (all years from 1912 to 1938); *Annual
Reports of the Agent of Government of India in Malaya* (all years from 1926 to
1940).

67   AN: *The Perak Pioneer*, January 5, 1910. Section 323 of the Malayan Penal
Code states that whoever causes voluntary hurt to another shall be
punished with imprisonment for a term which may extend to twelve
months or a fine, or both.

68   Free coolies were coolies recruited under the *kangany* system or those who
came to Malaya without any assistance by paying for their own passage.
Free coolies had different contractual terms with their employers and
enjoyed greater liberty than indentured coolies in terms of mobility and
employment, being free to leave the estate they worked on for better-
paying jobs on other estates. This freedom enabled them to negotiate
higher pay than indentured coolies.

69   AN: *The Perak Pioneer*, January 5, 1910.

70   Ibid.

71   AN: *Malay Mail*, January 7, 1910.

72   NAI: *New India*, January 5, 1923

73   AN: *The Law Reports of Federated Malay States, 1939* (Kuala Lumpur:
Government Printing Office, 1940), 50–51.

74   Ibid.

75 As Michele Foucault explained, subject position highlights the productive nature of any disciplinary power by revealing how the power structures name and categorize people into different hierarchies. See Michel Foucault, *The Order of Things: An Archeology of the Human Sciences* (London: Routledge, 1973).

CHAPTER 3

1 Leopold Ainsworth, *Confessions of a Rubber Planter in Malaya* (London: H.F. & G. Witherby, 1933), 49.

2 National Archives of United Kingdom, London (NAUK), File: 5079/99; Fiji Colonial Secretary Office, 1903.

3 Prabhu Mahapatra, "Restoring the Family: Wife Murders and the Making of Sexual Contract for Indian Immigrant Labor in the British Caribbean Colonies, 1860–1920," *Studies in History* 11, no. 2 (1995): 227–260.

4 For the term "household" I use the definition by Marcel van der Linden and Lee Mitzman. While discussing relations within labor families, they use the term "household" to refer to a varied number of situations and relations created amongst members of the family to aim toward mutually accepted goals of security, respectability, and justice in society. Nonetheless, Linden and Mitzman caution that socioeconomic, cultural, and political contexts, in which such household relations are performed, may even at times end in conflict between accepted goals. Thus, in using the term "household" I do not refer to any gender-specific spaces within the family, but rather the collaborative arrangements and agreements that took place within the coolie families. See Marcel van der Linden and Lee Mitzman, "Connecting Household History and Labor History," *International Review of Social History* 38, supplement S1 (April, 1993): 163–173.

5 Mahapatra, "Restoring the Family"; Margaret Mishra, "Between Women: Indenture, Morality and Health," *Australian Humanities Review* 52 (May 2012): 57–70; Rheddock, "Indian Women and Indentureship in Trinidad and Tobago 1845–1917"; Bahadur, *Coolie Woman*; David Trotman, "Women and Crime in Late Nineteenth Century Trinidad," *Caribbean Quarterly*, 30,

nos. 3–4 (1984): 60–72; Beall, "Women under Indentured Labor in colonial Natal"; Moses Seenarine, "Indentured Women in Colonial Guyana," in *Sojourners to Settlers*, ed. Mahin Gosine and D. Narine (New York: Windsor Press, 1999), 36–66; Lal, "Kunti's Cry."

6   Arondekar, *For the Record*.

7   Veena Das, *Life and Words: Violence and the Descent into the Ordinary* (Berkley, Los Angeles and London: University of California Press, 2007).

8   NLS: *The Straits Times*, June 24, 1937.

9   AN: P. N. Gerrard, "On the Hygienic Management of Labor in the Tropics," *Agricultural Bulletin of Straits and FMS* 6, no. 3 (1907): 72–90. The coolie lines as a general rule were raised 5–6 feet from the ground and the vacant space underneath these structures were used by coolies for their cooking activities. See Carruthers, "Report of the Director of Agriculture FMS for 1906," 281.

10   NAUK, CO 275/41: *Report of the Commissioners Appointed to Enquire into the State of Labor in Straits Settlement and Protected Native States, 1890* (Singapore: Singapore Government Printing Office, 1981), 4, 8.

11   Ibid.

12   Ibid.

13   AN: *Selangor Journal of Planters* 2, no. 6 (1894), 90.

14   Arunima Datta, "'Immorality', Nationalism and the Colonial State in British Malaya: Indian 'Coolie' Women's Intimate Lives as Ideological Battleground," *Women's History Review* 25, no. 4 (2016): 584–601. Frequent dialogues and negotiations concerning these issues are visible in the *Annual Reports of the Labor Department of the Government of Malaya* and the *Annual Reports of the Agent of Government of India in Malaya*; see BL, IOR V/24/1184–85.

15   Jackson, *Immigrant Labor and the Development of Malaya, 1786–1920*, 111–112.

16   BL, IOR L/PJ/6/1481, File 1420: N. E. Marjoribanks and Ahmad Tambi Marakkayer, *Emigration of Indian Labor to Ceylon and Malaya* (Madras Government, 1916); BL, IOR V/27/820/31: V. S. Srinivasa Sastri, *Report on the Conditions of Indian Labor in Malaya* (Delhi, 1937). See also NLS: *The Straits Times*, March 21, 1917, 12.

17   BL, IOR V/24/1184: *Annual Report of the Agent of Government of India in Malaya 1927*, 13–14.

18   BL, IOR V/24/1184: *Annual Report of the Agent of Government of India in Malaya 1935*, 10. See also BL, IOR V/24/1184: *Annual Report of Labor Department*, 1936, 46. Such colonial administrative concerns with privacy of coolie couples should not be misread as a colonial drive to really ensure privacy to coolie couples; rather, it would not be wrong to speculate that this was yet another strategy to demonstrate that conditions for 'privacy' were provided to coolies and yet coolie families remained infested with problems, thus proving that all intimate problems and chaos within coolie households were their responsibility and not the Empire's.

19   Sara Mills, *Gender and Colonial Space* (Manchester: Manchester University Press, 2005), 43–70.

20   As gathered from the *Annual Health Department Reports* and *Annual Crime and Prison Reports of FMS* (1920–1938).

21   Personal interview with Alex Cuthbert, May 2012, Collindale, UK.

22   See Arunima Datta, "Social Memory and Indian Women from Malaya and Singapore in the Rani of Jhansi Regiment," *Journal of the Malaysian Branch of the Royal Asiatic Society* 88, no. 309 (2015): 77–103.

23   Ibid.

24   BL, 20088.c.38.: The Central Indian Association of Malaya Kuala Lumpur, *Memorandum on "Toddy in Malaya,"* 1 (1937).

25   Michel R. Troulliot, *Silencing the Past: Power and the Production of History* (Boston: Beacon Press, 1995).

26   Arondekar, *For the Record*.

27   On some estates, room for married coolies had an en-suite cooking space, while in others, kitchens were communal.

28   AN: *Malayan Labor Commission Report*, 1916.

29   See G. W. Earl, *Topography and Itinerary of Province Wellesley* (Pinang: Pinang Gazette Printing Office, 1861).

30   Some planters even suggested that bachelors messing with married couples must pay the couple 2–3.50 dollars (depending on the location of the estate, which would influence the living expenses incurred by the coolies) per month and hand over the rice issued to them during the month. See *Interim Report of the Special Labor Committee on Matters Relating to Wages for Indian Estate Labor* (Kuala Lumpur: Planters Association of Malaya, 1928).

193

31 Datta, "'Immorality', Nationalism and the Colonial State in British Malaya."
32 Das, *Life and Words*.
33 AN: *Times of Malaya*, January 5, 1932.
34 Datta, "'Immorality', Nationalism and the Colonial State in British Malaya."
35 AN: *Times of Malaya*, January 23, 1935
36 NLS: *The Singapore Free Press and Mercantile Advertiser*, July 18, 1934. See also NLS: *The Straits Times*, July 17, 1934.
37 NLS, NL 1482: *The Straits Times*, December 7, 1933.
38 AN: *Times of Malaya*, April 5, 1935. See also NLS: *The Singapore Free Press and Mercantile Advertiser*, January 25, 1935.
39 NLS: *The Straits Times*, November 5, 1924.
40 NLS: *The Singapore Free Press and Mercantile Advertiser*, January 21, 1935.
41 AN: *Case Files*, Case 59/1940, 1940.
42 NLS: *The Straits Times*, June 24, 1937.
43 Jeffery Weeks, *Sex, Politics and the Society* (Essex: Pearson Publications, 1989).
44 Anna Clark, *The Struggle for the Breeches: Gender and the Making of the British Working Class* (Los Angeles: University of California Press, 1995).
45 Johan Galtung, "Violence, Peace and Peace Research," *Journal of Peace Research*, 6, no. 3 (1969): 167–191.

CHAPTER 4

1 As discussed in Chapter 1, in order to migrate, many aspiring single women resorted to illegal liaisons with migrant men, which were often referred to in Tamil as "certu-k-kolu-tali" (informally joined together). Such marriages were not based on customary rites and were often contracted at ports to escape background checks and interrogations carried out by Protectors of Emigrants, officials appointed by the Government of India to check whether women had been kidnapped or were running away from marriages. Inspections were less rigorous for women who were part of a married couple, and for that reason labor recruiters in some cases arranged marriages. See Heidemann, *Kanganies in Sri Lanka and Malaysia*.

2   BL: *Perak Pioneer*, January 17, 1910, 4–5; BL: *Perak Pioneer*, January 31, 1910, 4–5.

3   Most migration of overseas labor tended to be primarily male, with a few exceptions, such as Ceylon, where the sex ratio of migrants was equal owing to the requirement of female laborers to work on tea plantations. Furthermore, plantation colonies, which imported labor from other colonies, did not keep a record of the marriages, nor did they verify marriages contracted by migrants before entry. This dysfunctionality of colonial administration in both source and destination colonies made the status of migrant marriages ambiguous.

4   BL, IOR V/27/820/29–30: James Mc Neil and Chimman Lal, *Report on the Conditions of Indian Immigrants in the Four British Colonies: Trinidad, British Guiana or Demerera, Jamaica and Fiji, and in the Dutch Colony of Surinam or Dutch Guiana* (1915), 319.

5   BL, IOR P/V 160: C. F. Andrews and W. W. Pearson, *Report on the Indentured Labor in Fiji* (Calcutta: The Star Printing Works, 1916).

6   Walter Gill, *Turn North-East at the Tombstone* (Adelaide: Rigby, 1970), 71.

7   French Reunion was one of the non-British plantation colonies to which British India supplied laborers. Tinker, *A New System of Slavery*, 204.

8   BL: Rev. H.V. P. Bronkhurst, *The Colony of British Guayana and Its Laboring Population* (London: Wolmer, 1883), 136.

9   Ibid., 403. See *Demerara Daily Chronicle*, May 16, 1882.

10 BL: Bronkhurst, *The Colony of British Guayana and Its Laboring Population*, 403–404, 406.

11 BL, Parliamentary Papers, Cd Paper 7744–7745: James McNeill and Chimman Lal, *Report to the Government of India on the Conditions of Indian Emigrants in Four Colonies and Surinam, 1914* (London, 1915); Brij V. Lal, "Veil of Dishonor: Sexual Jealousy and Suicide on Fiji Plantations," *The Journal of Pacific History* 20, no. 3 (1985): 139.

12 G. A. Nateson, *Speeches of Gopal Krishna Gokhale* (Madras, 1920), 528.

13 BL, IOR V/24/1184–85: *Annual Report of the Agent of the Government of India in Malaya 1929*, 21; *Annual Report of the Agent of the Government of India in Malaya 1931*, 20–21; *Annual Report of the Agent of the Government of India in Malaya 1932*, 20–21; *Annual Report of the Agent of the Government of India in Malaya 1934*, 20.

14 BL, IOR V//24/1184: *Annual Report of the Agent of the Government of India in Malaya 1936*, 22.

15 NLS: *The Straits Times*, 29 August 1935, 7; Cornell University Kroch Library, Film 9186, *Report of the Commissioner of Police for FMS*, 1937; NLS: *The Straits Times*, September 19, 1938, 3.

16 Kelly, *A Politics of Virtue*; Jain and Rheddock, *Women Plantation Workers*; Ramachandran, *Indian Plantation Labor in Malaysia*; Sandhu, *Indians in Malaya*; Sinnappah, *Indians in Malaysia and Singapore*; R. K. Jain, *South Indians on the Plantation Frontier in Malaya*; Jackson, *Immigrant Labor and the Development of Malaya, 1786–1920*; Mahajani, *The Role of Indian Minorities in Burma and Malaya*; Kaur, "Indian Labor, Labor Standards." There has been a marked absence of work on Indian coolies in Malaya since the 1970s and this is reflected in Kaur's 2006 work ("Indian Labor, Labor Standards"), as even she does not refer to any recent literature.

17 Ann Laura Stoler, "Making Empire Respectable: The Politics of Race and Sexual Morality in 20th-Century Colonial Cultures," *American Ethnologist* 16, no. 4 (1989): 634–660; Jeffery Weeks, "Invented Moralities," *History Workshop* 32, no. 1 (1991): 151–166.

18 Indrani Sen, *Woman and Empire: Representations in the Writings of British India, 1858–1900* (New Delhi: Orient Longman, 2002); I. Chatterjee, *Unfamiliar Relations*.

19 Ibid.

20 While husband desertion was not specifically identified as an act of immorality, it was used to present women as victims of violence (perpetrators being their possessive partners) in marital and intimate relations.

21 Interestingly, such marriages were anathema to Victorian ideals of marriage involving virgin brides and "faithful wives" and arguably they could hardly admit the existence of depot marriages without admitting that the nationalists were right and that it was the colonial context which forced Indians into "immorality."

22 Vizenor, *Manifest Manners*.

23 AN: *Times of Malaya*, August 17, 1932, 3; NLS: *The Straits Times*, August 20, 1932, 16. Therasama lived with Periasamy as his mistress along with her son from her previous marriage.

24 In no way can such incidents of domestic violence be supported or excused, but recognition of the coolie women's situational agency reveals a crucial aspect of the everyday lives of coolie women in estate societies.

25 As discussed in Chapter 2.

26 NLS: *The Straits Times*, September 21, 1933, 12.

27 Weeks, "Invented Moralities."

28 NLS: *The Singapore Free Press and Mercantile Advertiser*, February 16, 1935, 3.

29 NLS, Reel 3575, *The Singapore Free Press and Mercantile Advertiser*, December 21, 1933, 2.

30 BL, IOR V/24/1184: *Annual Report of the Agent of the Government of India in Malaya 1931*, 21.

31 BL, IOR V/24/1184: *Annual Report of the Agent of the Government of India in Malaya 1934*, 20.

32 NLS: *The Straits Times*, August 19, 1930, 19.

33 Ibid.

34 BL: *Perak Pioneer*, October 22, 1908, 4; NLS: *The Singapore Free Press and Mercantile Advertiser*, October 27, 1908, 8; AN: *The Times of Malaya*, October 25, 1908, 4. Upon trial, the judge sentenced the husband to "extreme penalty of the law with no recommendation of any kind" as there was no "severe provocation" for him to kill his wife. BL: *Perak Pioneer*, November 14 and 18–19, 1908, 4–5.

35 NLS: *The Singapore Free Press and Mercantile Advertiser*, October 23, 1930, 12.

36 NLS: *Malaya Tribune*, June 8, 1937, 14; AN: *Times of Malaya*, July 10, 1937, page number not visible.

37 AN: *Times of Malaya*, April 23, 1935, 9, *Times of Malaya*, May 2, 1935, 9, *Times of Malaya*, July 12, 1935, 9.

38 NLS: *The Straits Times*, August 31, 1934, 12.

39 NLS: *The Straits Times*, November 16, 1934, 3.

40 BL: *Perak Pioneer*, March 22, 1907, 5; CUKL: *Annual Report of the Police Force, FMS for 1907*, 19.

41 John G. Butcher, *The British in Malaya, 1880–1941: The Social History of a European Community in Colonial South-East Asia* (Kuala Lumpur: Oxford University Press, 1979).

42 As comprehended from the many causes of suicide enlisted in the *Annual Labor Department Reports of FMS, 1912–1940*.

43 NLS: *The Straits Times*, January 12, 1917, 10; BL, IOR V/24/1184: *Annual Report of the Agent of the Government of India in Malaya 1931*, 20–21; BL, IOR V/24/1184: *Annual Report of the Agent of the Government of India in Malaya 1932*, 20–21; BL, IOR V/24/1184: *Annual Report of the Agent of the Government of India in Malaya 1934*, 20.

44 NLS: *The Straits Times*, January 12, 1917, 10.

45 BL, IOR V/24/1184–85: *Annual Reports of the Agent of the Government of India in Malayas*, 1926–1941.

46 BL, IOR V/24/1184–85: *Annual Reports of the Agent of the Government of India in Malaya*, 1930–1941.

47 Jackson, *Immigrant Labor and the Development of Malaya*; *The Selangor Journal* 6 (1894): 90.

48 Ibid.

49 Weeks, *Sex, Politics and Society*.

50 NUSL: *The Indian*, February 8, 1936, no page numbers, not visible on the microfilm.

51 NUSL: *The Indian*, May 6, 1936.

52 Tambe, "Gandhi's 'Fallen' Sisters."

53 Gandhi, *The Collected Works of Gandhi*.

54 BL, IOR L/E/7/1532: Extract from *Official Report of Madras Legislative Council Debates in Indians in Malaya*, Public Record Department (Parliament Branch), 1929, 218–220.

55 Nijhawan, "Fallen through the Nationalist and Feminist Grids of Analysis."

56 Antoinette Burton, *Burdens of History: British Feminists, Indian Women and Imperial Culture, 1865–1915* (Chapel Hill, University of North Carolina Press, 1994); Mrinalini Sinha, "Refashioning Mother India: Feminism and Nationalism in Late Colonial India," *Feminist Studies* 26, no. 3 (2000): 623–644; Barbara Ramusack, "Cultural Missionaries, Maternal Imperialists, Feminist Allies: British Women Activists in India, 1865–1945," in *Western Women and Imperialism: Complicity and Resistance*, ed. Nupur Chaudhuri and Margaret Strobel, 119–136 (Bloomington: Indiana University Press, 1992).

57 G. W. De Silva, ed., *Selected Speeches by S. N. Veerasamy* (Kuala Lumpur: Kyle, Palmer & Company, 1938).

58 Andrew Karmen, *Crime Victims: An Introduction to Victimology* (Belmont: Wadsworth Publishing, 2003).

59 Lata Mani, *Contentious Traditions: the Debate on Sati in Colonial India* (Berkeley: University of California Press 1998); Mytheli Sreenivas, *Wives, Widows, Concubines: the Conjugal Family Ideal in Colonial India* (Bloomington: Indiana University Press, 2008); Stoler, "Making Empire Respectable."

CHAPTER 5

1 Personal interview with Meenachi Perumal, June 18, 2016. Born in Bukit Keming estate, a rubber plantation in Selangor in Malaya, Meenachi Perumal joined the Rani of Jhansi Regiment (RJR) at the age of sixteen and was one of the youngest RJR recruits. She was already married then but had sworn to dedicate her life to the RJR and proud to be a member of the Jan Baz unit. Meenachi Perumal passed away in November 2017.

2 Paul Kratoska, *The Japanese Occupation of Malaya: 1941–1945* (London: C. Hurst & Co., 1998), 4–5. See also Cheah Boon Kheng, "Japanese Army Policy toward the Chinese and Malaya–Chinese Relations in Wartime Malaya," in *Southeast Asian Minorities in the Wartime Japanese Empire*, ed. Paul J. Kratoska, (London: Routledge Curzon, 2002), 97–110.

3 Winston Churchill, *The Second World War* (New York: Random House, [1959] 2011).

4 Lord Moran, *Winston Churchill: The Struggle for Survival 1940–1965* (London: Constable, 1968).

5 The Indian Independence League (IIL) was the political organization formed by Indian nationalists with the motive of overthrowing the British Empire from India. Founded in 1928, the IIL aimed at gathering Indian expatriates living outside India, mainly in Southeast Asia, to support the extremist Indian national movement from outside of India. Although it was formed in 1928, it was only after the Japanese occupation of Malaya that the IIL gained prominence and could amass a large number of recruits and

participants. The Japanese supported the league with political and logistical support and also encouraged Indians in Southeast Asia to join the IIL or the Indian National Army* (that is, the second Indian National Army [INA]; INA was the military wing of the IIL). The main participants or the recruits came from Singapore, Malaysia, Philippines (mainly Manila), and Burma.

The recruits from Burma were especially different from those from Malaya. They mostly belonged to middle-class families (usually were daughters or wives of educated Indians engaged in administrative tasks in colonial India) who had migrated from Bengal to Burma. Further, they maintained constant connections with family and friends in India and often visited Bengal—the most revolutionary society in colonial India.

See Lakshmi Sahgal, "The Rani of Jhansi Regiment," *The Oracle* 1, no. 2 (April1979): 17.

Note: The First INA was formed in February 1942 but it dissolved by December of the same year. Mohan Singh was the head of the first INA and had received Japanese support to recruit Indian prisoners of war in Singapore and Malaya. However, soon Singh and other officials of the INA had a fallout regarding the intentions of the Japanese toward Indians and India's freedom struggle and the first INA dissolved. Eventually, with the arrival of Bose in Singapore during 1943, the INA was revived under his leadership and is generally known as the second INA.

6   T. N. Harper, *The End of Empire and the Making of Malaya* (New York: Cambridge University Press, 1998), 47.

7   Carol Hills and Daniel C. Silverman, "Nationalism and Feminism in Late Colonial India: 1943–1945," *Modern Asian Studies* 27, no. 4 (1993): 741–760; Tobias Rettig, "Recruiting All-female Rani of Jhansi Regiment: Subhash Chandra Bose and Dr. Lakshmi Swaminadhan," Research Collection of School of Social Science, Singapore Management University, Singapore, 2013; Joyce Chapman Lebra, *Women Against the Raj: The Rani of Jhansi Regiment* (Singapore: Institute of Southeast Asian Studies, 2008).

Dato' Rasammah Bhupalan: Born in 1927, Dato' Bhupalan joined the RJR along with her sister at the age of sixteen and was one of the youngest RJR recruits. After the war, she became involved in Malaysian politics, especially with regard to women's issues, and was a founding member of the National Council of Women's Organizations. Rasamah received many accolades for her service to the nation. Dato', an honorary state title, was conferred on her for her contributions to the nation. Even in her late eighties, Dato' Bhupalan serves as an active member of the Young Women's Christian Association of Malaysia.

Interviews with Dato' Rasammah Bhupalan, May 11, 2011, March 23, 2012, and October 10, 2013.

8   Lebra, *Women Against the Raj*; Hills and Silverman, "Nationalism and Feminism"; Rettig, "Recruiting All-female Rani of Jhansi Regiment"; Nilanjana Sengupta, *A Gentleman's Word: The Legacy of Subhash Chandra Bose in Southeast Asia* (Singapore: Institute of Southeast Asian Studies, 2012).

9   Lebra, *Women Against the Raj*; Sengupta, *A Gentleman's Word.*

10 "Rani of Jhansi Regiment: Fighting for India" Episode, History Channel, Asia, February 16, 2012.

11 Aruna Gopinath, *Footprints on the Sands of Time: Rasammah Bhupalan: A Life of Purpose* (Kuala Lumpur: Arkib Negara, 2007).

12 Trouillot, *Silencing the Past.*

13 Lebra, *Women Against the Raj*; Sengupta, *A Gentleman's Word*; Rettig, "Recruiting All-female Rani of Jhansi Regiment"; Sahgal, *A Revolutionary Life.*

14 Lebra, *Women Against the Raj*, 60; Hills and Silverman, "Nationalism and Feminism."

15 Personal interview with Dato' Rasammah Bhupalan (May 11, 2011) and Dr Lakshmi Sahgal (June 15, 2011). The same has been quoted by Dr Sahgal in her autobiography. See Sahgal, *A Revolutionary Life*, 169.

16 The history of nationalist movements includes many examples of the politicization of gender and women's identities. See, for example, Anne McClintock, "Family Feuds: Gender, Nationalism and the Family," *Feminist Review*, 44 (Summer 1993): 61–80; Nira Yuval-Davis and F. Anthias, "Introduction" in *Woman—Nation—State*, ed. Nira Yuval-Davis and F. Anthias (Basingstoke: Macmillan, 1989), 1–15; Zilla Eisentein, *The Color of Gender: Reimagining Democracy* (Berkeley: California University Press, 1994); Mary Tetreault, "Justice for All: Wartime Rape and Women's Human Rights," *Global Governance* 3 no. 2 (1997): 197–212.

17 Subhash Chandra Bose, "Empire That Rose in a Day Will Vanish in a Night," in *Chalo Delhi: Writings and Speeches—Subhash Chandra Bose 1943–*

1945, ed. Sisir Kumar Bose and Sugata Bose (Calcutta: Netaji Research Bureau, 2007), 52–59.

18 McClintock, "Family Feuds"; Yuval-Davis and Anthias, 'Introduction'; Eisentein, *The Color of Gender*; Tetreault, "Justice for All."

19 Sita is the wife of Lord Rama in Hindu mythology. She is often idealized by Indians as the perfect Indian woman, someone who is selfless and makes innumerable sacrifices as a daughter, wife, and mother.

20 Ketu Katrak, "Women's Texts," *Modern Fiction Studies* 35, no. 1 (1992): 157–179; Geraldine Forbes, "Mothers and Sisters: Feminism and Nationalism in the Thought of Subhas Chandra Bose," *Asian Studies* 2, no. 1 (1984): 23–32; Geraldine Forbes, "The Politics of Respectability: Indian Women and the INC," in *The Indian National Congress*, ed. Anthony Low (Delhi: Oxford University Press, 1988), 54–97; Suresh R. Bald, "Politics of Gandhi's 'Feminism': Constructing 'Sitas' for Swaraj," in *Women, States, and Nationalism: At Home in the Nation?* ed. Sita Ranchod-Nilsson and Mary Ann Tétreault (London, New York: Routledge, 2000), 83–100.

21 G. J. Douds, "Indian POWs in the Pacific, 1941–1945," in *Forgotten Captives in Japanese-occupied Asia*, ed. Kevin Blackburn and Karl Hack (London: Routledge, 2008), 73–93.

22 NAUK, CO 273/669/5577/7: *British Intelligence Reports, FIR 8, Conditions of Malaya*, September, 1942, 4.

23 Michael R. Stenson, *Class, Race, and Colonialism in West Malaysia: The Indian Case* (St. Lucia: University of Queensland Press, 1980), 93.

24 Ibid., 9.

25 On estates, *kanganies* functioned as heads of the coolie groups under the European planters and supervised laborers on the estates. Also, from time to time *kanganies* were sent to India to recruit more coolies from their home villages. The *kangany* doubled as a supervisor and a recruiter for the European planters in Malaya.

26 R. K. Jain, *South Indians on the Plantation Frontier in Malaya*.

27 Labour Inspector, *Report on the Conditions of the Labor Force in the State of Kelantan Before and After Hostilities.* See NAUK, CO 273/669/50744/7, November 3, 1943. The report also mentions that many coolies sustained themselves by begging on the streets. Also see Appendix F in the same collection.

28 NUSL, CO 273/669/5577/7: *British Intelligence Reports, FIR 14, Reports of Four Respondents Who Escaped from Malaya in January 1943 and Arrived in China in April 1943*, December 9, 1944, 2.

29 NAUK, CO 273/669/5577/7: *British Intelligence Reports, FIR 8, Extracts from Daily World Broadcast*, 10.

30 AN: *Annual Medical Report of the Medical Department, 1946* (Kuala Lumpur: Government Printing Office, 1947).

31 Stenson, *Class, Race, and Colonialism in West Malaysia.*

32 Labour Inspector, *Report on the Conditions of the Labour Force in the State of Kelantan Before and After Hostilities*, November 3, 1943. See also CO 273/669/50744/7 Appendix F; *Annual Medical Report of the Medical Department, 1946* (Kuala Lumpur: Government Print Office, 1947); Stenson, *Industrial Conflict in Malaya*, 90; *British Intelligence Reports, FIR 8, Extracts from Daily World Broadcast*, 10 (CO 273/669/5577/7); *British Intelligence Reports, FIR 14, Reports of Four Respondents Who Escaped from Malaya in January 1943 and Arrived in China in April 1943* (December 9, 1944), 2 (CO 273/669/5577/7); *British Intelligence Reports, FIR 8, Extracts from Daily World Broadcast*, 10 (CO 273/669/5577/7).

33 AN: Labor Inspector, *Report on the Conditions of the Labor Force in the State of Kelantan Before and After Hostilities*, November 3, 1943. See also NAUK, CO 273/669/50744/7 Appendix F.

34 Personal communication with Pachaimmal, the wife of Marimuthu Sabapathy, on May 10, 2011, at her residence near Kelana Jaya. As stated previously in Chapter 2, Pachaimmal migrated to Malaya as an infant with her parents in the 1930s. She, like her husband, was employed as a coolie at Sungai Buaya estate, Selangor. She was eighty-four years old at the time of interview.

35 R. K. Jain, *South Indians on the Plantation Frontier in Malaya*, 302.

36 Ibid.

37 Kratoska, *The Japanese Occupation of Malaya*, 118.

38 Oral History Interviews (OHI), National Archives of Singapore (NAS), Acc. No: 000204/2: Abdealli K. Motiwalla, "Japanese Occupation in Singapore."

   Similarly, Vilasini Perumbulavil, who lived in Singapore during the occupation, recalled that her father allowed Japanese soldiers billeted nearby to take provisions from their kitchen. On one occasion a few soldiers ordered her mother to cook for them, and there was an argument when her mother declined. Worried about possible repercussions, her father immediately contacted friends in the INA who asked senior officers in the Japanese military to discipline the soldiers. The next day a senior officer came to the house and warned the soldiers not to disturb the people living there as the family was treating the soldiers kindly. See OHI, NAS, Acc No.: 002437/3: Vilasini Perumbulavil, "The Public Service—A Retrospection."

39 Tan Sri S. Chelvasingam MacIntyre, *Through Memory Lane* (Singapore: University Education Press, 1973), 120, 127, 284.

40 Laura Sjoberg and Caron E. Gentry, *Mothers, Monsters, Whores: Women's Violence in Global Politics* (London and New York: Zed Pub., 2007); Miranda Alison, *Women and Political Violence: Female Combatants in Ethno-National Conflict* (London and New York: Routledge, 2009); Dubravka Zarkov, *The Body of War* (Durham and London: Duke University Press, 2007).

41 Temma Kaplan, "Female Consciousness and Collective Action: The Case of Barcelona, 1910–1918," *Signs* 7, no. 3 (1982): 545–566.

42 OHI, NAS, Acc No. 01182/2: Lakshmi Sahgal, "Japanese Occupation of Singapore." Also, personal interview with Dr Lakshmi Sahgal, 2011.

43 Personal interview with Dato' Rasammah Bhupalan, 2011, 2012, 2013.

44 Ibid.

45 Rohini Gawankar, *The Women's Regiment and Captain Lakshmi of INA* (New Delhi: Devika Publications, 2003), 156, 189; personal interview with Dr Lakshmi Sahgal, 2011.

46 Sahgal, "The Rani of Jhansi Regiment."; Sahgal, *A Revolutionary Life*, 168–169.

47 Ibid.

48 As seen in previous chapters.

49 OHI, NAS, Acc. No. 000418/6: Seva Singh, "Communities of Singapore." Sahgal also validated the fact that many families were joining. Sahgal explains, first the men joined and then their wives and sisters joined the RJR. See OHI, NAS, Acc. No. 001182/2: Lakshmi Sahgal, "Japanese Occupation of Singapore."

50 OHI, NAS, Acc. No. 000392/5: Ban Cheng Tan, "Japanese Occupation of Singapore."

51 Personal interview with Dato' Rasammah Bhupalan, 2011, 2013, and Dr Lakshmi Sahgal, 2011.

52 Sahgal, *A Revolutionary Life*, 168. See also Gawankar, *The Women's Regiment and Captain Lakshmi of INA*, 190–191.

53 Personal communication with Dato' Rasammah Bhupalan (2013). See also Gawankar, *The Women's Regiment and Captain Lakshmi of INA*, 191.

54 OHI, NAS, Acc. No. 000025/7: K. R. Menon, "Japanese Occupation of Singapore."

55 Personal interview with Pachaimmal, May 9–10, 2011.

56 Interestingly, Pushpa and Pachaimmal, who lived on different estates and were born in different times, perceived the British colonialism vis-à-vis the Japanese differently.

57 Personal interview with Pushpa and Dave, May 10, 2011. David (Dave) Anthony was born to an Indian estate owner in 1939. Although very young at the time of the Japanese occupation, he has memories of experiences of the estate people—especially through his conversations with his family and friends. He is an active novelist and also produces video magazines and docu-dramas. Anthony also works extensively with the rubber-tapping community throughout Malaysia.

58 Stenson, *Class, Race, and Colonialism in West Malaysia*, 93, 97; MacIntyre, *Through Memory Lane*, 120, 127, 284.

59 Personal interview with Meenachi Perumal, 2016.

60 Sahgal, *A Revolutionary Life*, 171; also, as discussed in Chapter 2.

61 Personal interview with Dato' Rasammah Bhupalan, 2013.

62 Personal interview with Dato' Rasammah Bhupalan, 2011.

63 Mrinalini Sinha, *Colonial Masculinity: The "Manly Englishman" and the "Effeminate Bengali" in the Late Nineteenth Century* (New Delhi: Kali for Women, 1997).

64 Personal interview with Dato' Rasammah Bhupalan, 2011.

65 Personal interview with Dato' Rasammah Bhupalan, 2011, 2012.

66 Raymond A. Callahan, *Triumph at Imphal–Kohima: How the Indian Army Finally Stopped the Japanese Juggernaut* (Lawrence KS: University Press of Kansas, 2017).

67 McClintock, "Family Feuds"; Yuval-Davis and Anthias, *Woman–Nation–State* (Basingstoke: Macmillan, 1989); Eisentein, *The Color of Gender*; Tetreault, "Justice for All."

68 McClintock, "Family Feuds."

69 Yuval-Davis and Anthias, *Woman–Nation–State*, 7.

70 OHI, NAS Acc No. 000025/7: K. R. Menon, "Japanese Occupation of Singapore." K. R. Menon worked for the IIL as a secretary for several years and his recollection of the RJR recruits is very clear.

71 OHI, NAS, Acc. No: 000204/2: Abdealli K. Motiwalla, "Japanese Occupation in Singapore."

72 Mamoru Shinozaki, *Syonan—My Story: The Japanese Occupation of Singapore* (Singapore: Marshall Cavendish, 2011), 66.

73 *The Syonan Shimbun*, "Need for Women's Movement in Syonan Emphasized," November 19, 1943.

74 Sahgal, "The Rani of Jhansi Regiment," 17–18.

75 OHI, NAS, Acc: 000127/5: Damodaran s/o Kesavan, "The Japanese Occupation of Singapore."

76 Personal communication with Dato' Rasammah Bhupalan, 2011. The same has been quoted by Dr Sahgal in her autobiography. See Sahgal, *A Revolutionary Life*; Amritlal Seth, *Jai Hind: The Diary of a Rebel Daughter of India with the Rani of Jhansi Regiment* (Bombay: Janmabhoomi Prakashan Mandir, 1945).

77 Lal, "Kunti's Cry; Pool and Singh, "Indentured Indian Women of the Empire"; Kelly, "Fear of Culture";Kelly, *Politics of Virtue*; Kelly, "Gaze and Grasp," and many other similar works.

EPILOGUE

1 Interview with Pachaimmal, May 10, 2011, Selangor.

2 Interview with Selvaraju Sandrakasi, May 5, 2011, Kuala Lumpur.

3 Interview with Selvaraju Sandrakasi, September 24, 2015, Kuala Lumpur.

4 Andrew C. Willford, *Cage of Freedom: Tamil Identity and the Ethnic Fetish in Malaysia* (Ann Arbor: University of Michigan Press, 2006); Andrew C. Willford, *Tamils and the Haunting of Justice: History and Recognition in*

NOTES

Malaysia's Plantations (Manoa and Singapore: University of Hawaii Press/ Singapore University Press, 2014).

5   Personal interview, May 9–10, 2011.

6   *Fleeting Agencies* joins the efforts of anthro-historians like Andrew C. Willford and Carl Vadivella Belle to bring past and present histories closer and historicize the current situation on the estates in Malaysia through stories of "coolie" women of past and present. See Willford, *Cage of Freedom*; Willford, *Tamils and the Haunting of Justice*; Carl Vadivella Belle, *Tragic Orphans: Indians in Malaysia* (Singapore: Institute of Southeast Asian Studies, 2015).

7   Most of the rubber estates of the past have now been transformed into palm oil estates. Hence, some of the estates I visited were rubber estates, but most were palm oil estates. Today, large corporations such as Sime Darby own most of the larger estates, access to which is extremely difficult as a researcher. In contrast, most of the smaller estates I visited were owned by local Chinese entrepreneurs.

8   Interview with Saroja, October 4, 2011, Dunedin Estate, Putrajaya.

9   K.S. Jomo and Josie Zaini, *Meena: A Plantation Child Worker* (Kuala Lumpur: INSAN, 1985); K. S. Maniam, *Between Lives* (Pertaling Jaya: Maya Press, 2003).

10   Jomo and Josie, *Meena* (1985).

11   Peter Lee-Wright, *Child Slaves* (Oxon, New York: Earthscan, James & James, 1990, 2009), 107–108.

12   Interviews with Sundara Rajan, Semenyih, April 4 and 5, 2011. Rajan is the secretary of the Parti Socialis Malaysia, Semenyih branch. When I asked Rajan to describe his engagement with the estates, he explained, "I and my comrades work closely with the estate laborers in Semenyih to voice their grievances and demand rights for them from the government."

13   Interview with estate watchman (and gatekeeper) Abdul Khalek, at the Abaco rubber estate in Semeyenih, September 16, 2011.

14   Interview with women estate workers, Uma, Jaya, Mariammal, September 16, 2011, Abaco Rubber estate in Semeyenih.

15   In conversation with students at the University of Malaysia who were studying the current situation of Indian estate workers in the country, I found they were completely oblivious of the history of coolie women in

Malaya. Many of them even said they are using a gender studies approach to study the life of women on the estates. But when I asked them how far in the past they are going, they said, "but women estate workers don't have history here." Such ignorance about the past, while shocking, reflects the extent of silencing and erasure of coolie women's history. Students' requests for anonymity have been respected by not naming them here.

BIBLIOGRAPHY

ARCHIVES AND ABBREVIATIONS USED

INDIA

National Archives India, New Delhi (NAI)
National Library, Kolkata (NLK)
Tamil Nadu State Archives, Chennai (TNSA)
West Bengal State Archives, Kolkata (WBSA)
Netaji Research Bureau, Kolkata

MALAYSIA*

Arkib Negara, Kuala Lumpur (AN)
* *Federated Malay States is mentioned as FMS.*

SINGAPORE

National Archives Singapore (NAS)
National Archives Singapore Oral History Center (NAS OHC)
National Library of Singapore (NLS)
National University of Singapore Library (NUSL)

BRITAIN

British Library (BL)

British Library, India Office Records (IOR)
National Archives of United Kingdom at Kew (NAUK)

UNITED STATES OF AMERICA

Cornell University Kroch Library, Ithaca (CUKL)

JOURNALS, MAGAZINES, AND NEWSPAPERS

Agricultural Bulletin of Straits and FMS, 1907
Bengalee, 1913
British Colonist, 1861
British Malaya, 1930
Demara Daily Chronicle, 1882
Journal of the Indian Archipelago and East Asia, 1862
Journal of the Straits Branch of the Royal Asiatic Society, 1861
Malay Mail, 1911, 1913, 1927
Malay Weekly Mail, 1922
New India, 1923
Perak Pioneer, 1901, 1904, 1905, 1907, 1908, 1910–1912
Selangor Journal of Planters, 1894
Straits Settlement Gazette, 1880
The Guardian, 2012, 2013
The Indian, 1936
The Law Reports of FMS, 1939, 1940
The Malayan Law Journal, 1938
The Oracle, 1979
The Planter, 1923, 1930
The Singapore Free Press and Mercantile Advertiser, 1908, 1914, 1918, 1923, 1929–
        1931, 1933–1936, 1939
The Straits Times, 1901, 1908, 1911, 1917, 1922, 1924, 1926, 1929, 1930, 1933–1935, 1937
The Syonan Sinbun, 1942, 1943
Times of Malaya, 1908, 1909, 1911, 1913, 1932, 1935
Tolong Lagi, 1933

ORAL HISTORY ARCHIVES

Kesavan, Damodaran s/o. 1981. "Japanese Occupation of Singapore" (NAS, OHC, Acc: 000127/5).

Menon, K.R. 1982. "Japanese Occupation of Singapore" (NAS, OHC, Acc No. 000025/7).

Motiwalla, Abdealli K. 1982. "Japanese Occupation in Singapore" (NAS, OHC, Acc. No. 000204/2).

Natesan, Palanivelu. "Communities of Singapore" (NAS, OHC Acc. No. 00058/5).

Perumbulavil, Vilasini. 2000. "The Public Service—A Retrospection" (NAS, OHC, Acc No. 002437/3).

Sahgal, Lakshmi. 1990. "Japanese Occupation of Singapore" (NAS, OHC Acc. No. 001182/2).

Singh, Seva. 1984. "Communities of Singapore" (NAS, OHC, Acc. No. 000418/6).

Tan, Ban Cheng. 1984. "Japanese Occupation of Singapore" (NAS, OHC Acc. No. 000392/5).

PRINTED PRIMARY SOURCES

INDIA

Government of India. *Indian Emigration, 1910* (NAI Department of Commerce and Industry. Emigration Branch. April, 1910. File No. 3, Part B).

———. *Indians Emigration Rules 1923 and Special Rules to Ceylon and Malaya* (NLK Ministry of External Affairs, G.P. 325. 254 IN 2 Cem).

———. *Indians Emigration to Malaya, 1925* (TNSA Law Department, GO. No. 2383).

———. *Question and Answer in the Legislative Council Regarding the Deputation of Mc Neil and Chiman Lal to Enquire into the Condition of Indian Labour in Colonies* (NAI Department of Commerce and Industry. Emigration Branch. February, 1914. File No. 13, Part B).

———. *Special Report on the Conditions of Indentured Indian Labour Employed in the Federated Malay States* (NAI Department of Commerce and Industry. Emigration Branch. April, 1911. File No. 6–7, Part A).

———. "Terms of Agriculture, Wages and Conditions of Service." Department of Revenue and Agriculture. Emigration and Immigration, India. 1894 (NLK G.P. 325.254).

———. *The Indian Emigration Act, 1883* (NLK G.P. 325.254 IN 2e).

———. *The Indian Emigration Act, 1922* (NLK G.P. 325.254 IN).

———. *Treatment of Indian Labourers in Federated Malay States* (NAI Department of Commerce and Industry. Emigration Branch. June, 1913. File No. 3–4, Part B).

———. *Treatment of Indian Labourers in the Federated Malay States* (NAI Department of Commerce and Industry. Emigration Branch. March,1914. File No. 41–45, Part B).

Government of Malaya. *Federated Malay States Immigration Report* (NAI Department of Commerce and Industry. Emigration Branch. December, 1913. File No. 1–2, Part B).

Madras Devadasi Association. "The Dedication Bill." In *Manifesto of Madras Devadasi Association* (Madras: Aurora Press 1927) (NLK).

MALAYSIA

De Silva, G. W. ed. *Selected Speeches by S. N. Veerasamy.* Kuala Lumpur: Kyle, Palmer & Company, 1938.

Earl, G. W. *Topography and Itinerary of Province Wellesley.* Pinang: Pinang Gazette Printing Office, 1861.

Government of Malaya. *Addition of a New Section to the Penal Code Relating to Punishment for the Commission by a Male Person of An Act of Gross Indecency with any Male Person* (AN 1957/0271521).

———. *Annual Report of Labour Department 1913* (AN 1957/ 0175698).

———. *Annual Report of Labour Department 1914* (AN 1957/ 0181247).

———. *Annual Report of Labour Department 1915* (AN 1957/ 0187600).

———. *Annual Report of Labour Department 1919* (AN 1957/ 0209393).

———. *Annual Report of Labour Department 1936–1937* (AN 1957/0209393).

———. *Back to Back Coolie Lines for Accommodation of Indian Labourers on Pahi Estate* (AN 1957/0511984).

———. *Ban on Immigration of Indian Labourers to Malaya* (AN 1957/0568771).

———. *Correspondences Regarding Recruiting of Indian Labour from Northern India.* 1902 (AN 1957/0103354).

———. *Free Pardon to Mrs. Proudlock* (Appeal to Court, Selangor). 1911 (AN 1957/0158354).

———. *Death Rate amongst Free and Indentured Labourers* (AN 1957/0592394).

———. *High Mortality in July and August 1918 among Indian Labourers in Estates* (AN 1957/0445134).

———. *Indian Immigration Committee Meetings Minutes (Book No. 6), February 1932– February 1938* (AN2006/0019647).

———. *Interim Report of the Special Labor Committee on Matters Relating to Wages for Indian Estate Labor.* Kuala Lumpur: Planters Association of Malaya, 1928.

———. "Letter from A.S. Jelf. (Acting Undersecretary, FMS) to Secretary to the High Commissioner for the Malay States" (AN 1957/0610415).

———. *Licensing the Recruiters of Indian Labour: Forwards Correspondence for Information and Guidance.* 1902 (AN 1957/0429173).

———. *Line Ayahs, Crèches, Attendants and Education of Children of South Indian Labourers by Government* (AN 1957/0259526).

———. *Mr. William Steward Shot Dead at the Quarters of Mr. Proudlock, Voctoria Institution.* 1911 (AN 1957/0157353).

———. *Pamphlets on Toddy Drinking by Indian Labourers* (AN 1957/0423053).

———. *Permanent Exemption of Malaya from the Operation of Rule 23 of the Immigration Rules* (AN 1957/0516564).

———. *Petition by the Indian Community, Singapore: Free Pardon to Mrs. Proudlock.* 1911. (AN 1957/0158624)

———. *Petition by the Malay Community of Kuala Lumpur for Free Pardon to Mrs. Proudlock.* 1911 (AN 1957/0158587).

———. *Petition by the Old School Boys of the Victoria Institute for Free Pardon to Mrs. Proudlock.* 1911 (AN 1957/0158313).

———. *Policy Regarding Sale of Liqour to South Indian Labourers* (AN1957/0298677).

———. *Prohibition of the Sale of Toddy to Indian Women* (AN 1957/0409212).

———. *Recruiting of Labour in India, 1915* (AN 1957/0599212).

———. *Registration of Marriages of Indian Labourers* (AN 1957/0213817).

————. *Report of the Commission Appointed to Enquire into the Conditions of Indentured Labour in the Federated Malay States*. Kuala Lumpur: Government Print Office (AN 1957/0286315).

————. *Report of the Executive of the General Labour Committee, British Malaya on Indian Labour and Labourers*. 1920 (AN 1957/0610040).

————. *Report on Labour Commission 1890–1900: SS and FMS*. 1901 (AN 272/1896).

————. *Returns of Criminal Prosecutions for Enticing Away Married Indian Women* (1928–1929) (AN 1957/0513715).

————. *Returns of Criminal Prosecutions for Enticing Away Married Indian Women* (1930). (AN 1957/0516208).

————. *Returns of Criminal Prosecutions for Enticing Away Married Indian Women* (1931–1933) (AN 1957/0348832).

————. *Returns of Criminal Prosecutions for Enticing Away Married Indian Women* (1934) (AN 1957/0421129).

————. *Returns of Criminal Prosecutions for Enticing Away Married Indian Women* (1935) (AN 1957/0613562).

————. *Returns of Criminal Prosecutions for Enticing Away Married Indian Women* (1936) (AN 1957/0485188).

————. *Supply of Indian Labour for Estates in Malay Peninsula* (1917) (AN 1957/0604485).

————. *Toddy and Estate Labourers* (1916) (AN 1957/0603043).

————. *Toddy Commission and Report, 1917* (AN 1957/0604152).

————. *Visit of Mr. N. E. Marjoribanks to the Federated States of Malaya to Enquire into Labour Conditions* (1916) (AN 1957/0603357).

Parr, C.W. *Report of the Commission Appointed to Enquire into the Conditions of Indentured Labor in the Federated Malay States*. Kuala Lumpur: Government Print Office, July 13, 1910.

Planters' Association of Malaya. *Interim Report of the Special Labor Committee on Matters Relating to Wages for Indian Estate Labor*. Kuala Lumpur: Planters Association of Malaya, 1928.

SINGAPORE

Government of Malaya. "Dr. M. Watson's Report on Toddy in Districts of Selangor." *Proceedings and Reports of the Toddy Commission, FMS, 1916* (NUSL).

———. "Health and Sanitation on Estates." *Proceedings of the First Agricultural Conference, Malaya*, 1917 (NUSL).

Hare, George Thompson. *FMS Census of the Population, 1901.* Kuala Lumpur: Government Print Office, 1902. (NUSL)

Mukkarains, A. (Officer of the Honorary Commissioner for Depressed Class for SS and FMS). *Report on the Traffic between South Indian Ports and Malaya, 1925.* Kuala Lumpur: Government Print Office, 1926 (NLS RCLOS 959.51).

Poutney, A. M. *FMS Review of the Census Operations and Results, 1911.* London: Darling and Son, 1912 (NUSL).

Ridley, H. N. *The Story of the Rubber Industry.* London: Waterlow and Sons, 1911 (NUSL).

Santry, Danis and Claude Wilson. *Salubrious Singapore.* Singapore: Kelly and Walsh, 1920 (NLS).

Vlieland, C. A. *British Malaya: A Report on the 1931 Census and on Certain Problems of Vital Statistics.* London: Malayan Information Agency, 1932 (NUSL).

Weiss, J. Bernard. 'Case 59/1940. PP vs Periabuchi at Court of Senior Magistrate, Selangor'. In *Manual for Magistrates in Malaya.* Singapore: Lithographers, 1940 (NUSL).

BRITAIN

Bronkhurst, Rev. H.V. P. *The Colony of British Guayana and Its Laboring Population.* London: Wolmer, 1883.

Carruthers, J. B. "Report of the Director of Agriculture FMS for 1906." *Agricultural Bulletin of Straits and FMS* 6, no. 9 (1907).

Census Commissioner of India. *Census of India 1891: Madras—The Report on the Census.* London: Her Majesty's Stationery Office, 1893 (BL W7870/20).

Edgar, A. T. *Manual of Rubber Planting.* London: Incorporated Society of Planters, 1947.

Government of India. *Annual Report of the Agent of Government of India in British Malaya (1926–1940).* Calcutta: Government of India Central Publication Branch, 1927–1941 (IOR V/24/1184–85).

———. Extract from *Official Report of Madras Legislative Council Debates, 1929: Indians in Malaya* (IOR L/E/7/1532).

———. *E. N. Marjoribanks Report on Indians in Malaya.* 1917 (IOR V/27/820/12).

————. "Mr. Gokhale's address to the Council, 'Indentured Labour.'" In *Proceedings of the Council of the Governor General of India*. March 4, 1912 (IOR V/9).

————. *Srinivasa V.S. Sastri Report on the Conditions of Indian Labour in Malaya.* (IOR V/820/31).

Government of Malaya. *Annual Report of the Labour Department (FMS)* (1922–1927). Kuala Lumpur: Government Print Office, 1922–1927 (IOR L/E/7/1341).

————. *Annual Report of the Labour Department (FMS)* (1928–1929). Kuala Lumpur: Government Print Office, 1928–1929 (IOR L/E/7/1532).

————. *Annual Report of the Labour Department (FMS)* (1930–1936). Kuala Lumpur: Government Print Office, 1930–1936 (IOR L/PJ/8/ 258–259).

————. *British Intelligence Reports, FIR 8. Conditions of Malaya.* 1942 (CO 273/669/5577/7).

————. *British Intelligence Reports, FIR 14. Conditions of Malaya.* 1942–1943 (CO 273/669/5577/7).

————. *Census of British Malaya, the Straits Settlements, Federated Malay States and Protected States of Johore, Kedah, Perlis, Kelantan, Trengganu and Brunei, 1921*, compiled by Julius Ernest Nathan. London, 1922 (BL).

————. *Census of the Population, 1901, Federated States of Malaya*, compiled by George Thompson Hare. Kuala Lumpur: Government Press, 1902 (BL).

————. "Memo of Mr. S.W. Jones. April, 1937." *Labour Disputes in Malaya* (CO 273/632/9).

————. *Report on the Conditions of the Labour Force in the State of Kelantan Before and After Hostilities.* November, 1943 (CO 273/669/50744/7).

————. *Report of the Commissioners Appointed to Enquire into the State of Labour in Straits Settlement and Protected Native States, 1890* (CO 275/41).

House of Commons. *Hansard Parliament Debates, 3rd Series, 7 June, 1842.* London: His Majesty's Stationery Office, 1842 (BL).

————. *Emigration from India to Crown Colonies and Protectorates, June 1910.* London: His Majesty's Stationery Office, 1910 (BL Cd. 5192).

Mc Neill, James and Chimman Lal (Government of India). *Report to the Government of India on the Conditions of Indian Emigrants in Four Colonies and Suriname, 1914.* London: His Majesty's Stationery Office, 1915 (Cd Paper 7744–7745).

The Central Indian Association of Malaya Kuala Lumpur. *Memorandum on "Toddy in Malaya".* Kuala Lumpur: Malayan Printers, 1937.

UNITED STATES OF AMERICA

Government of British Malaya. *Annual Reports on the State of Crime and the Administration of the Police Force, Federated Malay States* (1919–1938) (CUKL).

———. *Annual Report of Director of Agriculture, FMS, 1906.* Kuala Lumpur: Government Print Office, 1907 (CUKL).

———. *Annual Report of the Police Force, FMS, 1907.* Kuala Lumpur: Government Print Office, 1908 (CUKL).

———. *Annual Report on Indian Immigration and Emigration, FMS, for the year 1908.* Kuala Lumpur: Government Print Office, 1909 (CUKL).

PERSONAL INTERVIEWS

Anthony, Dave. May 10, 2011, Kuala Lumpur, Malaysia.

Pachaimmal. May 10, 2011, Selangor, Malaysia.

Bhupalan, Dato' Rasammah. May 11, 2011, Petaling Jaya, Malaysia; July 5, 2012, Petaling Jaya, Malaysia; October 10, 2013, Kuala Lumpur, Malaysia.

Sahgal, Lakshmi. June 5, 2011, Kanpur, India (via phone).

Cuthbert, Alex. May, 2012, Collindale, UK.

Pushpa. May 10, 2011, Selangor, Malaysia; October 15, 2013, Selangor, Malaysia.

Perumal, Meenachi. June 18, 2016, Selangor, Malaysia.

DISSERTATIONS

Jain, Ravindra K. "Migrants, Proletarians or Malayans?" PhD dissertation, Australian National University, 1966.

Ramanathan, S. "Social Reform Movements in South India and Mahatma Gandhi: A Critical Study." PhD dissertation, Shivaji University, 2011.

SECONDARY SOURCES

Abadia, Oscar Moro. "The History of Archaeology as a 'Colonial Discourse.'" *Bulletin of the History of Archaeology* 16, no. 2 (2006): 4–17. Accessed March 15, 2014. doi: http://dx.doi.org/10.5334/bha.16202.

Abrams, Kathryn. "From Autonomy to Agency: Feminist Perspectives on Self-determination." *William and Mary Law Review* 40, no. 3 (1999): 805–817.

Abu-Lughod, Lila. *Writing Women's Worlds: Bedouin Stories.* Berkeley: University of California Press, 2008.

———. "Return to Half-ruins: Memory, Pastmemory and Living History in Palestine." In *Nakba: Palestine, 1948 and the Claims of Memory,* edited by Lila Abu-Lughod and Ahmad Sa'adi, 77–106. New York: Columbia University Press, 2009.

Ainsworth, Leopold. *The Confessions of a Planter in Malaya: A Chronicle of Life and Adventure in the Jungle.* London: H. F. & G. Witherby, 1933.

Alison, Miranda. *Women and Political Violence: Female Combatants in Ethno-National Conflict.* London and New York: Routledge, 2009.

Allen, Richard B. "Review of *Women Plantation Workers: International Experiences.*" *The Historian* 62, no. 2 (2000): 432.

Amrith, Sunil. *Crossing the Bay of Bengal: The Furies of Nature and Fortunes of Migrants.* Cambridge: Harvard University Press, 2013.

———. "Indians Overseas? Governing Tamil Migration to Malaya, 1870–1941." *Past and Present* 208, no. 1 (2010): 231–261.

———. "South Indian Migration, 1800–1950." In *Globalising Migration History: The Eurasian Experience,* edited by Leo Lucassen and Jan Lucassen, 122–150. Leiden: Brill, 2013.

Anagol, Padma. "From the Symbolic to the Open: Women's Resistance in Colonial Maharashtra." In *Behind the Veil: Resistance, Women and the Everyday in Colonial South Asia,* edited by Anindita Ghosh, 21–57. Hampshire and New York: Palgrave Macmillan, 2007.

Anderson, Clare. *Subaltern Lives: Biographies of Colonialism in the Indian Ocean World 1790–1920.* Cambridge: Cambridge University Press, 2012.

Arondekar, Anjali. *For the Record: On Sexuality and the Colonial Archive in India.* Durham: Duke University Press, 2009.

Arooran, K. Nambi. *Tamil Renaissance and Dravidian Nationalism.* Madurai: Koodal Publishers, 1980.

Ayer, S. A. *Story of the INA.* New Delhi: National Book Trust, 1997.

Azhagappan, R. *Periyar EVR.* New Delhi: Sahitya Academy, 2006.

Bahadur, Gaiutra. *Coolie Woman: The Odyssey of Indenture.* Gurgaon: Hachette Book Publishing, 2013.

Bald, Suresh R. "Politics of Gandhi's 'Feminism': Constructing 'Sitas' for Swaraj." In *Women, States, and Nationalism: At Home in the Nation?* edited by Sita Ranchod-Nilsson and Mary Ann Tétreault, 83–100. London; New York: Routledge, 2000.

Barlow, Colin, Sisira Jayasuriya, and C Suan Tan, eds. *The World Rubber Industry.* Oxon: Routledge, 1994.

Bayly, Christopher and Tim Harper. *Forgotten Armies: Britain's Asian Empire and the War with Japan.* London: Penguin Books, 2005.

Beall, Jo. "Women under Indentured Labor in Colonial Natal, 1860–1911." In *Women and Gender in Southern Africa,* edited by C. Walker, 146–167. Cape Town: David Philip.

Behal, Rana P. and Marcel van der Linden. *India's Laboring Poor: Historical Studies c.1600–c.2000.* Delhi: Cambridge University Press, 2007.

Belle, Carl Vadivella. *Tragic Orphans: Indians in Malaysia.* Singapore: Institute of Southeast Asian Studies, 2015.

Birla, Ritu. "Postcolonial Studies: Now That's History." In *Can the Subaltern Speak? Reflections on the History of an Idea,* edited by Rosalind C. Morris, 87–99. New York: Columbia University Press, 2010.

Blackburn, Susan. "Gendered Nationalist Movements in Southeast Asia." In *Women in Southeast Asian Nationalist Movements,* edited by Susan Blackburn and Helen Ting, 1–22. Singapore: National University Press, 2013.

Bose, Subhash Chandra. "Empire That Rose in a Day Will Vanish in a Night." In *Chalo Delhi: Writings and Speeches—Subhash Chandra Bose 1943–1945,* edited by Sisir Kumar Bose and Sugata Bose, 55–60. Calcutta: Netaji Research Bureau, 2007.

Boulle, Pierre. *Sacrilege in Malaya.* Translated by Xan Fielding. Kuala Lumpur: Oxford University Press, 1958.

Bradford, Helen. "Women, Gender and Colonialism: Rethinking the History of the British Cape Colony and Its Frontier Zone, c.1806–1870." *The Journal of African History* 37, no.3 (1996): 351–370. Accessed March 15, 2011. http://www.jstor.org.libproxy1.nus.edu.sg/stable/182498.

Breman, Jan. *Labour, Migration and Rural Transformation in Colonial Asia.* Amsterdam: Free University Press, 1990.

Brownfoot, Janice. "Memsahibs in Colonial Malaya: A Study of European Wives in a British Colony and Protectorate, 1900–1940." In *The Incorporated*

Wife, edited by Hillary Callan and Shirley Ardner, 186–210. London: Croom Helm, 1984.

Burton, Antoinette M. *Burdens of History: British Feminists, Indian Women and Imperial Culture, 1865–1915*. Chapel Hill: University of North Carolina Press, 1994.

———. *Dwelling in the Archive: Women Writing House, Home and History in Late Colonial India* (Oxford: Oxford University Press, 2003).

Bush, Willard C. *Pahang: The Saga of a Rubber Planter in the Malay Jungle*. New York: The Macmillan Company, 1938.

Butcher, John G. *The British in Malaya, 1880–1941: The Social History of a European Community in Colonial South-East Asia*. Kuala Lumpur: Oxford University Press, 1979.

Butler, Judith. *The Psychic Life of Power*. Stanford: Stanford University Press, 1997.

———. *Vulnerability in Resistance*. Durham and London: Duke University Press, 2016.

Butler, Sara M. "Runaway Wives: Husband Desertion in Medieval England." *Journal of Social History* 40, no.2 (2006): 337–359. Accessed March 15, 2011. http://muse.jhu.edu/journals/jsh/summary/v040/40.2butler.html.

Callahan, Raymond A. *Triumph at Imphal–Kohima: How the Indian Army Finally Stopped the Japanese Juggernaut*. University Press of Kansas: Lawrence KS, 2017.

Carter, Marina. *Lakshmi's Legacy*. Stanley, Rose Hill, Mauritius: Editions de l' Océan Indien, 1994

———. *Women and Indenture: Experiences of Indian Labor Migrants* (London: Pink Pigeon Press, 2012).

Chatterjee, Indrani, ed., *Unfamiliar Relations: Family and History in South Asia*. New Brunswick: Rutgers University Press, 2004.

Chatterjee, Partha. *Nationalist Thought and the Colonial World: A Derivative Discourse?* London: Zed Books, 1986.

———. "The Nationalist Resolution of the Women's Question." In *Recasting Women*, edited by K. Sangariand and S. Vaid, 233–253. New Delhi: Kali for Women, 1989.

Chatterjee, Piya. *A Time for Tea: Women, Labor, and Post-colonial Politics on an Indian Plantation*. London: Duke University Press, 2002.

Churchill, Winston. *The Second World War*. New York: Random House, [1959] 2011.

Clark, Anna. *The Struggle for the Breeches: Gender and the Making of the British Working Class*. Los Angeles: University of California Press, 1995.

Cronin, Stephanie. *Subalterns and Social Protest: History from Below in the Middle East and North Africa*. London and New York: Routledge, 2012.

Das, Veena. *Life and Words: Violence and the Descent into the Ordinary*. Berkley, Los Angeles and London: University of California Press, 2007.

Datta, Arunima. "'Immorality', Nationalism and the Colonial State in British Malaya: Indian 'Coolie' Women's Intimate Lives as Ideological Battleground." *Women's History Review* 25, no. 4 (2016): 584–601.

———. "Social Memory and Indian Women from Malaya and Singapore in the Rani of Jhansi Regiment." *Journal of the Malaysian Branch of the Royal Asiatic Society* 88, no. 309 (2015): 77–103.

De, Aparajita, Amrita Ghosh, and Ujjwal Jana, eds. *Subaltern Vision: A Study in Postcolonial Indian English Texts*. Cambridge: Cambridge Scholars Publishing, 2012.

De Silve, G. W., ed. *Selected Speeches by S. N. Veerasamy*. Kuala Lumpur: Kyle, Palmer and Company Ltd., 1938.

Douds, G. J. "Indian POWs in the Pacific, 1941–45." In *Forgotten Captives in Japanese-occupied Asia*, edited by Kevin Blackburn and Karl Hack. London: Routledge, 2008.

Drabble, John. *Rubber in Malaya: 1876–1922*. Kuala Lumpur: Oxford University Press, 1973.

Dubbois, Abbe. *Hindu Manners, Customs and Ceremonies*. New York: Cossimo Classsics, 2007.

Edgar, A. T. *Manual of Rubber Planting (Malaya)*. London: Incorporated Society of Planters, 1947.

Eisentein, Zilla. *The Color of Gender: Reimagining Democracy*. Berkeley: California University Press, 1994.

Eng, Lai Ah. *Peasants, Proletarians and Prostitutes: A Preliminary Investigation into the Work of Chinese Women in Colonial Malaya*. Singapore: Institute of Southeast Asian Studies, 1986.

Faruquee, Ashrufa. "Conceiving the Coolie Woman: Indentured Labour, Indian Women and Colonial Discourses." *South Asia Research* 16, no.1 (1996): 61–76. Accessed March 15, 2011. http://sar.sagepub.com/content/16/1/61.

Fay, Peter Ward. *The Forgotten Army*. Ann Arbour: University of Michigan Press, 1995.

Flather, Amanda. "Space, Place and Gender: The Sexual and Spatial Division of Labour in the Early Modern Household." *History and Theory* 3, no. 52 (2013): 344–360. Accessed August 12, 2014. doi: 10.1111/hith.10673.

Forbes, Geraldine. *Women in Modern India*. Cambridge: Cambridge University Press, 1996.

———. "Mothers and Sisters: Feminism and Nationalism in the Thought of Subhas Chandra Bose." Asian Studies 2, no. 1 (1984) 23–32.

———. "The Politics of Respectability: Indian Women and the INC." In *The Indian National Congress*, edited by Anthony Low, 54–97. Delhi: Oxford University Press, 1988.

Foucault, Michel. *The Order of Things: An Archeology of the Human Sciences*. London: Routledge, 1973.

Freedman, Maurice. "The Growth of a Plural Society in Malaya." *Pacific Affairs*, 33, no. 2 (1960): 158–168.

Frye, Marilyn. *The Politics of Reality: Essays in Feminist Theory*. California: The Crossing Press, 1983.

Galtung, Johan. "Violence, Peace and Peace Research." *Journal of Peace Research* 6, no. 3 (1969): 167–191.

Gandhi, M. K. *The Collected Works of Gandhi*. Delhi: Publications Division, Ministry of Information & Broadcasting, Govt. of India, 1958.

Gaw, Kenneth. *Superior Servants: The Legendary Cantonese Amahs of the Far East*. Oxford: Oxford University Press, 1989.

Gawankar, Rohini. *The Women's Regiment and Captain Lakshmi of INA*. New Delhi: Devika Publications, 2003.

Gergen, Marry McCanney. "Toward a Feminist Meta-theory and Methodology in the Social Sciences." In *Feminist Thought and the Structure of Knowledge*, edited by Mary McCanney Gergen, 87–104. New York: New York University Press, 1998.

Ghosh, Durba. *Sex and the Family in Colonial India: The Making of Empire*. Cambridge: Cambridge University Press, 2006.

Gill, Walter. *Turn North-East at the Tombstone*. Adelaide: Rigby, 1970.

Gillon, Kenneth O.L. *Fiji's Indian Migrants: A History to the End of Indenture in 1920*. Berkeley: University of California Press, 1962.

Gopinath, Aruna. *Footprints on the Sands of Time: Rasammah Bhupalan—A Life of Purpose*. Kuala Lumpur: Arkib Negara, 2007.

Gramsci, Antonio. *Selections from Prison Notebooks*. Edited and translated by Quinn Hoare and Geoffery Nowell Smith. London: Lawrence and Wishart, 1971.

Guha, Ranajit. "The Prose of Counterinsurgency." In *Selected Subaltern Studies*, edited by Ranajit Guha and Gayatri Spivak, 45–86. New York: Oxford University Press, 1998.

Hanlon, Rosiland O. "Recovering the Subject Subaltern Studies and Histories of Resistance in Colonial South Asia," *Modern Asian Studies* 22, no. 1 (1988), 189–224.

Hanson, Susan and Geraldine Pratt, eds. *Gender, Work and Space*. New York and London: Routledge, 1995.

Harper, T. N. *The End of Empire and the Making of Malaya*. New York: Cambridge University Press, 1998.

Heidemann, Frank. *Kanganies in Sri Lanka and Malaysia*. Munchen: Anacon, 1992.

Hills, Carol and Daniel C. Silverman. "Nationalism and Feminism in Late Colonial India: 1943–45." *Modern Asian Studies* 27, no. 4 (1993): 741– 760.

Hiralal, Kalpana. "Rebellious Sisters: Indentured Women and Resistance in Colonial Natal, 1860–1911." In *Resistance and Indian Indenture Experience: Comparative Perspectives*, edited by Mauritz Hassankhan et al., 241–270. New Delhi: Manohar Publications, 2014.

Hobswam, Eric. *Age of Capitalism, 1848–1875*. London: Abacus, 1975.

Igra, Ana R. *Wives without Husbands: Marriage, Desertion and Welfare in New York, 1900–1935*. Chapel Hill: University of North Carolina Press, 2007.

Jackson, James C. *Planters and Speculators: A Chinese and European Agricultural Enterprise in Malaya (1786–1921)*. Kuala Lumpur: University of Malaya Press, 1986.

Jackson, R. N. *Immigrant Labour and the Development of Malaya, 1786–1920*. Kuala Lumpur: Government Press, 1961.

Jain, Ravindra K. *South Indians on the Plantation Frontier in Malaya*. New Haven: Yale University Press, 1970.

——— *Indian Transmigrants: Malaysian and Comparative Essays*. Gurgaon: Three Essays Collective, 2009.

Jain, Shobita. "Gender Relations and the Plantation System in Assam, India." In *Women Plantation Workers: International Experiences*, edited by Shobita Jain and Rhoda Rheddock, 107–128. Oxford: Berg, 1998.

Janmohamed, Abdul. "Between Speaking and Dying: Some Imperatives in the Emergence of the Subaltern in the Context of U.S. Slavery." In *Can the Subaltern Speak? Reflections on the History of an Idea*, 139–155. New York: Columbia University Press, 2010.

Jayathurai, Dashini. "Labouring Bodies, Labouring Histories: Malayan Estate Girl." *The Journal of Commonwealth Literature* 47, no.3 (2012): 303–323.

Jomo, K.S. and Josie Zaini. *Meena: A Plantation Child Worker*. Kuala Lumpur: INSAN, 1985.

Kale, Madhavi. *Fragments of Empire: Capital, Slavery, and Indian Indentured Labor Migration in the British Caribbean*. Philadelphia: University of Pennsylvania Press, 1998.

Kaplan, Temma. "Female Consciousness and Collective Action: The Case of Barcelona, 1910–1918." *Signs* 7, no. 3 (1982): 545–566.

Karmen, Andrew Karmen. *Crime Victims: An Introduction to Victimology*. Belmont: Wadsworth Publishing, 2003.

Katrak, Ketu. "Women's Texts." *Modern Fiction Studies* 35, no. 1 (1992): 157–179.

Kaur, Amarjit. "Tappers and Weeders: South Indian Plantation Workers in Malaysia 1880–1970." *South Asia* 73, no. 1 (1998): 73–102. Accessed October 8, 2010. doi: 10.1080/00856409808723351.

———. "Indian Labour, Labour Standards and Worker's Health in Burma and Malaya, 1900–1940." *Modern Asian Studies* 40, no. 2 (2006): 425–475. Accessed October 8, 2010. doi:10.1017/S0026749X06001788.

———. "Malaysia." In *The Encyclopedia of the Indian Diaspora*, edited by Brij V. Lal, Peter Reeves, and Rajesh Rai, 156–167. Singapore: Editions Didier Millet in association with National University of Singapore, 2006.

Kelly, John D. "Fear of Culture: British Regulation of Indian Marriage in Post-Indenture Fiji." *Ethnohistory* 36, no. 4 (1989): 372–391. Accessed October 9, 2010. http://www.jstor.org.libproxy1.nus.edu.sg/stable/482653.

———. *Politics of Virtue: Hinduism, Sexuality and Counter-colonial Discourse in Fiji*. Chicago: University of Chicago Press, 1991.

———. "Gaze and Grasp: Plantations, Desires and Colonial Law in Fiji." In *Sites of Desire or Economies of Pleasure: Sexualities in Asia and Pacific*, edited by M. Jolly and Lenore Manderson, 72–98. Chicago: Chicago University Press, 1997.

Kelly, John D. and U. K. Singh, eds. *My Twenty-one Years in the Fiji Islands, and the Story of the Haunted Line.* Suva: Fiji Museum, 2003.

Kelly, Rita Mae et al. "Liberal Positivistic Epistomology and Research on Women and Politics." *Women and Politics* 7, no. 3 (1987): 12–27.

Khan, Yasmin. *India at War: The Subcontinent and the Second World War.* Oxford and New York: Oxford University Press, 2015.

Kheng, Cheah Boon. "Japanese Army Policy toward the Chinese and Malaya–Chinese Relations in Wartime Malaya." In *Southeast Asian Minorities in the Wartime Japanese Empire* edited by Paul J. Kratoska, 97–110. London: Routledge Curzon, 2002.

Knight, G. Roger. "Gully Coolies, Weed-Women and Snijvolk: The Sugar Industry Workers of North Java in the Early Twentieth Century." *Modern Asian Studies* 28, no. 1 (1994): 51–76.

———. *Commodities and Colonialism: The Story of Big Sugar in Indonesia, 1880–1942.* Leiden and Boston: Brill, 2013.

Kobayashi, Audrey, Linda Peake, Hal Benenson, and Katie Pickles. "Introduction: Placing Women and Work." In *Women, Work and Place*, edited by Audrey Kobayashi, ix–xliii. Quebec: McGill-Queen's University Press, 1994.

Kolsky, Elizabeth. *Colonial Justice in British India: White Violence and the Rule of Law.* Cambridge: Cambridge University Press, 2010.

Kratoska, Paul. *The Japanese Occupation of Malaya.* London: Hurst, 1998.

Krishnan, R. B. *Indians in Malaya: A Pageant of Greater India.* Singapore: The Malayan Publishers, 1936.

Kumar, Ashutosh. *Coolies of the Empire: Indentured Indians in the Sugar Colonies, 1830–1920* (Delhi: Cambridge University Press, 2017).

Kurian, Rachel. "Tamil Women in Sri-Lankan Plantations: Labour Control and Patriarchy." In *Women Plantation Workers: International Experiences*, edited by Shobita Jain and Rhoda Rheddock, 67–88. Oxford: Berg, 1998.

Lal, Brij V. *Chalo Jahaji: On a Journey through Indenture in Fiji.* Canberra: Division of Pacific and Asian History, Australian National University and Fiji Museum, 2000.

———. "Kunti's Cry: Indentured Women on Fiji Plantations." *The Indian Economic and Social History Review* 22, no. 1 (1985): 55–71.

————. "Veil of Dishonor: Sexual Jealousy and Suicide on Fiji Plantations." *The Journal of Pacific History* 20, 3 (1985).

Lebra, Joyce Chapman. *Women against the Raj: The Rani of Jhansi Regiment.* Singapore: Institute of Southeast Asian Studies, 2008.

Levine, Philippa. *Prostitution, Race, and Politics: Policing Venereal Disease in the British Empire.* New York: Routledge, 2003.

Linden, Marcel van der and Lee Mitzman. "Connecting Household History and Labour History." *International Review of Social History* 38, no. S1 (1993): 163–173. Accessed October 8, 2011. doi:http://dx.doi.org/10.1017/S0020859000112350.

Low, Kelvin E. Y. *Remembering the Samsui Women: Migration and Social Memory in Singapore and China.* Vancouver: University of British Columbia Press, 2014.

MacIntyre, Tan Sri S. Chelvasingam. *Through Memory Lane.* Singapore: University Education Press, 1973.

Mackenzie, Donald and Judy Wajcman, eds. *The Social Shaping of Technology: How the Refrigerator Got Its Way.* Milton Keynes: Open University Press, 1985.

Madhok, Sumi. *Rethinking Agency: Developmentalism, Gender and Rights.* New Delhi: Routledge, 2013.

Madhok, Sumi, Anne Phillips, and Kalpana Wilson. *Gender, Agency, and Coercion, Thinking Gender in Transnational Times.* New York: Palgrave Macmillan, 2013.

Mahajani, Usha. *The Role of Indian Minorities in Burma and Malaya.* Bombay: Vora, 1960.

Mahapatra, Prabhu. "Restoring the Family: Wife Murders and the Making of Sexual Contract for Indian Immigrant Labor in the British Caribbean Colonies, 1860–1920." *Studies in History* 11, no. 2 (1995): 227–260.

Majumdar, Shanti. "Netaji's Rani of Jhansi Regiment." *The Oracle* 2, no. 3 (1980): 21–26.

Manderson, Lenore. *Sickness and the State: Health and Illness in Colonial Malaya, 1870–1940.* New York: Cambridge University Press, 1996.

Mani, Lata. *Contentious Traditions: The Debate on Sati in Colonial India.* Berkley: University of California Press, 1998.

Maniam, K. S. *Between Lives.* Petaling Jaya: Maya Press, 2003.

McClintock, Anne. "Family Feuds: Gender, Nationalism and the Family." *Feminist Review* 44 (Summer 1993): 61–80.

McDonald, Lynn. *The Women Founders of Social Sciences*. Ottawa: Carleton University Press, 1994.

McDowell, Linda. "Beyond Patriarchy: A Class-based Explanation of Women's Subordination." *Antipode* 18, no. 3 (1986): 311–321.

Meerkerk, Elise van Nederveen. *Women, Work and Colonialism in The Netherlands and Java, 1830–1940: Comparisons, Contrasts, Connections*. Palgrave Macmillan 2019.

Mies, Maria. "Towards a Methodology for Feminist Research." In *Theories of Women's Studies*, edited by Gloria Bowles and R.D. Klein, 117–140. London: Routledge and Kegan Paul, 1983.

Mills, Sara. *Gender and Colonial Space*. Manchester: Manchester University Press, 2005.

Mishra, Margaret. "Between Women: Indenture, Morality and Health," *Australian Humanities Review*, 52 (May 2012): 57–70.

Moran, Lord. *Winston Churchill: The Struggle for Survival 1940–1965*. London: Constable, 1968.

Morgan, Jennifer L. *Laboring Women: Reproduction and Gender in New World Slavery*. Philadelphia: University of Pennsylvania Press, 2004.

Nag, Prithvish, ed. *Census and Mapping Survey*. Delhi: Concept Publishing, 1984.

Nair, Janaki. "On the Question of Agency in Indian Feminist Historiography." *Gender and History* 6, no. 1 (1994): 82–100. Accessed March 8, 2012. doi: 10.1111/j.1468–0424.1994.tb00196.x.

———. *Women and Law in Colonial India: A Social History*. New Delhi: Kali for Women, 1996.

Nateson, G. A. *Speeches of Gopal Krishna Gokhale*. Madras: G. A. Nateson, 1920.

National Archives of Singapore and National Archives of Malaysia. *Reminiscences of the Straits Settlements through Postcards*. Kuala Lumpur; Singapore: National Archives of Malaysia; National Archives of Singapore, 2005.

Netto, George. *Indians in Malaya: Historical Facts and Figures*. Singapore: George Netto, 1961.

Nijhawan, Shobna. "Fallen through the Nationalist and Feminist Grids of Analysis: Political Campaigning of Indian Women against Indentured Labour Emigration." *Indian Journal of Gender Studies* 21, no. 1 (2014): 111–133. Accessed September 25, 2014. http://ijg.sagepub.com/content/21/1/111.

Ortner, Sherry B. *Anthropology and Social Theory: Culture, Power and the Acting Subject*. Durham, NC: Duke University Press, 2006.

Parmer, J. N. *Colonial Labour Policy and Administration: A History of Labour in the Rubber Plantation Industry in Malaya, 1910–1941*. New York: Association of Asian Studies, 1960.

Pool, Gail R. and Hira Singh. "Indentured Indian Women of the Empire: Between Colonial Oppression and the Brahmanical Tradition." *Journal of Plantation Society in the Americas* 6, no.1 (1999): 1–46.

Prakash, Gyan. "Postcolonial Criticisms and History: Subaltern Studies." In *The Oxford History of Historical Writing: Volume 5: Historical Writing Since 1945 to the Present*, edited by Axel Schneider and Daniel Woolf, 74–92. Oxford and New York: Oxford University Press, 2011.

Rai, Rajesh. *Indians in Singapore, 1819–1945: Diaspora in the Colonial Port City*. Oxford University Press, 2014.

Ramachandran, Selvakumaran. *Indian Plantation Labour in Malaysia*. Kuala Lumpur: S. Abdul Majeed & Co., 1994.

Ramusack, Barbara. "Cultural Missionaries, Maternal Imperialists, Feminist Allies: British Women Activists in India, 1865–1945." In *Western Women and Imperialism: Complicity and Resistance*, edited by Nupur Chaudhuri and Margaret Strobel, 119–136. Bloomington: Indiana University Press, 1992.

Ranchod-Nilson, Sita and Tetreault, Mary Ann, eds. *Women, States and Nationalism: At Home in the Nation?* London: Routledge, 2000.

Reid, Donald. "Reflections on Labor History and Language." In *Rethinking Labor History*, edited by Lenard R. Berlanstein, 39–54. Urbana and Chicago: University of Illinois Press, 1993.

Rettig, Tobias. "Recruiting All-female Rani of Jhansi Regiment: Subhash Chandra Bose and Dr. Laxshmi Swaminadhan." *Southeast Asia Research* 21, no. 4 (2013), 627–638. Accessed March 5, 2014. http://ink.library.smu.edu.sg/soss_research/1388.

Rheddock, Rhoda. "Indian Women and Indentureship in Trinidad and Tobago 1845–1917: Freedom Denied." *Caribbean Quarterly* 54, no.4 (2008): 41–68. Accessed March 15, 2012. http://www.jstor.org.libproxy1.nus.edu.sg/stable/40654698.

Rheddock, Rhoda and Shobita Jain. "Introduction: Plantation Women: An Introduction" In *Women Plantation Worker: International Experiences*, edited by Shobita Jain and Rhoda Rheddock, 1–16. Oxford: Berg, 1998.

Rimmer, P. J. and Lisa M. Allen, eds. *The Underside of Malaysian History: Pullers, Prostitutes, Plantation Workers*. Singapore: Singapore University Press, 1990.

Roopnaraine, Lomarsh. "Review of Coolie Woman: The Odyssey of Indenture." *Journal of Intercultural Studies* 35, no. 4 (2014): 464–466.

Rose, Sonya O. *What Is Gender History?* Cambridge: Polity Press, 2010.

Ruberto, Laura E. *Gramsci, Migration, and the Representation of Women's Work in Italy and the U.S.* Lanham: Lexington, 2007.

Rudnick, Anja. *Working Gendered Boundaries: Temporary Migration Experiences of Bangladeshi Women in the Malaysian Export Industry from a Multi-Sited Perspective.* Amsterdam: University of Amsterdam Press, 2009.

Sahgal, Lakshmi. "The Rani of Jhansi Regiment." *The Oracle* 1, no. 2 (1979): 17–19.

———. *A Revolutionary Life: Memoirs of a Political Activist.* New Delhi: Paul's Press, 1997.

Sandhu, Kernial Singh. *Indians in Malaya: Some Aspects of Their Immigration and Settlement (1786–1957).* London: Cambridge University Press, 1969.

Saunders, Graham. *The Development of a Plural Society in Malaya.* Kuala Lumpur: Longman Malaysia, 1977.

Scott, James C. *Domination and the Arts of Resistance: Hidden Transcripts.* New Haven: Yale University Press, 1990.

———. *Weapons of the Weak: Everyday Forms of Peasant Resistance.* New Haven: Yale University Press, 1985.

Scott, Joan. *Gender and the Politics of History.* New York: Columbia University Press, 1999.

Scott, William Henry. *Cracks in the Parchment Curtain and Other Essays in Philippine History.* Quezon City: New Day Publishers, 1982.

Seenarine, Moses. "Indentured Women in Colonial Guyana." In *Sojourners to Settlers*, edited by Mahin Gosine and D. Narine, 36–66. New York: Windsor Press, 1999.

Sen, Indrani. *Woman and Empire: Representations in the Writings of British India, 1858–1900.* New Delhi: Orient Longman, 2002.

Sen, Samita. "Offences Against Marriage: Negotiating Custom in Colonial Bengal." In *A Question of Silence: The Sexual Economies of Modern India*, edited by Janaki Nair and Mary E. John, 77–110. London: Zed Books, 1998.

———. *Women and Labour in Late Colonial India: The Bengal Jute Industry*, Cambridge Studies in Indian History and Society. Cambridge: Cambridge University Press, 1999.

Sengupta, Nilanjana. *A Gentleman's Word: The Legacy of Subhash Chandra Bose in Southeast Asia*. Singapore: Institute of Southeast Asian Studies, 2012.

Seth, Amritlal. *Jai Hind: The Diary of a Rebel Daughter of India with the Rani of Jhansi Regiment*. Bombay: Janmabhoomi Prakashan Mandir, 1945.

Sewell, William H. "Toward a Post Materialist Rhetoric for Labor History." In *Rethinking Labor History*, edited by Lenard R. Berlanstein, 15–38. Urbana and Chicago: University of Illinois Press, 1993.

Shah, Nayan. *Stranger Intimacy: Contesting Race, Sexuality and the Law in the North*. Berkley: University of California Press, 2011.

Shameen, Shaista. "Migration, Labour and Plantation Women in Fiji: A Historical Perspective." In *Women Plantation Workers: International Experiences*, edited by Shobita Jain and Rhoda Rheddock, 49–66. Oxford: Berg, 1998.

Shepherd, Verne A. "Indian Migrant Women and Plantation Labour in Nineteenth and Twentieth Century Jamaica: Gender Perspectives." In *Women Plantation Workers: International Experiences*, edited by Shobita Jain and Rhoda Rheddock, 89–106. Oxford: Berg, 1998.

Shinozaki, Mamoru. *Syonan-My Story: The Japanese Occupation in Singapore*. Singapore: Marshall Cavendish Editions, 2011.

Siang, Song Ong. *One Hundred Years' History of the Chinese in Singapore*. Singapore: John Murray Publishers, 1923.

Sinappah, Arasaratnam. *Indians in Malaysia and Singapore*. Bombay: Oxford University Press, 1970.

Sinha, Mrinalini. *Colonial Masculinity: The "Manly Englishman" and the "Effeminate Bengali" in the Late Nineteenth Century*. New Delhi: Kali for Women, 1997.

———. *Specters of Mother India: The Global Restructuring of an Empire*. Durham: Duke University Press, 2006.

———. "Refashioning Mother India: Feminism and Nationalism in Late Colonial India." *Feminist Studies* 26, no. 3 (2000): 623–644.

Sjoberg, Laura and Caron E. Gentry, *Mothers, Monsters, Whores: Women's Violence in Global Politics*. London and New York: Zed Pub., 2007.

Spivak, Gayatri Chakravorty. "Can the Subaltern Speak?" In *Marxism and Interpretation of Culture*, edited by Carl Nelson and Lawrence Grossberg, 271–316. London: Macmillan, 1988.

———. *In Other Worlds: Essays in Cultural Politics*. New York: Methuen, 1987.

———. "The Rani of Sirmur: An Essay in Reading the Archives," *History and Theory* 24, no. 3 (1985): 242–272.

Sreenivas, Mytheli. *Wives, Widows, Concubines: The Conjugal Family Ideal in Colonial India*. Bloomington: Indiana University Press, 2008.

Stenson, Michael R. *Class, Race, and Colonialism in West Malaysia: The Indian Case*. St. Lucia Australia: University of Queensland Press, 1980.

———. *Industrial Conflict in Malaya: Prelude to the Communist Revolt of 1948*. London: Oxford University Press, 1970.

Stoler, Ann L. "Making Empire Respectable: The Politics of Race and Sexual Morality in 20th-Century Colonical Cultures." *American Ethnologist* 16, no. 4 (1989): 634–660. Accessed July 19, 2011. http://www.jstor.org.libproxy1. nus.edu.sg/stable/645114.

———. *Along the Archival Grain: Epistemic Anxieties and Colonial Common Sense*. Princeton and Oxford: Princeton University Press, 2009.

———. "Archival Dis-Ease: Thinking through Colonial Ontologies." *Communication and Critical/Cultural Studies* 7, no. 2 (2010).

Subramaniam, P. *Social History of the Tamils (1707–1947)*. New Delhi: D. K. Printworld, 2005.

Tambe, Ashwini. "Gandhi's 'Fallen' Sisters: Difference and the National Body Politic." *Social Scientist* 37, no. 1 (2009): 21–38.

Tilly, Louise Tilly and Joan Scott, eds. *Women, Work and Family*. New York: Methuen, 1987.

Tinker, Hugh. *A New System of Slavery*. London: Oxford University Press, 1974.

Tetreault, Mary. "Justice for All: Wartime Rape and Women's Human Rights." *Global Governance*, 3/2 (1997): 197–212.

Trouillot, Michel-Rolph. *Silencing the Past: Power and the Production of History*. Boston: Beacon Press, 1995.

Trotman, David. "Women and Crime in Late Nineteenth Century Trinidad." *Caribbean Quarterly* 30, 3–4 (1984): 60–72.

Tsurumi, Patricia E. *Factory Girls: Women in the Thread Mills of Meiji Japan.* New Jersey: Princeton University Press, 1990.

Tully, John. *The Devil's Milk: A Social History of Rubber.* New York: Monthly Review Press, 2011.

Varma, Nitin. *Coolies of Capitalism: Assam Tea and the Making of Coolie Labor.* Berlin and Boston: Walter de Gruyter GmBh, 2017.

Vizenor, Gerald. *Manifest Manners: Narratives on Postindian Survivance.* Lincoln: Nebraska, 1999.

Warren, James Francis. *Ah ku and Karayuki-san: Prostitution in Singapore, 1870–1940.* Singapore: Singapore University Press, 2003.

———. *Rickshaw Coolie: A People's History of Singapore 1880–1940.* Singapore: Singapore University Press, 2003.

Weeks, Jeffery. "Invented Moralities," *History Workshop* 32, no. 1 (1991): 151–166.

———. *Sex, Politics and Society.* London: Longman Group Ltd., 1989.

Willford, Andrew. *Cage of Freedom: Tamil Identity and Ethnic Fetish in Malaya.* Ann Arbour: University of Michigan Press, 2006.

———. *Tamils and the Haunting of Justice: History and Recognition in Malaysia's Plantations.* Manoa and Singapore: University of Hawaii Press/Singapore University Press, 2014.

Wright, Arnold and H. A. Cartwright, eds. *Twentieth Century Impressions of British Malaya: Its History, People, Commerce, Industries and Resources.* London: Llyod's Greater Britain Publishing Company Ltd, 1908.

Wright, Peter Lee. *Child Slaves.* Oxon, New York: Earthscan, James & James, [1990] 2009.

Yuval-Davis, Nira. *Gender and Nation.* London: Sage, 1997.

Yuval-Davis, Nira and F. Anthias. "Introduction." In *Woman – Nation– State*, edited by Nira Yuval-Davis, and F. Anthias, 1–15. Basingstoke: Macmillan, 1989.

Zarkov, Dubravka. *The Body of War.* Durham and London: Duke University Press, 2007.

INDEX

marriage
  contractual marriages, 43, 46, 92,
    109–110
  Marriage Registration Act, 119
  registration, 18, 47, 100, 119
maternal health, 61–62
Maternity allowance, 61, 65
Menon, Gopala, 122
messing, 82, 86, 91–93, 95, 100
midwives, 61
migration, 2, 33, 39
  India to Malaya, 28
Montague Chelmsford Reforms, 37
*munsif*s, 31

Nehru, Nandrani, 43
nurses, 140, 148,

patriarchy, 3, 11, 16, 23–24, 69, 101, 138,
  152
partner desertion, 105–106, 110, 118, 153
  husband, 13, 103
  in Indian coolie communities, 105
  mistress, 110
  retribution for, 114
  Victorian ideals, 108–109
  wife, 109
payrolls, 48, 63, 64
Periyar, Ramasamy, 44
piecework system, 56–58, 65
plantation, 33
laborers, 8, 12
economy, 10, 80, 92, 103
  society, 1–4, 10, 19, 60, 80, 94, 102
planters,

discipline of coolie men, 19
economic concerns, 32–33
European, 31, 78, 104, 132
gendered labor migration, 32
immoral practice allegations, 68
memoirs, 48–50, 78
moral outrage, 104
payment by results, 56
Planter's Association, 61
political concerns, 33–36
pregnant workers, 61–62
recruitment strategies, 27, 29–30,
  38–39, 63
response to domestic violence, 82, 92,
  96–97
Selangor Journal of Planters, 84
shaping coolie identities, 90, 99
tension in Malaya, 36–38
treatment of women laborers, 59,
  60–61, 64, 91
Victorian categorizations, 100
port marriages, 46
primary workers, 50, 59
privacy, 25, 83, 84–85, 91, 120
proletarization, 66, 69, 70
prostitutes, 14, 42–43, 47, 68
Protectors of Emigrants, 42, 45, 47

Rani of Jhansi Regiment (RJR), 89,
  125, 129–131, 135–150, 152, 156
activity of women members, 140
elite members, 138, 142, 145
formation, 129–131
memoirs, 26, 144
military plans, 126

For EU product safety concerns, contact us at Calle de José Abascal, 56–1°, 28003 Madrid, Spain or eugpsr@cambridge.org.

www.ingramcontent.com/pod-product-compliance
Ingram Content Group UK Ltd.
Pitfield, Milton Keynes, MK11 3LW, UK
UKHW010250140625
459647UK00013BA/1771